SPEECHES ON INDIAN QUESTIONS

SPEECHES ON INDIAN QUESTIONS

By

The Rt. Hon. Mr. MONTAGU

GYAN

Published by

Gyan Publishing House
5, Ansari Road
Daryaganj, New Delhi-110002
Phone: 011-47034999, 9811692060
E-mail: books@gyanbooks.com

Distribution Network
gyanbooks.com
India, USA, Canada, UK, Australia, France

ISBN: 978-81-212-6855-4 (PB)
First Published, 1917

2nd Impression 2023

Printed at: Gyan Press, Delhi.

SPEECHES ON INDIAN QUESTIONS
Author: The Rt. Hon. Mr. MONTAGU

SPEECHES

ON

INDIAN QUESTIONS

BY

The Rt. Hon. Mr. MONTAGU

FIRST EDITION
PRICE RE. 1-8

"But I am positive of this, that your great claim to continue the illogical system of government by which you have governed India in the past is that it was efficient. It has been proved to be not efficient. It has been proved to be not sufficiently elastic to express the will of the Indian people ; to make them into a warring nation as they wanted to be. The history of this war shows that you can rely upon the loyalty of the Indian people to the British Empire —if you ever before doubted it! If you want to use that loyalty you must take advantage of that love of country which is a religion in India, and you must give them that bigger opportunity of controlling their own destinies, not merely by councils which cannot act, but by control, by growing control, of the Executive itself. Then in your next war—if we ever have war—in your next crisis, through times of peace, you will have a contented India, an India equipped to help. Believe me, Mr. Speaker, it is not a question of expediency, it is not a question of desirability. Unless you are prepared to remodel, in the light of modern experience, this century-old and cumbrous machine, then I believe, I verily believe, that you will lose your right to control the destinies of the Indian Empire."

MR. MONTAGU in the *House of Commons*.

PREFACE.

This book contains all the important speeches on Indian affairs, of the Rt. Hon'ble Mr. E. S. Montagu, the present Secretary of State for India. It is a fitting companion volume to the "Indian speeches" of Lord Morley, under whom Mr. Montagu served as Under Secretary of State between 1910 and 1913. One feature of this volume is the reproduction from *Hansard* of Mr. Montagu's speeches on the Indian Budget, made in the House of Commons in four successive years, as Under Secretary of State. The collection also includes his Guildhall speech on "Indian Affairs," on "Indian Land Policy" delivered at the Liberal Colonial Club, London, and his well-known speech on the Report of the Mesopotamian Commission delivered recently in the House of Commons. Under the Indian Constitution, the Secretary of State possesses such vast powers of control and supervision over the Government of India that the speeches of any Secretary of State are bound to be of interest to Indian readers. But when, as in the case of Mr. Montagu, the holder brings, to his high office, knowledge and experience based on work as Under Secretary of State for India, and travel and intercourse with all shades of Indian opinion in this country, his utterances are bound to have additional interest. Even more than this, Mr. Montagu has not allowed the springs of his liberal enthusiasm to be dried up by office, and his pronouncements breathe the true spirit of liberal statesmanship. That Mr. Montagu is visiting India as the special representative of His Majesty's Government in order to discuss with the authorities and the representatives of the people the various questions in regard to "the development of self-governing institutions with a view to the progressive realization of responsible Government in India" is additional reason why Indians should like to know what manner of man this Secretary of State is, who has got to solve one of the most important problems of the British Empire. To some people language is given to conceal their thoughts; but Mr. Montagu's speeches ring true and reveal the man as he is. This up-to-date and comprehensive collection of Mr. Montagu's speeches will, it is hoped, be cordially welcomed by the public at large.

THE PUBLISHERS.

CONTENTS.

MONTAGU'S INDIAN SPEECHES.

THE INDIAN BUDGET, 1910.

On the motion to go into Committee on the East India Revenue Accounts.

Mr. Montagu said : This motion would not sound to a stranger to our proceedings as a highly controversial one, but the discussion which will arise upon it is rather inaccurately known as the Debate on the Indian Budget, and it gives the House an opportunity, somehow markedly inadequate—(hear, hear)—for a review of the whole circumstances of Indian government and conditions. In the very large draft which I shall have to make upon the patience of hon. members I trust they will make all allowance for certain obvious disadvantages under which I labour. My noble friend, Lord Morley, has now been Secretary of State for five years. It was only during the first two of them that he was able to make his own annual statement in the House, and for the last two years and on this occasion the House has to listen to what I believe it will agree is a story of conspicuously successful administration from different spokesmen, each one of whom—and I hope I shall not be guilty of any disrespect to my predecessors when I say it—has felt the almost insuperable difficulty of adequately representing not only a great administrator, but so gifted and individual a personality as Lord Morley of Blackburn. (Hear, hear.) Concerning my own predecessor (Master of Elibank) I can only say that I regret, and never more than at this moment, the fact that he has been translated from the India Office, with those gifts of lucidly expounding any case he has to defend, and has gone to another sphere of action.

FOREIGN AFFAIRS.

I do not think it is necessary for me to say much this year about the foreign affairs of India. The North-West Frontier has been in a peaceful and undisturbed condition during the year that has just closed. There have been a few small raids which are the ordinary features of frontier life. The Amir of Afghanistan has appointed Afghan representatives to the Joint Commission which has been appointed to consider with a view to settlement various boundary disputes and claims of many years' standing. The Commission met for the first time last month, and the attitude of the Afghan representative was such that I do not think it is too sanguine to expect that the Commission will soon be able to arrive at a satisfactory settlement. On the North-East Frontier the chief events of the year have been the conclusion of a new treaty with Bhutan and the flight of the Dalai Lama from Tibet. With regard to the treaty with Bhutan, the effect is to give Great Britain control over the foreign relations of the State. It may be taken as an indication of the firm determination of His Majesty's Government in no circumstances to allow foreign interference in the frontier States of Nepaul, Sikkim and Bhutan—a determination which I am glad to be able to say is fully shared by the rulers of those States themselves. The flight of the Dalai Lama from Lhassa was due to the despatch to that city of Chinese troops. Hon. members will find a complete account of all the events in the Blue Book on Tibetan affairs which has just been presented to the House. His Majesty's Government have found nothing in them to necessitate a departure from their policy and the policy of their predecessors of non-interference in the internal affairs of Tibet, or, with the domestic relations between Tibet and China, but they have made it clear to China that they will require a strict conformity with the provisions of the Anglo-Tibetan Convention of 1904 and with the Anglo-Chinese Convention of 1906, and they have no reason to doubt the good faith of the assurances which have been received from the Chinese Government. The reason for the despatch of troops to Lhassa was to maintain order in that city and at the trade marts.

THE AGRICULTURAL OUTLOOK.

Then, coming to internal affairs, I am not in the position of my predecessor, who described India in March, 1909, as still under the effects of famine and distress. The autumn rains of 1909 were eminently satisfactory, and the autumn harvest has been followed by an equally fine spring harvest. Almost all the crops have been exceptionally productive. The cotton crop gathered in the winter months of 1909 was one of the best on record. The estimated yield is 4,500,000 bales, being an increase of 22 per cent. on the yield of the previous year. The rice crop has been equally good. In the province of Bengal, where rice is the staple article of food, the yield is put at 78 per cent. better than that of the previous year, and 47 per cent. better than the average for the previous five years. The wheat crop of 1910 now coming into the market is one of the best of recent years. In 1908 the yield was 6,000,000 tons. In 1909 it was 7,600,000 tons. This year the final estimate is no less than 9,500,000 tons. The agricultural prosperity of India may thus be said to be completely re-established, and it immediately begins to have an effect on the increase of exports and of imports, and a diminution of prices of the commoner food grains. The export trade has increased from £100,000,000 sterling in 1908-09 to £123,000,000 sterling in 1909-10. Should wheat and seeds continue to be exported through the autumn and winter months to the extent anticipated, the export trade of 1910-11 will be on a very large scale indeed.

Trade Prospects.

Of course, the import trade has been slower to move because there was a great accumulation of stocks, and the slump of 1908 was so severe that recovery cannot be expected very quickly. In 1909-10 the imports fell from £86,000,000 to £82,000,000, but in the closing months of the year there was a considerable upward movement. The third sign of improvement, the fall in general prices, is in some degree of great importance to large portions of the population of India, particularly those who dwell in towns, and is the most gratifying sign of improvement, when we recollect that the common food grains are 20 per cent. cheaper now than they were a year ago. But, of course, it must not be forgotten that the agriculturists of India have benefited very largely by the increase in prices of what they have sold, while the land revenue and other taxes have remained stationary. Twenty years ago it took 40lb. of wheat to pay the land revenue on an acre of land in the Punjab ; now it takes only 29lb., and meanwhile the average sale price has risen from 38 to 98 rupees in the Punjab. It is a much higher figure in the irrigated provinces.

PLAGUE AND MALARIA.

This picture that we have been able to sketch of a practically wholly agricultural community is a very satisfying one, but I have got something rather less optimistic to say upon two subjects which have always got to be mentioned in Debates on Indian affairs—they are the plague and the malaria. Last year my predecessor was able to say that the plague was decreasing, that it had shown decreasing virulence in 1908 and 1909. Experts thought that the worst had been seen of this disease before 1906, which had shown the biggest rate of disappearance of its great virulence. The mortality in that year dropped from 1,000,000 to 157,000. In 1907 it rose again to 1,200,000. In 1908 it decreased to 156,000, and in 1909 the mortality was only 175,000. But this year it has flared up once more, and to the end of June the mortality was 374,000, and, as in former years, the death-rate has been most severely felt in the United Provinces and the Punjab. It is a local disease in the sense that it seems always to recur in particular provinces and in particular districts of particular provinces. But, on the other hand, scientific evidence all seems to show that it is unconnected with any peculiarities of local circumstances such as drains, and is wholly unconnected with the comparative wealth or poverty of the inhabitants. The extermination of rats and fleas, the prevention of their importation from an infected district to a district not infected seems to be now agreed as the essential way of tackling the disease. Inoculation, and the temporary evacuation of infected premises are used as subsidiary measures. Although the statistics are not hopeful, it is satisfactory to think that the population of India are getting more and more to realise the necessity for co-operating in the administration of laws for enforcing remedial measures and carrying on the continual war which the Government of India have undertaken against the ravages of the plague. But I may point out that in British India with a population of 230,000,000 the death-rate annually is 8,000,000, so that in all the year the contribution which the plague makes to the death-rate is a very small one. Malaria is far more important to the population of India at large, and it is very difficult to gauge accurately the ravages of this disease, because the death returns under the heading "Fevers" in India are not very scientific; but, of course, in regions where malaria is active, the death-rate under the heading "Fevers" in British India shows its activity. In 1908, when malaria was very severe in Upper India, the death-rate from fever rose from 4,500,000 to 5,424,000, or an increase of 900,000, which may roughly be set down to the ravages of this disease. The causes which bring about epidemics are obscure. They seem to be connected with excessive rainfall that floods the country and increases the faclilities for the breeding of the infecting mosquito. In October, 1909, a Committee was convened by the Viceroy at Simla, and the results of this Conference are such that when they are adopted we may hope for a very profitable and satisfactory effect. In the towns site improvements may be made that will have the effect of limiting the breeding places of the mosquito. I fear that we must still have resort to active measures such as the distribution of quinine, which has always been provided by means of plantation as widely and cheaply as possible, though since the Conference the production of quinine has been still more facilitated, and its distribution at a still cheaper price as widely as possible is being helped—and by grants in aid of various municipal bodies for drainage and improvement of sites, while at the same time remedies are being attempted in the towns where the malarial mosquito abounds and breeds.

INDIA'S FINANCIAL POSITION.

So much for a general view of the material conditions of the people of India. Up to now I have dealt with matters affecting the condition of large masses of the population of India, but, as the subject of this Debate is, officially at least, the accounts and estimates of the Government of India, it is my duty to say something of the financial position of the Government of India in 1909-10 and 1910-11. I shall endeavour not to weary the House with an unnecessary display of figures. I have so much to say, and I recognise so clearly that the longer I take to say it the less time there is for members of the House to say what they want to say, that I propose to deal very briefly with the financial statement for the year. The Blue Books which have been laid before the House on the subject contain a full account of it, and for the first time this year they contain, in addition to the financial statement of the financial member of the Viceroy's Council, and the ordinary tabular statement, the very instructive debates in the Viceroy's enlarged Council, and I would recommend to all students of Indian affairs a perusal of these books. They will find them of exceptional and absorbing interest. At the beginning of the year 1910-11 the chief topic of interest is how far the results of the past year actually coincide with the Budget Estimate of March, 1909. This Estimate shows a surplus of £230,000, while the revised Estimate shows a surplus of £289,000, and I am happy to say that later figures show the surplus as £526,000, so that the difference between this final figure and the £230,000 estimated for is not a very serious matter, having regard to the large amount of expenditure involved. But the resemblance is only superficial, and the discrepancies between the results of the year and the Budget Estimate are very large indeed. There was, as the Budget had anticipated, a great improvement in revenue as compared with the preceding year, but, with the exception of opium, the improvement fell very short of what had been anticipated. Land revenue, taxation and commerical undertaking produced together £476,300 less than the Budget Estimate, and a deficit was only avoided for two reasons. First, expenditure on both civil and military work was kept well within the Budget Estimate. Having regard to the very great importance of economy in India, this is not only satisfactory in itself, but augurs very well for the future of the finances of the country. The second reason was that owing to the good results of the opium sales in the year, and the higher prices paid than was expected, opium produced £900,000 more than the Budget Estimate. The House will agree that this sum, exceptional as it was, was rightly treated by the Government of India as a windfall, and a large portion of it was expended in making grants to those local Governments whose finances had been depleted by the famine arrangements of three years ago. After making these grants to local Governments they are able to show, as I was saying, a surplus for the year 1909-10 of £526,400.

A Comparison with Past Years.

As regards the present financial year, 1910-1911, new taxation is necessary for the first time in sixteen years. Since 1894-95 there has been no new taxation in India, while the relief granted to the tax-payer in land cesses in 1905-6 and the reduction of the Salt Tax in 1903, and again in 1905, and again in 1907, and the reduction of the Income Tax have relieved the tax-payer and have cost the State no less than £4,500,000 a year. This year, in order to show a balance of £376,000, additional taxation to bring in £1,126,000 is being imposed. The main cause of this additional taxation is that while the revenue, owing to the remission of taxation under certain heads, has not expanded, there has been a very large increase in the expenditure under certain heads with which the revenue has not been able to keep pace. I will not make a comparison with the revenue of 1907-8, because that was a year of famine, or of 1908-9, which was a year of exceptional depression in trade, or of the year 1909-10, in which there were abnormally high opium prices. The last normal year was 1906-7, and if I compare the Estimate for the year 1910-11 with that year, I find that while Land Revenue, Stamps, Excise, and Customs have increased, Railways, Salt, Post Office and Irrigation have decreased by almost the same amount, so that if there was no increase in taxation the revenue would be very nearly the same as in 1906-7.

Railways and Salt Revenue.

Let me explain for one minute, briefly, this question of the decrease in revenue. First, as to railways. The gross receipts have increased by £3,000,000, but the working expenses and interest charges have increased by £4,750,000, leaving a net decrease of £1,750,000. These increases and expenses were fully explained by the Chairman of the Railway Board during the discussion in the Viceroy's Council. They are attributable partly to increases in wages and salaries, partly to improvements in facilities, and to a large expenditure in strengthening and doubling lines and improving and enlarging stations. Such expenditure is not immediately productive, but there is every reason to hope that, in course of time, its value will be very great. I am spared the necessity of developing further the subject of railways, because a few months ago I was able to lay before the House, in introducing the Loans Act of this year, an account of the convenience and profit to India of this, which is one of the best examples of Socialistic undertakings which the world has to show. As regards salt, the loss of revenue is due to the reduction of the duty in 1907-8 from 1½ rupees to 1 rupee per maund. If the reduction of the duty has caused the revenue to fall in the same proportion the loss would have been £1,365,000, but there has been a considerable increase in consumption in this necessary of life, reducing the loss to £967,000. Of the £481,000 loss under the heading of "Post Office, Telegraph, Mint and Exchange" there was a reduction in postal rates in 1907-8 which cost £208,000 a year.

The Growth of Expenditure.

When I turn to the expenditure figures I find an increase for 1906-7 of £2,485,000. Nevertheless, I would point out that there is a decrease under the heading of "Military Services" of no less a sum than £463,900, although the figures for 1910-11 include the cost of the increase granted to the pay of the Native Army, £426,000. The chief cause of this economy is that the expenditure on Lord Kitchener's scheme for the improvement of the Indian Army has been greatly reduced, owing to the completion of some measures, the modification of others, and the improvement of the international situation. As regards the increases, expenditure in the Education Service has increased by half a million, in the Medical Service by £300,000, in the Scientific and Agricultural Departments by £224,000, and in buildings and roads by £185,500. I do not think I need defend these increases. In addition to this, there has been an increase of £881,300 in the cost of the police force, in accordance with the recommendation of the Police Commission of 1903. There have been also increases in the pay of subordinate establishments employed on the collection of the land revenue and in other departments, necessitated in some cases by the general upward movement of prices and wages. There is one aspect of the growth of expenditure which I ought to mention, because it was referred to at some length in the financial statement of India—I mean the increased amount assigned to the Government of Eastern Bengal and Assam. The income assigned to the Province in 1906 was found to be inadequate for its needs ; the Province was somewhat backward in educational facilities, in medical establishments, in means of communication, and so on, and the experience of the last four years has shown the necessity for increasing the funds available for its development. The Government of India has, accordingly, made to it a grant of about £255,000 a year, with effect from 1910-11, and this is the charge which has to be met in this year's Budget.

Opium and the Chinese Agreement.

The Finance Member of the Viceroy's Council also laid especial stress upon the prospective loss of revenue from opium, compared with 1908-9 and 1909-10. It is a fact well-known to members in all parts of the House that new sources of revenue will have to be discovered to replace the opium revenue which is to be lost to India during the next ten years. Actual receipts for any particular year may vary, because the reduction in the output may lead to an increase in price, but the larger the receipts in any year the greater the loss that will be felt when the trade is ultimately stopped and that source of revenue disappears. During the five years 1901-5 the average total annually exported from India to countries beyond the seas was 67,000 chests, of which China took 51,000, and this amount the Government of India undertook, with effect from January 1, 1908, to reduce by 5,100 chests per year for three years. The Chinese Government on their part undertook to reduce progressively in the same way the production of opium in China. There are no returns as to the amount of this production, but recent estimates put it at eight or ten times the amount of the Indian import. It was further agreed that if the Chinese would fulfil their share of the agreement, the

Indian Government would continue to reduce their export by 5,100 chests annually for seven years more. The present year is the third year of the agreement. The Indian Government have limited the export of opium, and the Imperial Chinese Government on their part claim to have reduced production by more than three-tenths of the area formerly under poppy. Although this cannot be substantiated by statistics, there is no reason to doubt that this is true. But the Foreign Office, before agreeing to the renewal of the agreement, have deputed Sir Alexander Hosie, lately Consul-General at Tientsin, to make enquiry. The condition that statistical proof should be furnished has been waived, and the Chinese Government have been offered an extension of the existing agreement for another three years.

THE EFFECT ON INDIA.

As regards the average annual net revenue, before the agreement with China it was £3,500,000 sterling. In 1908-9, the first year of the agreement, it rose to £4,645,000 ; in 1909-10 it was £4,432,000. This improvement, despite the reduction of export, is due to the higher prices obtained for Bengal opium, to the decrease on expenditure in Bengal, owing to reduced operations, and the fact that Pass Duties on Malwa opium have been received in advance on opium that will be exported up to the end of 1911. In 1910-11 there will be no receipts from Pass Duties, but a higher price has been estimated for Bengal opium, and the revenue budgeted for is £3,500,000 sterling. In 1911-12, receipts on account of duty on Malwa opium will not commence until January, 1912, and there will then be monthly sales from that date of the rights to export the fixed number of chests of Malwa opium. Assuming that Bengal opium will continue to fetch Rs. 1,750 a chest, a net revenue of about £3,000,000 a year may be hoped for in 1911-12 and 1912-13. It will thus be seen that the first half of the agreement with China will pass without injury to the Indian revenue, but the second half will be more serious. Now, the Secretary of State is receiving representations from members of this House urging the shortening of the ten years' period. (*Hear, hear.*) This period was proposed by the Chinese Government themselves, and the Chinese have suggested no alteration. I can only say that any alteration would lead to serious financial and administrative questions. I would urge members to be satisfied with the very satisfactory arrangement that has been made, and to forbear to ask that an excessive strain should be placed either on the finances of India or on the temper of the opium cultivators, the tax-payers, both in British Provinces and in Native States, and the relations of the Indian Government with those of the Native States. It is generally known that the United States Government have issued an invitation to His Majesty's Government to take part in a proposed International Opium Conference to be held at the Hague, in order to give effect to the recommendations of the Shanghai Commission and to consider otherwise the opium question. His Majesty's Government, in examining in a friendly spirit the tentative programme which the United States

Government have suggested, is inclined to think that it may require some revision before it can usefully serve as a basis for a conference, and that some preliminary understanding between the Powers as to the subjects to be discussed may be desirable. His Majesty's Government, for instance, could not agree to submit to discussion at the proposed conference the diplomatic relations subsisting between this country and China, and it may probably desire to know whether the Powers, accepting the principle of a conference, will assent to the conference dealing fully with the cognate question of regulating the export of morphia and cocaine to the East, and will undertake to have the necessary information collected if it is to arrive at a useful decision. However that may be, the fact remains that despite the prosperity of India, the increase in its expenditure on subjects such as I have mentioned, the condition of the revenue, owing to remission of taxes, the prospective loss of revenue from opium, account for the necessity for new taxation this year. To meet a deficit of £750,000 and to turn that deficit into a surplus of £376,000, the Government have proposed new taxation amounting to £1,126,000.

The New Taxes.

This money is to be found by increasing the Customs Duties on imported liquors, to iyeld £135,000 with a corresponding excise on beer manufactured in India to yield £ 33,000 ; an increase in the duty on silver to yield £307,000 ; on petroleum to iyeld £ 105,000, and on tobacco to yield £ 420,000, with an increase on

Stamp Duties to yield £126,000. No increase, it will be seen, has been proposed on any necessary of life, and the easy expedient of once again increasing the Salt Tax or the land rates has been very properly avoided. There has been little discussion of the Liquor Duties, an increase in which will have satisfactory results if it stops some of the import of cheap foreign spirits with their corrupting and demoralising effects on the natives in some parts of India. The duty on silver has been seriously canvassed, and the debate thereon in the Council is one of the most valuable and instructive. The duty was formerly five per cent., but the increased duty is 16 per cent., or a rise from about 1¼*d.* to 4*d.* per ounce. One incidental effect of the duty will be to raise the value in India of the large amounts of savings held by the Indians as silver. It was expected in some quarters that, in consequence of the imposition of the Indian duty, the prices of silver outside India would fall, and this would involve a fall in Indian exchange on China. It was argued that, in consequence of this, the exportation of goods from India to China would become less profitable, while the Chinese producer, not being exposed to this same disadvantage, would gain. I will not go now into the question as to whether the trade of one country is permanently fostered, or that of another injured by the rise or fall in the rate of exchange; but these objections to a very good revenue-producing duty have been answered, and the question has become academic only because the prices of silver and the Indian exchange on China have risen since the imposition of the increased duty. The price has risen from 23 $\frac{7}{16}$*d.* per oz. to 25$\frac{1}{8}$*d.*, and the China exchange has risen from Rs. 129$\frac{1}{2}$ to Rs. 132$\frac{3}{4}$ per $ 100. The increased tax on petroleum is not likely to cause much comment. The import of petroleum is increasing, and rose in India from 83,000,000 gallons in 1904-5 to 90,000,000 gallons in 1908-9. There has been considerable objection to the new duties on tobacco. These were imposed for revenue purposes only. The amount of tobacco imported into India in 1908-9 was five and a half million pounds. If duty had been paid on this import at the rate now in force in the United Kingdom it would have produced £1,449,000, instead of £39,000. It was only reasonable that, when in need of revenue, an attempt should be made, as in other civilised countries, to obtain from this source a substantial amount. The new duties are less than half those now in force in the United Kingdom. In so far as they will stop or reduce the importation of inferior cigarettes into India, cigarettes which sell for $\frac{3}{4}$*d.* per packet of ten, or even cheaper, and do something to check the growth of cigarette-smoking, no one will be sorry. If they were protective they would defeat the object of the Secretary of State, and the Government of India, in raising revenue. I may add that the Indian tobacco which is alleged to compete with the imported article is of very poor quality. The natural conditions in India are hostile to good curing, for the climate is too dry, and the fermentative changes necessary do not take place. The average value of such unmanufactured tobacco as is produced in, and exported from, India, is shown by the Trade Returns to be about $1\frac{3}{4}$*d.* per lb. As I have so often said, their effect has been watched, and is being watched, with the greatest care, and the desirability and possibility of a corresponding Excise will always be considered. I may say, before leaving finance, that the need for economy is obvious from what I have said. The Secretary of State is now considering what steps may be desirable in order to secure a more economic administration.

The Political Unrest and its Genesis.

I have now done my best to enable the House to form some opinion of the material condition of the people of India. There remains the even more important task of examining the political condition of the Empire. I say it is more difficult, because we, Western people, bred in the tradition of self-government, do not easily realise the complexities that involve the ruling power in India—(*Hear, hear*)—the diversities of interest through which the path of compromise must be found, the multifarious elements that must be welded into a large and steady policy. The conflicting claims of different classes may bulk largely at home, but underlying them there is, generally speaking, an essential unity of religion, of tradition, and, on the whole, of interests. In India are associated under a single rule varieties of races far wider than can be found in the whole of Europe, as many different religions as Europe contains sects of Christianity. Stages of civilisation range from the Hindu or

Mahomedan Judge on the Bench of the High Court to the naked savage in the forest. Grafted on to this diverse population, numbering nearly 300,000,000, is a European element, numerically insignificant, less than 200,000 in all, a population in no sense resident in the country, but of an importance in the spheres of education, commerce and administration wholly disproportionate to its numbers. The responsibility for the government of such a country rests ultimately on the people of Great Britain, and is exercised through the Secretary of State in his Council. The problem before us is to yoke a government, as complex and irresponsible to the peoples which it governs as the Government of India, to a democratic system in England which every year shows itself more determined to do its share in the government of this great dependency. The mechanism for performing this duty lies in this House. The views expressed in it on an infinite variety of subjects must be duly considered by the Secretary of State, who is, in effect, the servant of the House. To achieve this responsible task in the House requires dignity, reserve, and a sense of proportion which it is difficult to overrate. In the last Parliament there was one who was accustomed to take a prominent part in Indian and Imperial affairs, who differed widely from me and my friends in his views, whose methods might well be taken as a model for such discussions as these. I should like to add a word expressive of my personal sense of loss on the death of Lord Percy, which has already been widely lamented.

THE LARGER AUDIENCE.

I fully realise that my words, and, indeed, the words of all who follow me, are not only likely, but certain, to be overheard, and that our discussions are awaited thousands of miles away by people of little experience of political government, of growing political ambition, with inherent and acquired characteristics totally different from our own. Our words must be chosen not only for Englishmen accustomed to Parliamentary Debates, but for Englishmen impatient of Parliamentary Debate—not only for English audiences, but for Indian audiences. I know full well that recent changes in the Indian attitude are confined to a very small portion of the population. One must never lose sight of the remarkable fact that nine-tenths, or over 200,000,000 of the vast population of India are still uneducated and illiterate. All talk of unrest, of which one hears so much, is talk of that small fraction of a vast number of the people which education has reached, and within this small fraction are to be found all those divergent forces which are classed together as political unrest. We must remember, however, that the amount of yeast necessary to leaven a loaf is very small; when the majority have no ideas or views the opinion of the educated minority is the most prominent fact in the situation. (*Hear, hear.*) How much earnest thought and hasty judgment centres on the word "unrest." (*Hear, hear.*) Of course there is unrest. It is used by some, adorned by instances of the inevitable friction of complex government, as a proof of the failure of the British occupation. It is used by others, ornamented with details of crime statistics, as evidence of the lack of strength of British rule, of the lack of firmness of a particular political party in this country, and it is, of course, used by that portion of the Press which considers only its own circulation for sensational purposes. (*Cheers.*) May I say how strange it seems to me that a progressive people like the English should be surprised at unrest! We welcome it in Persia, commend it enthusiastically in Turkey, patronise it in China and Japan, and are impatient of it in Egypt and India! Whatever was our object in touching the ancient civilisation of the Indian Empire, whatever was the reason for British occupation, it must be obvious that Eastern civilisation could not be brought into contact with Western without disturbing its serenity, without bringing new ideas into play, without infusing new ingredients, without, in a word, causing unrest. And when we undertook the government of the country, when, further, we deliberately embarked on a policy of educating the peoples on Western lines, we caused the unrest because we wished to colour Indian ideals with Western aspirations.

THE REVOLT AGAINST AUTHORITY.

When we came into India we found that the characteristic of Indian thought was an excessive reverence for authority. The scholar was taught to accept the assurance of his spiritual teacher with unquestioning reverence; the duty of the subject was passive obedience to the rulers; the usages of society were invested with a divine sanction which it was blasphemy to question. To a people so blindly obedient to authority the teaching of European, and particularly of English thought, was a revolution. English literature is saturated with the praise of liberty, and it inculcates the duty of private and independent judgment upon every man. We have always been taught, and we all believe that every man should judge for himself, and that no authority can relieve him of the obligation of deciding for himself the great issues of right and wrong. The Indian mind at first revolted at this doctrine. Then one or two here and there were converted to it. They became eager missionaries of the new creed of private judgment and independence, and the consequence is that a new spirit is abroad wherever English education has spread, which questions all established beliefs and calls for orthodoxy, either political, social, economic, or religious, to produce its credentials. We are not concerned here, except in so far as they are important causes of political unrest, with either religious or social unrest. It is not necessary for me to do more than state the platitude that religious unrest produces among those who have experienced its political results. There can be no departure from religious orthodoxy without its being accompanied by its fierce reaction to orthodoxy. Side by side with the unrest produced directly by English example comes the indirect result of a religious revival. The activities of those who are questioning the teaching they have inherited call into action those who fiercely combat the new religious heterodoxies, abominate the

Western example producing them, emphasise the fundamental and, they say, the unconquerable differences between the East and the West, and demand freedom from alien influences. These two counter forces —the reform movement and the survival that opposes it—involve not only those directly affected, but their parents, relations, and friends, and cause political and social unrest.

The Work of Social Reform.

For an example of social unrest I would call the attention of the House to the social reformers who are devoting their attention to the education of women, the abolition of infant marriage, freedom of travel and sea voyage, and similar social work, with the far-reaching effects on the domestic sphere, and result in questioning the usages which claim divine sanction, and were hardly in olden times distinguishable from religion. Despite ostracism and sometimes boycott, pecuniary loss and moral obloquy, the efforts of the reformers are in a small degree bearing fruit. And just as religious reform produces religious revival, so social reform brings its counter movement. Those forming it resent interference with the old-established usage, disapprove of the reforms achieved and proposed, and hate the teaching which has produced them and those who gave the teaching. And then there is, of course, economic unrest—the necessary concomitant of an advance in the material well-being of the masses, indicative of impatience with the incommodities of life which were once accepted as inevitable, of changes in industrial conditions, of increasing wants and of quickened desires. There is a perceptible advance in the general well-being, but the start is from a very low point. The enlargement of the wants of people accustomed to an extraordinary simple standard of living is bound to manifest itself in ways which are indicative of economic unrest. Viewed broadly, India may be said to be passing from the stage of society in which agricultural and domestic industries of the cottage order have predominated, in which each village has been an isolated community, and each individual attached to a particular spot and hereditary occupation, to the stage of organised over-seas commerce and capitalised industry. As yet the transition is visible only in a few exceptional districts, where factories or coal-mining have taken hold, and in the maritime cities through which the commerce of India to other countries pours. Indirectly, the whole continent is affected; the demand for labour for the industrial centres penetrates to the most secluded villages, raising the local wage rates, and increasing the farmer's wage bill. The demand of foreign countries for the food grains, the oil seeds, the cotton and the jute of India raises local prices, widens the cultivator's market, and changes the crops he grows. The competition of machine-made goods with hand-loom industry impoverishes the village weaver, or converts him into a mill hand and drives him into a town. Of these three movements—the religious movement, the social movement, and the economic movement—each produces its quota of political unrest, and the counter movements of those who abominate the new teaching, resent the alteration of the time-honoured social customs, dislike any departure from orthodox religion, question the teaching that produces it, and also show resentment to those who teach it. All these things together make that curious, differently produced force in India which is known as political unrest.

The Handling of Political Agitation.

It would be very surprising indeed if the religious and social reform movements, such as I have described, together with the opposition to them, the desire for economic trade, the tendency to preserve uneconomic and ancient industries, together with the spread of education and the growth of the Native Press, the fermentation of new ideas, stopped short of the political sphere. Of all forms of liberty England has always shown the most jealous solicitude for political liberty, and I think we can regard political unrest in India as being but the manifestation of a movement of Indian thought which has been inspired, directly or indirectly, by English ideals, to which the English and the Government of India themselves gave the first impetus. It is constantly being nourished by English education given in Government schools and colleges. In so far as this political unrest is confined to pressing the Government to popularise the government of the country, so far as the conditions of India will permit, I do not believe that anybody in this House will quarrel with it. You cannot give to the Indians Western education from carefully chosen and carefully selected teachers, trained either in Europe or in India ; you cannot give to the Indians Western education either in Europe or in India and then turn round and refuse to those whom you have educated the right, the scope, or the opportunity to act and think as you have taught them to do. (*Hear, hear.*) If you do, it seems to me that you must cause another kind of unrest, more dangerous than any other, among those bitterly dissatisfied and disappointed with the results of their education, who use methods which have been taught them in Western countries to vent their disappointment. For this reason, it seems to me, if I may say so, that the condition of India at the moment is one which, handled well, contains the promise of a completer justification of British rule ; handled ill, is bound to lead to chaos. (*Hear, hear.*) English thought may be responsible for the fundamental principle of revolt against authority, but it cannot be responsible for all the changes which that principle has undergone in its adaptation to Oriental environment. It would be absurd to suppose that old beliefs can be unseated and old usages altered without some element of danger. There have been recently in India manifestations of political unrest with which no one can sympathise, and with regard to which difference of opinion is not legitimate. There have been assassinations and conspiracies to murder ; there have been incitements to murder ; there have been attempts to create hatred against certain sections of His Majesty's subjects. If this pernicious unrest were allowed to spread it would result in widespread misery and anarchy—(*Opposition cheers*);

it would produce a state of things in India which would be more inimical to progress than even the most stringent coercion. (*Hear, hear.*) It would spread chaos, from which society would seek refuge in a military dictatorship. For these reasons, if the Government was prevented from doing its duty in preventing this, it seems to me it would be a great step backwards, and a tragedy in history.

A Statement of Policy.

The majority of the Indians themselves, as the House well knows, realise fully the danger, and will exert themselves to suppress those extremists who are jeopardising their position. I do not want to risk any assurance which the conditions no not justify, but I can say that within the last six months there has been a considerable revulsion in our favour. Horror at the assassinations and political outrages, which are wholly repugnant to the true spirit of Hinduism; the strong line taken by the Government and the Rajas in regard to sedition ; the general feeling that political agitation carried on by students and school-masters is doing infinite injury to the rising generation, and attempts that have been made in public and private life to promote more intimate relations between the different races—all these, combined with the liberal policy pursued by the present Government in affording to Indians a wider entry into public life, have had their effect. But I would ask the House to consider what, in the face of these different spirits of unrest arising from the complex and contradictory causes that I have tried to show, should be the root principle of Government in India. The answer is easy to give, if difficult to act up to. True statesmanship, it seems to me, ought to be directed towards separating legitimate from illegitimate unrest. The permanent safeguard must be a systematic government, which realises the elements of good as well as the elements of danger, and which suppresses criminal extravagances with inflexible sternness. His Majesty's Government, acting upon this principle, are determined to arm and to assist the Indian Government in its unflinching war against sedition and illegitimate manifestations of unrest, while it shows an increasingly sympathetic and encouraging attitude towards legitimate aspirations.

THE PRESS LAWS.

I propose, if the House will permit me, to give the latest example of the two branches of policy which I have outlined. The latest example of the first part of the policy is the new Press Act. After full debate in the new Council the measure has become law, and has been in force for some months—I believe already with beneficial effects. Its object may be said to have been to create a responsible instead of an irresponsible Press. In this country public opinion may usually be trusted to produce this effect; but in India, with its differences of race, of creed, and of caste, public opinion in this sense can hardly be said to exist. Therefore something is required in the manner provided by this Act, which I propose to examine in some detail, because I recognise frankly that it is an exceptional measure which the House is justified in demanding should be thoroughly examined, and because I believe that a large amount of the criticism which has been directed against it is due to a misapprehension of its provisions. May I assume that it is common ground that a certain section of the Indian Press has done incalculable mischief during the last two years? It was certainly common ground in the Viceroy's Council when the Bill was under discussion. There was criticism of the remedy proposed by the Government, but nobody questioned the necessity for some remedy or the existence of the disease. I think it would be difficult to exaggerate the dangerous effect of seditious literature on the unformed and impressionable minds of students. I need not labour the point; it will be admitted by all who have a knowledge of Indian affairs, and terrible tragedies have brought it home to us. No one better realises than the Indian parents themselves the gravity of the evil, or more earnestly seek to remedy it. I would ask permission to read to the House a leaflet which has already been disseminated in Bengal :—

Dear Readers,—We have made our appearance at this juncture as the situation is one of extreme importance. Do not be led away by false hopes and temporary conciliations. Let not any conciliatory measure of the Government pacify you and scare you away from your path. Sacrifice white blood unadulterated and pour to your gods on the altar of freedom; the bones of the martyrs are crying for vengeance, and you will be a traitor to your country if you do not adequately respond to the call. Whites, be they men, women or children, murder them indiscriminately, and you will not commit any sin, but simply perform

the highest Dharma. We shall appear again with more details. Adieu !

The leaflet was signed " Editor, " and then follows a postscript : " The Editor will be extremely obliged to the readers if they translate this into all languages, and circulate it broadcast. " That being an example of the sort of thing that is sometimes circulated among schoolboys in village schools, it is absolutely necessary that the Government should seek some weapon with which to try and prevent the dissemination of such nauseous stuff. Of course, the question presents itself, " why not be satisfied with the existing law ? You can punish sedition under the Penal Code and you can prevent sedition under the Criminal Procedure Code. Two years ago you passed a very stringent Press Act, which enabled you under certain circumstances to crush newspapers out of existence." To this the reply must be that, notwithstanding careful trial, the existing law cannot cope with the evil which the new law is designed to meet.

THE FAILURE OF PAST REPRESSION.

The policy of prosecution under the Penal Code has been given a thorough trial during the last three years; its result has been to make martyrs of misguided and insignificant youths ; to advertise sedition, and to enhance the circulation of offending newspapers. Its deterrent effect on the worst class of papers has been negligible. The preventive clause in the Criminal Procedure Code is not much good. It empowers a magistrate to call upon a printer or publisher to furnish security to be of good behaviour. This is easily evaded.

The person bound over has only to cancel his registration as a publisher and to register a dummy publisher and the newspaper goes on all the same. The Act of 1908 has been successful in preventing the open advocacy of murder; but the Act only concerns itself with open incitements to violence. What we have now to deal with as well as that evil are methods which are just as dangerous even if less flagrant—incessant misrepresentation, the imputation to the Government of malevolent motives, incitements to revolution under the guise of religious exhortation, implied justification of assassination by reference to revolutions in other countries. This preaching by innuendo has proved just as mischievous to the Oriental imagination, as any direct incitement to murder which would have come under the Press Act of 1908. In these circumstances the Government determined to make an effort to create a sense of responsibility and to prevent rather than to punish. Let us see what the Act does. Instead of concerning itself with the individual, like the clause of the Criminal Procedure Code referred to above, it transfers the security to the newspaper or the Press itself. No security is exacted from any registered newspaper which was existing when the Act was passed, unless it is guilty of publishing seditious matter. All new publications alike, so that it does not involve any invidious distinction, furnish security varying from £33 to £133, unless the magistrate thinks fit to grant an exemption, owing to the fact that, in his opinion, the funds of the newspaper are not sufficient to find the money necessary. In the event of a newspaper which has given security against the publication of seditious matter, publishing seditious matter, the security and all the copies of the offending issue may be declared forfeit, and a new and larger security demanded. On a subsequent offence, subject to appeal to the High Court, the Press itself, as well as the security, is forfeit.

THE NEW ACT DEFENDED.

Such are the main provisions of the Act. I would submit to the House that this Act really provides a far more humane procedure than the procedure by prosecution, which some members seem to prefer. Instead of putting the offender to the ignominy of prosecution and imprisonment, he is, on the first offence, merely warned in a friendly manner. If he proceeds in his infringement of the law he does so with his eyes open. Even then he is only asked for a modest security, upon which he will be fined interest by the Government. Even after a further offence, if his security is forfeited, he has only to furnish a further security in order to have a further chance of doing well. Nobody can represent this as drastic ! It certainly would not prevent anarchy of which the Press is not the cause, but only the manifestation. We only hope that by this means we shall be able to check the contamination, by deliberate misrepresentation and inflammatory doctrine, of those who might otherwise be useful members of the community. The Press remains free to publish what it likes. Honest papers will not be affected by it. Those papers which have anything to fear from it have so abused the full measure of freedom, previously granted, that the continuation of their unfettered freedom will become impossible. The fear that the smaller concerns may be extinguished by their inability to find security has been met by the orders issued by the Government of India that in these cases the requirement should be waived, and no security should be taken. Personally, I am not impressed by the picture some have drawn of the nervous editor, not knowing whether he may have incurred the displeasure of a crouching Government. The Act enumerates very definitely the sort of writing that constitutes an offence, and it expressly exempts from its purview the honest expression of disapproval of the Government action. May I quote to the House a remark of Sir Fitz James Stephen, which was quoted in the debate in the Viceroy's Council? It runs :—" I do not believe that any man who sincerely wished not to excite disaffection ever wrote anything which any other honest man believed to be intended to excite disaffection." I believe there is nobody in this House who will not in his heart of hearts agree with that remark. I can only say that the Government of India have always kept prominently before them the necessity of avoiding, at all costs, what might impair the right, which is not less valuable to the Government itself, of frank and henest criticism of Government measures and action. They have issued Administrative Orders with a view of securing uniformity of obligations, and with a view of avoiding, if possible, hardships. In the circular in which they issue instructions to refrain from demanding security in the case of papers whose resources cannot supply it, it is also stated, or laid down, that existing newspapers should be warned before demanding security, and that the security should be fixed at the minimum that may reasonably be expected to enforce obedience to the law. I should like to quote one paragraph of the recent Order, because I do not think you can find better evidence of the determination of the Government not to use this Act in any harsh or oppressive way :—

> It is the earnest wish of the Governor-General in Council that the Act should be administered with careful discrimination between those newspapers and Presses which are generally well conducted and those which transgress from a deliberate intention to excite disaffection. No order of forfeiture should be passed without previous consultation with the Law Officers, and in coming to a decision due weight should be given to other articles published by the offending journal which indicate the nature and tendency of its writings.

THE APPROVAL OF INDIAN OPINION.

I am now going to ask the House's permission to quote an Indian paper on the way in which the Act is being administered. The editor of certain vernacular papers had been warned by the Deputy Commissioner of Lahore against continuing to publish matter which might excite disaffection and cause a disturbance of the peace between the Hindu and Mahomedan populations. The *Tribune*, a daily paper edited in English by an Indian gentleman, commented as follows :—

> Where the authorities think it necessary to move, it is certainly wise and far-sighted to put in friendly counsel before taking action under the law. The fact that the Deputy Commissioner of

Lahore has demanded an undertaking in the first instance, is a clear and welcome indication that the authorities have no desire to work the law in a harsh or rigorous manner.

That is a welcome tribute with which I trust the House will agree. Let no one imagine that this Act has been thrust upon an unwilling India. If there is anyone who thinks that, I would beg him to study an account of the debate in the Viceroy's Council, which has been issued as a White Paper, and note the way in which speaker after speaker arose and acknowledged the lamentable necessity for such action. I believe that the Act, taken in conjunction with the Seditious Meetings Act, will complete the armour necessary, so far as one can foresee, for the repression of the campaign of calumny and of sedition. It will, at any rate, prevent that horrible form of sedition-mongering which consists in disseminating cruel mis-statements among young boys at school.

WHAT IS "SEDITION?"

May I ask the House to consider for one moment how difficult it is by quoting words to decide what is and what is not seditious. Let me give an example. It is constantly said by seditious people that the English have caused malaria. There are apologists who say—and on one occasion I heard my hon. friend Mr. Ramsay MacDonald adopt this attitude—"But this is an interesting scientific fact. Canals are the breeding places of anopheles. The English build canals. It is a good wind that blows nobody ill; they, therefore, produce malaria. This statement, which is seditious in your opinion, is merely an attempt from the man who utters it to disseminate an interesting scientific result incontrovertible and remarkable." How harmless is the sentiment if this were all! But what sophistry all this is! When it is uttered with the deliberate attempt to make the ignorant believe that the British Government have introduced malaria deliberately, by building canals and even railroads to diminish the troublesome population, it ceases to be a scientific fact; it becomes a dangerous, libellous, and malignant calumny.

THE POLICE.

I will take again, as another example, the subject of the Indian police, and I will say, as I have so often said in the House, that no one can deny the imperfections of this force. But you cannot produce a complete reform of a faulty force in a year, a decade, or even fifty years. The improvement has been the most earnest attempt of the British Government—yes, and of the Indian people—during the last sixty years, during which the police have formed the subject of a series of Commissions of Enquiry, the last of which was appointed in 1902 by Lord Curzon. It recommended comprehensive reforms in all branches of the service, the annual cost of which was estimated at over £1,000,000 sterling. Its findings were adopted by Government Resolution, and effect has already been given to most of the proposals, and the work of reorganisation is still in progress. Let us consider for one moment the force with which the Report deals. The Civil Police in

British India number 176,000 men, who have to deal with a population of nearly 232,000,000, scattered over 1,000,000 square miles. Let me give a typical district. In a district of Bengal there is a European Superintendent of Police, with the assistance of an Indian Deputy Superintendent, who has to control nine Inspectors, seventy-nine Sub-Inspectors, eighty-three head constables, and 778 constables. The area of the district is 5,186 square miles, the population is nearly 3,000,000, there are twenty-six police stations and twenty-one outposts, some of them very difficult of access, and in 1908 4,170 cases of serious crime to investigate. These statistics illustrate, far more than any words of mine, the difficulties under which the police work is done in India ; and when one reflects that educated Indians regard police duties with abhorrence, that to work for a "confession," as it is euphemistically termed, has been inherited from pre-British times as the best mode of procedure in a criminal trial, that little help is obtained from the people in bringing criminals to book, some faint idea of the difficulties will be realised. Having regard to all these circumstances, it is not surprising that isolated instances of abuse may sometimes be found. But by improving the police, by the vigorous prosecution of malefactors, by the expenditure of money, reorganisation must be gradually effected, and is going on with a determination which no honest man can doubt. Let me ask the House to compare some extracts which I have taken from the Commission on Torture in Madras in 1885 with the Report of the Curzon Commission of

1902. The Commission of 1855 quotes and endorses the words of an official witness :—

> The so-called police of the Mofussil district is little better than a pollution. It is a terror to well-disposed and peaceable people, none whatever to thieves and rogues, and if it were abolished *in toto*, property would not be a whit less secure.

The Commission of 1902 says :—

> It is significant that a proposal to remove a police station from any neighbourhood is opposed by the people. They know that, on the whole, the police are for their protection.

The Commission on Torture in Madras in 1855 spoke of " the universal and systematic practice of personal violence," and said " it was still of enormous proportions, and imperatively calling for an immediate and effectual remedy." The Commission of 1902 wrote :—" Deliberate torture of suspected persons and other most flagrant abuses occur occasionally, but they are now rare." Again, I say, a marked improvement has been seen. Nevertheless, so keenly and rightly sensitive are the English people about reform in the police force that defects are quickly pointed out. To point out defects in the police force, if it is considered that they still require pointing out, and to suggest new remedies and palliatives which have not yet been discovered, if there be such, is useful work, demanding the sympathy of all men, but to collect instances of abuse, many unproved, some proved to be false, to take quotations from their context and garble them, to represent as findings of a Commission what is merely report of popular opinion, to quote a statement of an interested party as being "an account of what happened in the very words of the official resolution," to say that the

Indian Government has never prohibited torture, when it is punishable with seven years' penal servitude, to ignore any Government action to stop these abuses, and to represent the Government as ignorant or supine, callous, and tolerant of bad practices, I say, whether this be the work of a Hindu agitator or an ex-Member of Parliament, it is seditious, dangerous, and ought to be stopped.

Indian Students in England.

Turning now from these unpleasant subjects, I want to say that it is undoubtedly true that, hand in hand with any repressive measures designed to deal with manifestations or symptoms, the root causes must be dealt with too, and chief among these we must look for an improvement in the matter of education. The worst danger which threatens India is the lawlessness or disregard of authority which exists amongst students or schoolmasters. Now, I have described the political difficulties which exist to-day as largely the consequence of Western education. If there is a solution it is surely to be sought in some reconsideration of the system which caused it, both in India and England, even at the cost of other economies or new taxation and large expenditure from the revenues of India. Let me first deal with the position of the Indians who come to England for purposes of study. The number now in England cannot be less than 1,000; they are far removed from the influence of their parents and guardians; they often arrive wholly friendless and ignorant of Western customs. Their position is one of great difficulty and considerable danger, and they afford a problem urgently demanding solution. Last year my predecessor outlined the means by which we hoped to deal with the question, and the House will expect to hear what progress has been made. These measures are under three heads, namely: (1) The appointment of Educational Adviser to Indian students at the India Office ; (2) the appointment of an Advisory Committee; (3) the provision of a house for the National Indian Association and the Northbrook Society for the purpose of a joint clubhouse. The educational adviser, Mr. T. W. Arnold, was appointed in April, 1909. His duties are multifarious. He must be a store of information upon educational matters of every kind. He must advise students as to their residence if they do not become members of a residential university or college. He is a standing referee for educational institutions as to the qualifications of Indian applicants for admission. A doubt was entertained whether Indian students would be willing to avail themselves of the assistance of an official agency situated at the India Office. This doubt has been resolved in a most satisfactory manner. The students come in very large numbers, and the immediate problem is to cope with the very large amount of work with which the educational adviser has to deal. In the last twelve months his personal interviews with Indian students have numbered upwards of 1,300. In addition to the work which was originally assigned to him, he has been entrusted by parents in India with the guardianship of their sons in no less than seventy cases. This entails closer supervision than is attempted in ordinary cases, and involves, among other duties, the care of their money. The Advisory Committee, appointed in May, 1909, consists of Lord Ampthill as Chairman, six Indian gentlemen of standing, resident in this country, and two English members of the India Office, with correspondents in the various provinces in India. This Committee makes recommendations to the Secretary of State upon all questions referred to them regarding Indian students and holds receptions from time to time in the India Office of students recommended to them by the University Committees in India. The Committee, and especially the Chairman, have thrown themselves with ardour into their work, and have proved very useful to the Secretary of State. The Secretary of State has leased a house (No. 21) in Cromwell Road, facing the South Kensington Museum, to which the Northbrook Society and the National Indian Association will shortly be transferred. The educational officer will also have his office in this building. Bedrooms will be reserved for the use of Indian students upon their first arrival in this country. Arragements have been made for meeting students on their first arrival, and, instead of wandering about as at present in search of lodgings, they will be welcomed at the house in Cromwell Road, and given a bed and meals at once. Subsequently they will be given information about the many details which a stranger wants to know on arrival, and advice as to their studies, and they will be furnished, it is hoped, with introductions to English friends and see in fact that they are not friendless in London. The

Northbrook Society will run a social club in the rooms assigned to it. Both the societies give receptions at regular intervals, to which Indian and English ladies and gentlemen are invited, and where opportunities of making acquaintance are frequent. The house will be opened, it is hoped, in August, and will be available for students who come to this country at the beginning of the next academic year. A good start has been made on the right lines. The Secretary of State intends to proceed vigorously on these lines and, as time goes on and opportunity offers, to enlarge the scope of organised effort. Let me add one word, addressed not so much to those within these walls as to such audience as I may have outside them. Our efforts cannot bear real fruit unless we have the co-operation of those among whom the lives of Indian students are thrown. Many a friendless, sensitive lad looks back, I fear, on the period that he spent in England as one long spell of loneliness and unhappiness. Nothing that the India Office can do will remedy that. The remedy lies in the endeavours of those among whom their lives are spent to overcome insular reticence and prejudices, and to extend a real welcome which, if it is given in the spirit of true and frank comradeship, and not in patronising tolerance, will meet with warm-hearted reciprocation and will bear fruit of which the giver did not dream.

A MINISTER FOR EDUCATION.

Turning now to India, we must make the teaching more practical, encourage and extend technical instruction, for which there is a great demand, supervise and improve the hostels. The educational system now in existence has undoubtedly been successful in purifying the judicial service. It is capable of great extension in improving the moral tone of the country, spreading discipline and disseminating useful knowledge by means of well-paid and contented teachers. Now education is left to the Member in charge of the Home Department. He is over-burdened with work as it is, and his duties will be multiplied by the enlargement of the Council. Adequate consideration of educational questions touching the foundations of life in the many communities of India cannot be reasonably expected from a Department placed in such circumstances as these. A responsible Minister for Education has been an indispensable Member of a British Cabinet for some time, and there is no reason why the same necessity should not be just as strong in what I may call the Cabinet of the Government of India. Steps are needed to secure a coherent policy towards education, and to control the expenditure of the money allotted for this purpose. We have, therefore, decided to revive the sixth membership of the Council, dormant since the abolition of the Military Supply Department, and to appoint a member of Council for education. The head of an Education Department will be all the more likely to perform his work in a broad and comprehensive spirit if he is brought into living contact with the currents of Indian affairs, and this is most effectively secured by knowledge of the general deliberations on public business. It is no object of ours to take a step towards centralisation, but I would remind the House that the Decentralisation Commission have given their reasons for thinking that the general control of educational policy is within the legitimate sphere of the Government of India, and does not hamper development in accordance with local needs and conditions. I may say that such a man, it is confidently hoped and believed, has been found, and His Majesty has approved the selection of Mr. Butler—a man who has been occupying up till now the position of Foreign Secretary to the Government of India. He will, I am sure, become the head of a Department which will ensure to India one of its greatest needs—a better and co-ordinated system of education.

THE APPOINTMENT OF MR. CLARK.

Whilst I am on the subject of the Viceroy's Council, I desire to put an end to public anxiety by announcing that Mr. W. H. Clark, of the Treasury and the Board of Trade, has been appointed, and His Majesty has approved his appointment, as Member for Commerce and Industry. No one who knows his high attainments and conspicuous achievements in this country and in the East, and certainly no one among his friends, of whom I am glad to think he has many in this House, will question that he brings to a difficult and important task great qualifications which will be invaluable to the Government of India.

THE INDIAN COUNCILS ACT.

I pass now to deal with the other branch of the policy I have outlined, to give some account of the latest contribution in the direction of meeting legitimate aspirations by saying something of the Indian Councils Act the working of which has done much to improve the condition of affairs in India during the last six months. I think I may claim for the Indian Councils Act, the working of which has done much, as I have said, to improve the condition of affairs in India during the last six months, that it has been a great success. The House will expect me to make a few remarks, necessarily brief, on its working. It provided, it will be remembered, for a large increase in the number of the various Legislative Councils in India, introduced a true system of election, making its members more widely representative, and greatly widened their deliberative functions. At the same time, though they did not form part of the Act, it was decided to abolish for the future, in all Councils, save that of the Governor-General, the practice of maintaining a majority of official members. The Act also provided for the enlargement of the Executive Councils of the Governors of Madras and Bombay, and the establishment of an Executive Council to assist the Lieutenant-Governor of Bengal. Our proposals were subjected to much criticism, both here and in another place, and, although we met with no actual opposition in the Division Lobby—except on one point, which was eventually settled by compromise—the right hon. gentleman, the Leader of the Opposition deliberately disclaimed on behalf of his party any responsibility for the consequences that were likely to follow the passing of the Act. We are quite content to accept sole responsibility for the consequences, which so far —though it is early yet to speak—not only falsify the gloomy anticipations expressed in some quarters, but I might almost say actually surpass our expectations. The regulations that were necessary before the Act could come into operation were published on November 15 last. No time was lost in holding the elections, and the new Councils were able to meet early in the present year. Since then there has been no inconsiderable amount of legislation. In every Council a budget has been discussed and passed, and full use has been made of the newly-granted right to move resolutions on matters of public importance. So, although the time is short, the material for forming a judgment on the working of the Act is not wholly inadequate. There are two salient points in which particularly the fears of our more conservative critics have been falsfied. The one is the admirable dignity and sense of responsibility displayed by the non-official members; the other is the conspicuous and gratifying success with which the official members, after the manner of old Parliamentary hands, have explained and defended their policy in debate. Let me take one illustration—an excellent illustration, for it is drawn from a case in which the circumstances were such as to have strained the system to breaking point if it had possessed the defects that some saw in it. About a year ago, before the revised Councils had come into existence, a Bill to amend the Calcutta Police Act was introduced into the Bengal Council. It was largely uncontroversial, but certain of its provisions which in the opinion of the Government were needed for the efficient discharge by the police of the duty of maintaining order, excited the liveliest disapproval from a certain class of Indian politicians, and a certain section of the Indian Press ; disapproval which found an echo in this country and within these walls. Even after its stringency had been modified in certain respects this opposition continued and the Lieutenant-Governor wisely decided not to pass the measure at once, but to reserve its final stages for the reformed Legislative Council.

THE "SPIRIT OF INDEPENDENCE."

Now, of all the revised Councils, Bengal has the largest un-official majority, and, as everyone knows, what I may call, for want of a better term, the "spirit of independence" is more active in Bengal than anywhere else. We had therefore the interesting experiment of a Bill that had excited vehement protests as an encroachment on liberty being considered by a Council with a large un-official majority drawn from, politically, the most progressive province of India. What happened ? The Bill became law after a reasonable and temperate debate. Only one amendment was put to the vote, on a point which must, therefore, presumably be considered the most contentious in the Bill, namely, the proposal to empower the Commissioner of Police to prohibit processions if likely to cause a breach of the peace. The amendment was lost by thirty-six votes to five, nineteen non-officials voting with the Government.

I have dwelt upon this example because in it were present in a peculiar degree all the elements of danger that our critics apprehended and because a single actual instance is more illuminating than a profusion of generalities. Incidentally, I may observe how much stronger is the position of a Government when they rely on legislation passed in such a way than when their legislation bears the quasi-executive stamp of an official majority. As in legislation, so in non-legislative discussions the debates have, on the whole, been notable for moderation and reason. Such debates, especially the preliminary debates on the financial statement, have an educational value that must not be overlooked in that they bring home to non-official members the real difficulties of administration. Every question has been fully discussed ; all opinions have been represented, and the Government has had ample opportunity for stating its views, explaining its motives, and bringing out the difficulties of a particular line of action. And in these discussions there has been no sharp line of cleavage between officials and non-officials ; the old idea that non-officials must necessarily be in opposition seems to have disappeared. I would commend many of these debates—as, for instance, the debate on primary education in the Governor-General's Council on March 18—to the careful attention of students of Indian matters. The House is aware that in fulfilment of the other part of the Act of 1909—the part relating to Executive Councils—we have appointed Indian gentlemen to the Executive Councils of the Governors of Madras and Bombay. We have also sanctioned proposals for the establishment of an Executive Council for the Lieutenant-Governor of Bengal ; I hope an announcement will be made on this subject at a very early date. In effect, the Councils Act has resulted in producing excellent debates, creating opportunities for the ventilation of grievances and of public views, creating public opinion, permitting the Governors to explain themselves, giving to those interested in politics a better and a more productive field for their persuasive powers than the rather more sterile debates in Congress.

Disaffection and Reform.

I have now described not only the latest measure for dealing with disorder, the measure to create a responsible Press, but also the latest measure for an attempt to popularise the Councils Act. The material which I have now laid before the House will give the least imaginative member ample food for thought and profitable thought on the most difficult problems which the science of Government has ever offered to students. I am fully conscious of the impossibility of presenting a true picture, and of the audacity that I have been guilty of in endeavouring to analyse nations and attempting to assign causes for their emotions. Let me frankly tell the House that I could never have found the courage to make these attempts or to occupy the attention of those who have survived so long, did I not find strength, courage, and inspiration in the supreme importance, overwhelming interest and great complexities of my subject. The dangers that beset the future of India are the sources of its possibilities. They can only be avoided by acknowledging and fostering the germs of progress, and they can only be really aided to a healthy growth by war upon the internal evils in which they are embedded. Let me only point out frankly some of the dangers that I think I see first here in this House. Do not, on the one hand, oppose all agitation for reform because you are led astray to confuse it with seditious agitation. Do not use your murderer as an excuse for your conservatism. And I use that term in no party sense. The hon. member behind me (Sir J. D. Rees) does not sit on the benches opposite—but none the less he is a Conservative. (*Loud laughter.*) You cannot foster sedition more surely than by driving to it, or confusing with its advocates those who look to you with confidence for sympathy with their legitimate aspirations. You see clearly the seditious man and his seditious writings, and you are led to say: "This is Indian unrest; this House can have no sympathy with it. Let us put it from us, let us uproot it vehemently." But when you put it from you, do not put away with it the man who is deserving of your respect and sympathy. And aided by this, and because of this, the other danger comes into being. Do not fear that you are lacking in sympathy with the true reformer because you refuse sympathy to the anarchist. Of course, nobody in this House really sympathises with anarchy. But because you are afraid that some reformer may be called an anarchist, because you fear that you will be accused of refusing to assist those who are animated by some democratic ideals similar to your own, you are led sometimes to appear to throw a protecting cloak over the malefactor in order to proclaim aloud your sympathy with the reformer. To resist the efforts made to cope with the anarchist because you will not trust the Government of India to differentiate between the anarchist and the reformer; these divergent, contradictory, and equally dangerous tendencies would, either of them, if they prevailed, subvert order and dissipate the promise to be found in Indian affairs at the moment; and it is because of their existence that all parties in the House should help the Government in segregating violence and incitement to violence which mask, hinder, and might render impotent real efforts for reform. Remember, too, that every reform is irrevocable in India. Each reform opens out new activities, new spheres of thought, new views of life to those whom it affects. Each reform demands eventually, as its corollary, new and further reforms. These reflections ought to lead to ready acquiescence, on the one hand, in reforms that are justly demanded, tempered by the utmost caution, on the other hand, in taking steps irrevocable in themselves and inevitably leading to further steps.

THE ADMINISTRATIVE MACHINE.

What of those at the other end of the machine? I trust implicitly, from what I have seen of the public-spirited men who administer India on the spot, that they are determined to meet the changing spirit of the time generously and sympathetically. Paper reforms are useless if given grudgingly and made the excuse for tightened reins in administrative action—punitive measures become as dangerous as the evils they are to cure if used indiscriminately for repression and not for punishment, to drive honest men to despair instead of sinners to repentance. But I am positive—and this House will, I hope, find evidence of this in the study of Indian affairs on all hands—that lessons and examples of the past and the high purpose and loyalty which are the cherished possessions of the Service I am discussing, ensure the avoidance of such obvious dangers as these. The ranks of the Civil Service are, however, recruited yearly from our universities, and to those who are going to India to the responsible tasks they have chosen I am bold enough to say, mainly because I am fresh from the university and know vividly at what I am hinting, banish as quickly as you can the intolerance of boys and the prejudice of undergraduates, imbibe the traditions of the great Service you are joining, adapt them to modern demands, and go to administer a country in virtue and by the power of the sympathy you can implant in its people. Remember that the best intentions of the Government may be frustrated by the most junior members of the Service, called upon, as they are, immediately to assume great responsibilities. I can conceive no more important career than the Indian Civil Service, and I would urge that it should be the object of all those who enter it to permit not even the most unfriendly examination to detect any deterioration in the Service. This is a suitable moment for taking so comprehensive a survey as I have wearied the House with this afternoon.

THE VICEROY.

Lord Minto, after a difficult reign, is returning to England, and I believe will receive, when he returns to this country, the gratitude which he has so richly earned from those upon whom the ultimate responsibility for Indian Government rests. The relations of a Viceroy to the Secretary of State in Council are intimate and responsible. The Act of Parliament says: "That the Secretary of State in Council shall superintend, direct and control all acts, operations and concerns which in any way relate to or concern the Government or revenues of India, and all grants of salaries, gratuities and allowances, and all other payments and charges whatever out of or on the revenues of India." It will be seen how wide, how far-reaching, and how complete these powers are. The Secretary of State is separated from this task by the sea, hampered by the delays of communication, checkmated by the lapse of time. The cable and the steamer alone render them possible, and for a successful administration of India the most liberal-minded, hard-working Secretary of State is helpless without a loyal, conscientious and statesmanlike Viceroy.

A FIVE YEAR'S RECORD.

Lord Morley and his Council, working through the agency of Lord Minto, have accomplished much. Taxation has been lightened to the extent of millions of pounds ; famine has been fought and frontiers have been protected with unparalleled success and speed. Factory conditions, general health, education, the efficiency of the police, have all been improved ; the pay of the Native Army has been increased. Our relations with Native States have been improved and were never better. The rigidity of the State machine has been softened, while liberal measures of reform have opened to the educated classes of the Indian community a wider field for participation in the government of the country. This is a great record for five years, and contains many abiding results of a conspicuously successful administration of Indian affairs. I believe that men of all parties will be grateful that Lord Morley remains to carry out the policy he has initiated, and the new Viceroy, Sir Charles Hardinge, goes to India amid the almost universal welcome of those who recognise his high attainments and great qualifications. I cannot do better than close by addressing to him, with all respect, the words that were addressed to his grandfather on a similar occasion by Sir Robert Peel, because I believe they embody now as short as it is possible to put them the essential needs of the continued success of English government in India. The Prime Minister wrote, in 1844:—

If you can keep peace, reduce expenses, extend commerce, and strengthen our hold on India by confidence in our justice and kindness and wisdom, you will be received here on your return with acclaims a thousand times louder, and a welcome infinitely more cordial, than if you had a dozen victories to boast of.

THE INDIAN BUDGET, 1911.

On the motion to go into Committee of Ways and Means on the East India Revenue Accounts, Mr. Montagu made his annual statement in the House of Commons on July 26.

There is a regrettable custom which, if not unbroken and unbreakable, is at any rate nearly always respected—that the representative of the India Office should thrust himself and his department only once a year upon the attention of this House. And yet I am conscious that, this year the House has been asked to listen to me twice in one week, and this at a time when the notice and excitement of party strife is at its height, and when ominous clouds are hanging low over Europe. But I make no apology, for India is, and India will remain, among the first of England's responsibilities, among the first of England's glories. Her history and her future call for as much attention as we can give, and indeed far more than we can give to consider her problems. I have nothing personal to say save that I fear I have increased my own difficulties by the eagerness with which—like an explorer in a new country—I travelled so wide a field last year. I do not want, for obvious reasons, to repeat what I said then and I hope that, in turning my attention to other subjects, I shall not be accused of avoiding anything of difficulty. Before I turn to business, may I pay the customary tribute—customary and sincere—to those who have taken part in this debate in former years and who, since last year, have passed away ? I allude to two of my predecessors. Mr. Johns Ellis was a respected Parliamentary veteran, who showed his interest in Indian affairs by devoting to my office the last years of his Parliamentary activity, almost the last years of his life. Mr. Buchanan, whose share in the passage of the Indian Councils Bill through this House will, I hope, never be forgotten by India, won by his breadth of view, courtesy, and gentleness the respect and affection of all parties in the House, at a time when Indian affairs were more controversial than at present.

POPULATION.

Last year, it will be remembered, I gave the House some figures—always poor things by which to try to picture a country to show the numbers of the peoples with which we had to deal. I can give them more accurately this year, because in India, as in this country, a Census was taken last spring. It extended to all the Provinces and Feudatory States forming the Indian Empire—from the Shan States on the borders of Yunnan in the east to the desert of Baluchistan in the west ; from the snows of the Himalaya in the extreme north to Cape Comorin in the tropics. It embraced an area of one and three-fourth millions of square miles. With nine days of the enumeration the Government of India were able to announce the provincial figures of the Provinces and Feudatory States and principal towns. The corresponding provisional figures in this country were not announced for seven weeks. This is a remarkable instance of most careful preliminary organisation and attention to the minutest details. It would not have been possible, without the willing co-operation of many voluntary workers belonging to all classes of society. Census taking in India is not without its own peculiar difficulties. I am told, for instance, that on one occasion a certain tribe in Central India became firmly persuaded that the enumeration was preliminary to their being sold as slaves, and serious rioting or failure was threatened. The official in charge of the Census operations, being a man of resource, realised that some other hypothesis was required to account for the enumeration. He sought out one of the headmen and informed him that the tribe was quite under a misapprehension ; that the real object of the enumeration was to decide a bet that had been made after supper between Queen Victoria and the Czar of Russia as to who had the greater number of subjects. Not only the Queen's reputation, but also her fortune, was at stake. That tribe was enumerated to a man ! (*laughter*). The total population of India is returned at 315 millions, against 294 millions in 1901. But part of the increase (1,731,000) is due to the inclusion of new areas. Allowing for this, the net increase in the ten years comes to 6·4 per cent. The rate of increase shown by the recent Census in the United Kingdom was 9·06 per cent. Of the total population of 315 millions, 244 millions are included in British India and 71 millions in Native States.

With these figures, let me now turn to the real or ostensible purpose of my speech—the description of the Budget—the finances of India. It is here that I propose to compress my subjects as much as I can. Full information has already been given in the two Blue-books circulated to hon. members. It may be that some, at any rate, among us have looked at them, and it is certain that anybody who wants to can do so: so I propose to confine myself to a recapitulation of a few of the important facts and a brief explanation of certain features.

THE FINANCIAL SURPLUS.

In March, 1910, the Government of India budgeted for a surplus of £376,000. At the end of the year they found an improvement of £5,448,400, but of this improvement £402,000 went automatically to Provincial Governments. Thus the amount by which, the position of the Government of India was better than had been anticipated in March, 1910, was £5,046,400. Half this excess may, for the moment, be disregarded, because it arose from an exceptional and transient cause—the sensationally high price of opium. Apart from this, there was a saving of £811,600 on expenditure, and an increase of £1,912,900 in the yield of heads of revenue other than opium. On the side of economy the most important feature was a saving of £358,000 in military expenditure, partly due to a decline in prices. The improvement of £1,912,900 in the yield of heads of revenue other than opium was mainly the result of increased net receipts from customs, and commercial undertakings such as railways and canals; £494,300 occurs under customs. I will only mention two items—silver, which showed an increase of £450,000, and tobacco, which showed a decrease of £225,467. When the former duty was being increased last year, a cautious estimate was naturally framed of its probable yield, since it was necessary to allow for the possibility of some dislocation of trade consequent on the increase. But, as a matter of fact, the importation in silver in 1910-11 showed only a very small falling off from the very high level of the preceding year, and the revenue gained accordingly. It may be added that the fear expressed during the discussions in 1910 that the increased duty might depress the price of silver outside India and thus cause some disturbance of international trade has not been realised. The London price of silver just before the increase of the Indian duty was 23 $\frac{7}{16}$ *d.* per ounce; the present price is 24 $\frac{3}{8}$*d.* The effect of the increased duties imposed on tobacco last year has not been so satisfactory. The duties were fixed at the rates that were thought likely to be most productive, and the Government of India hoped that they would bring in £420,000. They effected the trade to a much greater extent than was anticipated; in fact, imports during the year showed a reduction of 75 per cent. in quantity and nearly 50 per cent. in value. Railways accounted for £1,272,000 of the surplus; irrigation £91,000, and telegraphs £104,000. The improvement in the profit of railways is the result of the increase in the gross traffic receipt—£674,500—and the decrease of working expenses, interest charges, and miscellaneous charges by £597,700. The shareholders, who are junior partners with the Government in some of the most important lines of railways, have benefited considerably by the improved traffic and cheaper working. The guaranteed companies received as surplus profits, or net earnings, over £100,000 more than in the preceding year. In the period from 1st June, 1910, to 1st June, 1911, although Consols fell from 82½ to 81½, the general trend of the prices of the stock of the chief Indian Railway Companies was upward, sometimes as much as 6½ points, as in the Bengal and North-Western and the Southern Punjab Railways.

IMPORTS AND EXPORTS.

It will thus be seen that the better financial position of the Government is not the outcome of the increased burdens on the people, but the indirect result of favourable conditions by which the general population benefits much more directly and in much fuller measure than the Government. The Government of India is not merely a Government. It is a vast commercial undertaking, sharing directly in the prosperity of its subjects, and directing many of their most profitable enterprises. How it came about that England—so distrustful of national or even municipal commercial enterprises—at a time when I suppose it was even more distrustful than it is now, gave to those who administered for it in India such wide commercial opportunities is a matter for speculation ; but not only in railways and in canals, but even in agriculture—the chief industry of India—the Government is a large and active partner. It is this situation which makes budgeting in India so difficult—the impossibility of predicting the conditions which may lead to large surpluses or great deficits. Empires may rise or fall, but the weather—here little more than a topic of banal conversation—is of paramount importance to the peoples and the Government of India. Of course the world's harvest is at the root of world trade, but in India failure of the harvest brings misery to millions, danger and difficulty to an overwhelming proportion of the population in her Provinces, and deficits to her Government. Success of the harvest brings overflowing coffers to the Government and prosperity to the people. Last year I was able to tell the House that, after two years of severe drought, the abundant rains of 1909 had re-established the agricultural prosperity of India. The crops of 1909-10 were heavy, the prices satisfactory, and the export trade generally brisk, I am thankful to be able to say to-day that there has been no check to this prosperity. The monsoon rains of 1910 were sufficient, and the harvests reaped at the end of the year and in the recent spring have been normal or above normal. The prediction that I made last year of expanding trade has also been fulfilled. The exports of Indian merchandise in 1908-09 were £100,000,000 ; in 1909-10 £123,000,000 ; and 1910-11 £137,000,000. (*Cheers*). A rise of 37 per cent. in the three years is a notable event, and imports of merchandise have increased too, though to a much less extent.

Thus, then, it is to this general prosperity of harvest and of trade that India owes its surplus. I turn now to the extraordinary improvement in the actual receipt from opium as compared with the Budget estimates. It is hardly necessary for me to assure the House that this is not the result of any deviation from the arrangements made with China in 1907. It is, on the contrary, the result of strict adherence to that Agreement ; for the restriction of supply, consequent upon the steady progress of the reduction of exports, has raised prices to an unexampled level. In 1908-09 the average price of a chest of opium sold in Calcutta for export was £92 ; in 1909-10 it was £107 ; and in 1910-11 it was £195. The consequence of this extraordinary rise was to give the Government of India last year £2,723,000 revenue from opium beyond what they expected, and this, added to the surplus with which I dealt just now, gave the total surplus of about £5,500,000.

The Disposal of the Surplus.

The uses to which this surplus were put are fully explained in the Blue-books. It will be seen that a million pounds has been granted to Local Governments for expenditure on projects of permanent value for the development of education and sanitation—two crying needs of India, about which I shall have more to say later. Of this amount £601,200 will be distributed between technical and industrial institutions, primary and secondary schools and colleges, hostels, girls' schools and European schools, and about £400,000 will be used for drainage and waterworks in towns. About £1,000,000 is granted for expenditure in the promotion of various administrative or municipal schemes; for instance, the City of Bombay Improvement Trust gets £333,300, Eastern Bengal and Assam, £183,600 for the re-organisation of the subordinate police; £1,000,000 has been retained by the Government of India as an addition to its working balance, and £2,000,000 has been set aside to be used towards the discharge of floating debt. Hon. members who read the report of the discussion on the Budget in the Viceroy's Legislative Council will find that the disposal of the surplus was received with general satisfaction. There was not, indeed, a tame unanimity of approval, because there is some feeling among the representatives of Indian opinion against the practice of devoting much money to the discharge of debt. In this House the opposite view is likely to be held, and the Government may perhaps be thought to have infringed the strictest canons of finance in not using the whole realised surplus for the discharge of debts; but, inasmuch as the non-productive debt amounted on 31st March 1911, to only £46,000,000, as against £71,000,000 ten years previously, so that, if the same rate of reduction were to continue the non-productive debt would be extinguished in about 18 years, the Government of India may claim to have displayed on the whole a combination of prudence and liberality in dealing with the surplus that good fortune placed at its disposal. It has intrenched its own financial position, discharged onerous liabilities, and has spent considerable sums on very deserving objects.

BUDGET PROSPECTS.

I must turn now for a moment to the Budget estimate for 1911-12. Our estimates have been based on the expectation that harvests and trade will be good and a surplus of £819,200 is anticipated. I trust that this expectation will be fulfilled but, as the prospects of the harvests give rise to some anxiety in places, I thought it desirable to obtain from the Government of India the latest information on the subject. The following telegram was received from them yesterday :—" Prospects are generally good in greater part of Eastern Bengal and Assam, Bengal, Madras, and Burma. In the rest of India, including the dry zone of Burma, sowings appear, generally speaking, to have been normal, but crops have begun to wither, and if no rain falls during the next ten days or so, the antumn crops will be imperilled. The situation (more especially in North-Western Deccan, North Gujarat, Berar, and west of Central Provinces and in North-West India) generally causes some anxiety, but stocks are in most places considerable and the condition of the population is reported good and prices show no abnormal movements." The only alteration of taxation that is provided for is in tobacco. The experience of last year seemed to indicate that a larger, or at any rate a more stable revenue would be derived from a lower duty and the rates have accordingly been reduced by one-third.

THE EXPENDITURE ON THE DURBAR.

But although taxation has not been reduced, provision has been made for the cost of the Durbar and the military review to be held at Delhi in December next, and for other incidents of the King's visit, without any extra taxation. The latest estimate of gross expenditure is £942,200, Imperial and £ 183,000 Provincial expenditure. Against this there will be a considerable set off in the shape of receipt from the Durbar Light Railway, visitor's camps, and sales of plant and material. It may be of interest to add that the Government of India have made the most careful arrangements to secure that the account of the cost of the Royal visit, which will be prepared in due course, shall show the whole of the expenditure on every description. There are few questions of greater difficulty than that of the scale on which expenditure of this kind should be incurred when the ratepayers are poor, but when at the same time there is among them a very general desire that the celebration shall be on a worthy and adequate scale. In this instance the scale of expenditure was fixed after very careful consideration by the Government of India and the Secretary of State, and when the financial provision was brought to the notice of the Legislative Councils, both Provincial and Imperial, it was received by the Indian representatives with what the Viceroy in his speech on March 27, described as "a tidal wave of enthusiasm." An Indian Member of one of the Provincial Councils expressed an opinion on the expenditure by saying "I wish it were more." I think we may assume that the decision of the Government represents fairly well the means between the possible mistakes of extravagance on the one hand and on the other hand failure to give suitable expression to the feelings of a population deeply moved by a great and indeed unique occurrence. I say unique occurrence, but although His Majesty is not going to be crowned again at Delhi, it would not be unprecedented that a King of England should undergo two coronation ceremonies. There are several instances, as the House no doubt knows. Richard I., who was crowned at Westminster in 1189, was crowned again at Winchester in 1194, much against his will, on his return from captivity in Germany after his ill-started crusade. Henry III had to be content with an initial coronation at Gloucester, as the French were in occupation of London—without a Crown too, as the Regalia had been lost with the rest of King John's baggage in the Wash—and it was not until four years later that a second ceremony was held in Westminster Abbey. But two centuries afterwards the tables were turned, when Henry VI was crowned both in Westmininster Abbey and in Notre Dame. Nor is it unprecedented that Delhi should witness the accession ceremony of an Emperor. This historic city has been the scene of many accession festivals, though the ancient ceremonies present points of dissimilarity from those which will be witnessed next winter. We do not, for instance, think it necessary to conclude the festivities, as did Aurangazeb, by the public decapitation of 500 thieves, "thereby," as the historian quaintly says "terrorizing the perverse." (*Laughter*). The unique nature of the present occasion lies in the fact that India has never before had the opportunity of receiving in person and doing honour to Her English Emperor and Empress.

An Hon. member :—British. (*Laughter.*)

Mr. Montagu :—Her British Emperor and Empress.

THE DURBAR ARRANGEMENTS.

It may interest the House to hear a brief description of the ceremonies of which the Durbar will consist. Our aim is to make them as popular as possible and to give every opportunity to the people of India of sharing in them. I am glad to be able to say that the outbreak of plague at Delhi, which caused some anxiety, has now subsided, and we may hope that there is no danger of any such untoward incident as marred the Coronation of James I, when the plague was raging in London, and the people were forbidden to come to Westminster to see the pageant. On December 7, Their Majesties will arrive at the Bastion of Delhi Fort, where 150 ruling Chiefs will be presented. Subsequently, they will go in procession with British and Indian escorts round the Great Mosque and through all the principal streets of the town. On the Ridge they will be received by the representatives of British India between 3,000 and 4,000 in number. On the two following days the King will receive visits from the Chiefs, and will lay the foundation-stone of the All-India Memorial to King Edward in Delhi. On December 11, colours will be presented to British and Indian troops. The Durbar ceremony itself will take place on December 12. In order to make it as popular as possible accommodation will be provided for 50,000 spectators in addition to the 12,000 officially invited guests and the 20,000 troops in the great arena; so that there will be space for about 100,000 persons to see the ceremony. On the following day, in the morning, the King will receive the officers of the Native Army, and in the afternoon, Their Majesties will attend a garden party at the Fort, while a huge popular *fete* will be held on the ground below the Fort, to which it is expected that about a million people will come to spend the day in the games and amusements that will be provided for them. It is anticipated that, following the custom of the Moghul Emperors, Their Majesties will show themselves to the people from the Bastion of the Fort. On the 14th, there will be a review of unprecedented size, in which British and Indian troops, numbering over 19,000, will be present, and I may add that this will have been preceded by four days manœuvres on a scale never before found possible. Thus the advantage of practical training will be combined with the delights of brilliant display. On the next day, the 10th, Their Majesties will depart in procession through the streets of Delhi, and this historic pageant will be over. (*Cheers*). We, who have crowned and welcomed with great joy our King this year, will wish him "God Speed" as he sets sail on his imperial mission, believing that he will receive a real and heart-felt welcome from all the people in India not only because news of his popularity and single purposed devotion to his imperial duties will have reached their shores, but because they will see in his visit, thus freshly crowned, an earnest that the passage of time and growing knowledge has increased the desire, which has always animated the British people, to help and serve their Indian fellow-subjects. (*Cheers*).

THE OPIUM REVENUE.

I must, however, get back to the subject of finance, because I want the House to look with me for a moment at the future beyond the year with whose finance we are at present concerned. We must now definitely face the total loss, sooner or later, of revenue derived from opium sold for export to China. As the House knows, a new agreement on this subject was concluded in May last between the United Kingdom and China. The Provisional Agreement of 1908, which arranged that the import of Indian opium and the production of Chinese opium should be progressively diminished year by year until 1917, import and production will entirely cease, was confirmed. His Majesty's Government have, moreover, agreed that the export of opium from India to China shall cease whenever clear proof is given of the complete absence of production of native opium in China. They have also agreed that Indian opium shall not be conveyed into any province which can establish by clear evidence that it has effectively stopped the cultivation and the import of native opium. It is sufficient to state, as I have the main terms of the agreement to make it clear that, in furtherance of the policy of sympathetic support of reform in China, and in recognition of the progress made there in reducing the production of native opium, the Indian Government have gone a long way towards the final extinction of their opium trade. (*Hear, hear.*) The Government of India will loyally and scrupulously carry out their share of the agreement and I claim the sympathy and admiration of the House of Commons for all who are doing their share, as I believe, because they have decided that opium growing and opium trading is an immoral and intolerable industry. First of all, there are the Chinese people who are showing so admirable a zeal in eradicating the vice which has laid them so long helpless in chains. There are the Indian people, the taxpayers, who are willingly and cheerfully sacrificing in this humane interest a valuable source of revenue. (*Cheers.*) There are the opium growers in the Native States, and there are His Majesty's Government and the Government of India, who, in 1906, found the opium trade flourishing and unlimited, and who have now succeeded in setting an end to this industry. And it is possible, as some prophets say in two years or less, that we shall have to face a loss of £3,000,000 approximately of net opium revenue which figures in the estimate for 1911 and 1912. Towards meeting this there is the estimated surplus for this year of £800,000 but there is also the non-recurring item of £ 1,000,000 for the King's visit. There is, therefore, a margin of nearly £ 2,000,000 of surplus revenue in the present year. It is not over-sanguine, I think, to hope that each future year may be expected to give a modest addition to the revenue of the Government, because, although it is difficult and undesirable to obtain sudden increases of revenue in India, there is nevertheless a steady upward movement due to the spread of cultivation, the growth of railway and irrigation systems and the general developement of the country. I am not forgetting that it is possible that a portion of the natural growth of revenue may be required to meet increased expenditure, especially on objects such as improved education and sanitation, which are commended by public opinion in India and in England, but there is also the possibility of economy in other branches of expenditure. I quote the promise which was made last January in the debate on the subject in Calcutta, when the Finance Member said that all the members of the Government of India will, during the current year, subject the expenditure for which they are individually responsible to close scrutiny with a view to effecting all possible economy. I have every reason to believe that this promise is being fulfilled. (*Hear, hear.*) It has, indeed, given rise to rumours founded on what information, obtained from where, I do not know. It is said that we propose to cut down the military forces in India. Well, what if we did? Is it suggested that when we are reviewing the expenditure in other departments, we should except the military department? If there were no army in India, no one would suggest that the army should be made anything but large enough, and only large enough, for the needs of the situation, but simply because, the army was devised and organised at other times it is seriously suggested that no modification should be made, and that even though you are searching for economy in every department, you should not be allowed to question your military expenditure. I can assure Hon. members that the Government does not share this illogical view, but that nothing is, or will be, contemplated that will impair the efficiency of our Army for defending and guarding the peace of our Empire. *(Hear, hear.)* However this may be, the question whether the loss of opium revenue will involve fresh taxation cannot be definitely answered. The present financial strength of the Government of India, the growth of its resources, and the growth or restriction of its expenditure, are all factors that have to be considered and reconsidered as financial plans for each successive year are made.

POLITICAL STATE OF INDIA.

I now reach that portion of my statement which is ordinarily devoted to a more general discussion of the political conditions of India. I hope I shall not be thought to fail in my duty if I say very little about political affairs this year. I dealt with them very fully last year, and in politics the year has been uneventful. That is all to the good. The North-West Frontier has been singularly free from disturbance. There have, of course, been raids and there will continue to be raids so long as an increasing population with predatory instincts presses more and more heavily upon the soil. The appointment of a special officer to take charge of our relations with the Waziris has undoubtedly been successful so far, and it is hoped that the recent Joint Commission of British and Afghan officials which disposed of an accumulation of cases of border crime will check frontier raids, especially if the Afghan authorities are firm in carrying out their agreement not to permit outlaws to reside within 50 miles of the frontier. The North-East Frontier, on the other hand, was the scene of a deliberate open attack by Abors on a small British party, in which Mr. Noel Williamson, Assistant Political Officer at Sadiya, lost his life. The outrage is one for which His Majesty's Government are taking steps to inflict punishment at the earliest possible moment. Mr. Williamson was a young and energetic officer who had done good service on the frontier, and to whom the Government of India are indebted for much valuable information about peoples whose confidence it is notoriously difficult to win. The House, I am sure, will wish to join the Government in an expression of regret at the loss of so valuable a life. (*Cheers.*) In the internal sphere of the political department an interesting event was the constitution of the State of Benares under the suzerainty of His Majesty the King-Emperor. This involves no change in the Constitutional theories of the Government of India, nor does it betoken any new policy in regard to such cessions in future.

POLITICAL CRIME.

Political crime has, I am sorry to say, shown its head once or twice. As long as there are men who lurk safely in the background to suggest these crimes (*cheers*) ; as long as there are tools, often half-witted and generally immature, to commit them, under the impression that they are performing deeds of heroism, so long, I am afraid, occasional outrages of this sort may occur. (*Hear, hear.*)

Do not think I am minimizing their horror. I can imagine nothing more tragic than that a devoted servant of the Government should have a career of utility to India cut short in this way. I should like to take this opportunity of expressing the deep regret that His Majesty's Government and the Government of India feel at the deplorable murder of Mr. Ashe and to tender the profound sympathy of all concerned with the relatives of this promising officer. But, horrible and deplorable as these crimes are in their individual aspect, it is a very common mistake, and a very great mistake to attach too much importance to isolated occurrences of this sort as indices of the political situation, or to make them the text for long jeremiahs in the most exalted journals. (*Laughter and cheers.*) With all respect to the admonition of an army of friendly critics, I adhere to everything that I said last year as to the progressive improvement of the general situation, though I shall probably again be told that my optimism is unjustifiable. I want to protest here against the ill-informed and unthinking pessimism of which we hear a good deal, accompanied by vague and unsubstantiated criticism of the present Government for being in some mysterious way responsible for the state of affairs which the critics regard with alarm. I wish that the people who talk like this would take pains to substantiate their views with something more than bare and vague assertions of general alarm. What do they mean, these prophets of woe, who shake their heads and say: "We do not like the news from India; India is in a dangerous state" adding something, as a rule, about a Radical Government ? *(Laughter.)* They write it to their friends, they print it in the newspapers, they whisper it over the fireside. What do they mean? Why, all that they mean, so I venture to assert, is that the Indian problem is a difficult one, and a complicated one, becoming as the country develops and its people are educated increasingly difficult and increasingly complicated. There is no need to tell that to us who are concerned with the administration of India. It is all the more reason why we should face the future bravely and thinkingly; all the more reason why we should avoid a mournful pessimism which begets the atmosphere of distrust in which it thrives. Whatever hysterics may be indulged in by arm-chair critics in the Press, the House may rest assured that the Indian Courts will not be deflected one jot from that adherence to strict justice which has won them the respect of all sections of the community, nor the Executive Government from exercising clemency where clemency will serve the best interests of the country. *(Cheers.)* The policy of Lord Crewe and Lord Hardinge is the policy of Lord Morley and Lord Minto—immovable determination to punish fitly anarchy and crime, with strict sympathy for orderly progressive demand for the peoples that they govern. *(Hear, hear.)* Indeed, this is no new principle of Indian Government, for the policy of the Great Moghul was two centuries ago thus described by Manucci :—" Liberality and generosity are necessary to a prince ; but, if not accompanied by justice and sufficient vigour, they are useless ; rather do they serve to the perverse as occasion for greater insolence."

A CHANGING INDIA.

I do not want to be dogmatic, but India is changing fast—as fast as, if not faster than the West, and our views must keep pace with the change. India has been given peace, unity, and an Occidental education, and they have combined to produce a new spirit. It is our duty to watch that movement, and to lead it, so far as it may be led from without, into right channels. When a change is produced in the political organization of a great Empire it must not be regarded as the result of an inspiration of a philosophic Secretary of State creating new condition of things out of a placid sea, anxious to modify the realm over which he presides in accordance with his whim, his fancy, or even his settled conviction. Political change in any country, I take it, results from causes very different from this. It must originate from within, not from without. Social conditions, slowly developing, stir public opinion and public demand which move unformed and uncertain at first, gathering strength and shape later, and it is the duty of those in charge of the machine of Government to lead them into the channels of altered policy by means of statutes, roders in Council, and so forth. These paper documents are the manifestation of the development of the country. They do not, of themselves, thrust the country either backwards or forwards. They only mark, as I understand it, and so help its movement forward with a success which depends upon the equipment and wisdom of those in whom the control is vested. That is where true statesmanship lies—to watch the manifold and complex currents, to diagnose aright the signs of the times, to await the moment, and when the moment comes, to step in and mould into proper shape aspirations and demands which are feeling and groping for expression.

LORD MORLEY'S WORK.

It is for this that the name of the great statesman who has recently left the India Office will be remembered in Indian history. Lord Morley with a keen and liberal understanding of Indian men and affairs, has set such a seal upon Indian progress as can fall to the lot of few Secretaries of State. The appointment of John Morley to the India Office stirred great hopes in India. He had the good fortune to find in Lord Minto one whose share in the events of the last five years have obtained for him the affection and gratitude of India. (*Hear, hear.*) The hopes were amply fulfilled. Liberal and generous reform, coupled with unflinching repression of crime, successfully met a situation that might well have broken the reputation of a lesser man. He put off his armour amid the universal regret of the whole of India, and, if I may take this opportunity of saying so on their behalf, to the regret of all who worked under his leadership. (*Hear, hear.*)

By Lord Morley's reform scheme I say that we have successfully marked the political development of India as it is at the moment, and have provided a channel along which India's political history may run. I hope contentedly and steadily for many years to come. May I say again what I said last year, that it is the opinion of all concerned in the Government of India that this scheme has been a complete success, and that the standard of work in the new Legislative Councils is worthy of the highest praise ? (*Hear, hear.*)

THE POLITICAL FUTURE.

And it is because of this that, when I ask myself the question, " What of the future ?," I am compelled to say frankly that a country cannot develop by political agitation alone. I say, as one who profoundly sympathizes with progressive opinion in India, that political agitation must not be allowed to outstrip development in other directions. Genuine political agitation must be spontaneous ; it must be the inevitable result of causes working within a nation, not fictitious importation from outside. It is not enough to admire and envy Western political institutions. They cannot be imported ready-made ; they must be acquired as the fitting expression of indigenous social conditions. If India desires—I use this condition because I know there are some in India who would retrace their steps and abandon Western influence, and go back to autocracy —but if she desires, as I believe the majority of educated Indians desire, to attain to Western political institutions, it must be by Western social development. The Indian educated fraction with democratic leaning is a tiny fraction. It must remove, if needs be by years of work this inevitable rejoinder to its demands, not by clamour or by political agitation, but by work, however patient, along the lines I am about to indicate. It cannot be removed in any other way.

The measures taken two years ago afford ample provision for the expression of public opinion, and for the more effective control by Indians over the government of their country. The time is not ripe for any further modification of the system of government, and so I say to India, with all respect :—" Work out your political destiny so far as you may under your existing Constitution ; find out its best possibilities, and improve, if you will its machinery ; but, for the moment, turn your attention more directly to other problems which make a far more urgent call upon your energies. The Government is ready, to play her part, but, without you, the Government can do nothing." Indians must turn their attention to organizing an industrial population which can reap the agricultural and industrial wealth of the country, and attain a higher level of education and a higher standard of living.

Industrial Progress.

India has developed from a series of isolated self-supported village communities, where the man's occupation was agriculture carried on to feed the community, where payments were made wholly in produce, and where such industry as there was, was mainly hereditary, and the products were distributed among the inhabitants of the village. Justice, law and order were enforced by the village itself, often by hereditary officials. An idyllic picture, perhaps marred only by the important consideration that such an India was wholly at the mercy of climatic conditions. Drought or tempest meant starvation and sometimes disappearance. In the famines of olden times, far, far older than the British occupation, millions died of hunger, just as thousands died in France in the 17th century. What has altered all this ? The same cause which altered similar conditions in England, in France, in Germany, in almost every European country—with this distinction, that what European countries acquired by centuries of evolution has been imported into India by zealous workers, profiting by the history of their own country. The huge development of railways in India is the work of little more than a score of years. The fit metalled roads were laid but 50 years ago. By these means of communication, with the post and the telegraph, the isolation of village communities has been broken down, money has been introduced as a means of exchange, competition has come in, and national and even international trade has been developed. India's manufacturers compete with the manufacturers of ths rest of the world and require, as they do, the latest developements of science and technical knowledge. Her agriculturists till the soil no longer merely to provide themselves with food, but to sell, perhaps at the other end of the world, the products of their labour. Famine no longer means starvation. Thanks to modern means of communication and to the greater security given by the irrigation system that the British Government has so largely developed, in times of scarcity in these days the numbers of deaths directly attributable to lack of food is insignificant.

But there are signs of a further development which also has its analogy in the industrial history of the West. The independence of all branches of industry, the concentration of labour in factories under expert management, the stricter division of labour, the use of mechanical power, and the employment of large amounts of capital are symptoms of this revolution. It is just what happened in this country when our great woollen and cotton industries were developed from the isolated hand-weavers. This period in a country's history brings with it many possibilities of evil unknown to a most archaic society, but it brings also possibilities of wealth and greatness. I hope the House will not pause to deplore the risks of evil, for, if the industrial revolution has begun, nothing can stop it. You might just as well try to stop the incoming tide in your outstretched hands. Our task is rather to guard against the evils that our Western experience enables us to foresee.

SIGNIFICANT FIGURES.

I do not want, to be accused of seeing in India an industrial revolution that does not exist, and so I may be permitted to read a very few figures. Twenty years ago, there were 126 cotton mills, employing 112,000 hands: there are now 232 mills employing 236,000. In the same time, the number of jute mills has likewise developed and the persons employed in them increased from 61,000 to 192,000. Altogether, there are now about 2,500 factories of all kinds worked by mechanical power, employing nearly a million persons. The tea industry gives employment to 600,000 persons, and exports annually 250 millions of pounds of tea, valued at nearly £8,000,000, an increase in ten years of nearly £2,000,000. As regards mineral production, the chief mineral worked is coal. The annual output, which has more than doubled in the last eight years is 12,000,000 tons, and the industry employs about 130,000 persons. Petroleum also has developed very rapidly. The output is now 177,000,000 gallons, which is quadruple that of ten years ago. Manganese ore is also a new and considerable mining industry. As yet there is no steel-making plant in India, but much is expected from Messrs. Tata Brothers undertaking, which is near completion. If we may add the *employees* on the railways, who number some half a million, to the numbers employed in factories, tea estates, and mining, the total comes to about 2¼ million persons.

There are 2,156 companies registered in India with a nominal capital of £70,000,000, and a paid-up capital of £40,000,000. These figures have been doubled in ten years. There are also many companies registered abroad which carry on business exclusively in India, mainly in tea growing, jute mills, cotton mills and rice mills. These companies (omitting railway companies); have a share capital of £36,00,000 besides debentures. The banking capital of India has increased in ten years from £20,000,000 to £ 43,000,000, and if they wanted further proof of this industrial revolution, it would be found in the fact that although four-fifths of the exports of India consist of raw materials and food-stuffs and four-fifths of the imports consist of manufactured goods, these proportions are being modified as time goes on. Raw material imports have increased at a more rapid rate than manufactured imports, whilst the rise in the exports of manufactured goods is more than twice as great as the rise in the exports of raw material. These are my evidences of the industrial revolution, and, in order to avoid the evils with which it is attended, India has need of the assistance of the best and wisest of her sons. What is wanted is the application of modern methods and modern science to Indian industry. We want to see a stream of educated young men entering industrial careers, and leaving alone the overstocked professions of the Bar and the public service: (*Hear, hear.*) May I quote an Indian economist, Mr. Sarkar, who says :—" The supreme need of to-day is managers of firms, pioneers and *enterpreneurs.* The highest intellect of the nation should be educated for industries, remember, the highest intellects are serving the industries in Europe, and capital and business experience are closely associated with brain power. " And again :—" Our recent industrial awakening has created a sudden demand for business managers; experienced men of this class are not available in sufficient numbers.

and so our new ventures are run by amateur managers, such as lawyers, retired public servants, and so forth, with the best intentions, are unfit to take the place of a trained business-man. For this reason many of new joint-stock companies have failed. That is the want in India ; technical education and people willing to profit by it." (*Hear, hear*).

THE NEW AGRICULTURAL WORLD.

I hope that the industrial development of India will not be confined strictly to industries. I hope this development will also extend to the new agricultural world which has been formed by the comparatively recent destruction of the isolation of the village. Division of labour has been introduced, the export of produce is growing, and the shares of the landlord, the Government, and the labourer are now being paid more and more by the cultivator in money. Government has modified, in the interest of the cultivator, the system of revenue assessment which it inherited from its predecessors, and which represents its partnership in the agricultural industry. Government has also been sedulous to protect tenants from the exaction of landlords. Its method of controlling landlords who added to fixed rents cases for fictitious services would, I fear, shock many conservatives in this country, and cause envy among the most advanced agricultural reformers. (*Laughter.*) In Bengal the tenency law provides that every cultivator who has held any land in a village, for twelve years acquires a right of occupancy, and is protected from arbitrary eviction and from arbitrary enhancement of rent. (*Hear, hear.*) He has got fixity of tenure and fair rent (*hear, hear*) and in Madras the cultivator is virtually a peasant proprietor, paying a judicial rent for the enjoyment of his land. (*Hear, hear.*) But the cultivator has two things always against him ; he is dependent of the seasons, and he is naturally improvident. He will spend, for instance, the equivalent of several years' income on a single marriage festivity. He must, therefore, turn to the money-lender, and once in his clutches, he is never free. This is not unique in India. The tale is just the same as the tale in Ireland, in Germany, and in France, and 140 per cent. and 280 per cent. are not uncommon rates of interest. The whole of the surplus produce goes to the money-lender as payment of interest. As for the payment of principal, that is nearly always impossible. Indian agriculture is going to be saved, as I believe, by the Raiffeisen system, a boon from the West, which is taking hold in India.

I want to see something of co-operative movement, because I believe that even England may have much to learn from India here. You cannot apply capital to agriculture in the same way that you can apply it to industry, for you cannot take your raw material, the land, and lump it together into a factory ; the size of an economic holding can never be greater or smaller than the local conditions of market, of soil, of climate make possible. Though aggregation is the essence of the manufacturing industry, and isolation is the essence of the agriculture industry, the principle of capitalisation governs both, but in agriculture resource must be had to co-operation. The law under which the societies are incorporated was passed in 1904, and some time elapsed after its enactment before the principles of co-operation could be made intelligible to the people by the Government officials to whom the work of organisation was entrusted. The principles were borrowed from Europe, was unfamiliar to the people, and required a certain amount of intelligence as well as a willingness to make trial of a new idea. The initiative had to come without ; the Government gave it by means of officers and funds. The officers' zeal and interest have repeatedly been acknowledged, but funds have been supplied sparingly, in order to make the movement from the outset a genuine one. (*Hear, hear*). Imperfectly though the figuers reflect progress, they are remarkable. In three years the number of societies has increased from 1,357 to 3,498. The number of members has increased from 150,000 to 231,000 ; the working capital has risen from £300,000 to £800,000. It is fair assumption that each member represents a family, and that the co-operative movement has beneficially affected no less than a million people. Of course the banks vary in detail in different provinces, but perhaps in Bengal, whether there is no share capital and no dividend, and all societies are organised on the strictest principles of unlimited liability, and members of the society pledge their joint credit, we get the most perfect application of the Raiffeisen principle.

PRACTICAL RESULTS.

It is from the accounts of the movement given by the provincial officers (and of the 28 officials at the last Conference of Registrars, 20 were Indians) that one realizes the capacity of the Indian rural population to respond to a beneficent idea and their latent powers to work for the common good. The initiative in the first instance had to come from the Government and its officers, but a Registrar and one assistant and two or three inspectors in a province of 20,000,000 or 40,000,000 people could do nothing unless they could count on the assistance of honorary helpers. This has been forthcoming; men of education and public spirit animated solely by enthusiasm for the movement have set themselves to learn the principle of co-operative credit societies, and in their several neighbourhoods have become organizers and honorary managers of banking. Even greater enthusiasm is to be found in the villagers among poor and the homely men of little education. It has been found, not by any means in every village, or equally in all parts of India, but to an extent which was not anticipated. In a poor village a credit bank was started with a capital of 20 rupees: it has now a working capital—chiefly deposits —of more than £3,000. The bank has also a scholarship fund to school, and an arbitration committee for settling local disputes. I have another example of a committee managing a credit bank, which, by denying membership to a man of bad character until he had shown proof of his reform, made a good citizen, out of a bad one. We read also of buried bags of rupees, crusted with mould, being produced and deposited in the bank. It seems as if we were in this way beginning to tap the hoarded wealth of India.

Several societies have bought agricultural machines, and some are occupying their spare time and capital in opening shops and doing trade in cattle and wood. Others, again, aim at land improvement, repayment of old debts, and in the improvement of the backward tenant, and even at the establishment of night and vernacular schools. In several districts the village societies have resorted to arbitration in village disputes, and in one or two cases they have taken up the question of village sanitation. One can almost see the beginnings of the rivals of old village communities. (*Hear, hear.*) But there is also another note struck in most of these reports. While villagers have shown a wonderful capacity for combination and concerted action and while enthusiastic workers of position and intelligence have here and there been enlisted in the cause, there is complaint of the apathy of the natural leaders of the Indian community and their apparent failure to realize the immense importance of the movement. There is no doubt that the field wants many more workers, and I hope it will not ask in vain.

THE PROBLEM OF EDUCATION.

There is, then, growing in India, this great two-sided organization of industrial and agricultural life. I do not think it can grow healthily for unless serious attention is given to one or two important matters to which I now want to draw attention. The first is education—general and industrial. I regret that I am not in a position to say much in detail on this subject, all the more because I see that my honourable friend the member for Hackney has a motion on the subject on the paper. The department constituted last year to take charge of education has been hard elaborating a policy, and I hope that the result of their labours will shortly be made public. We have to deal with 16 million boys of school-going age, the bulk of them widely scattered over an agricultural population.

There is no general demand at present for education among the people, who have borne their illiteracy very cheerfully. This is no reason, of course that there should be any reluctance in our efforts to spread education among them. But while it is the obvious duty of the Government to provide better buildings, better equipment, a better curriculum, and better teaching staffs, there is a duty on the other hand for Indian educational reformers to create a willingness to allow children to be educated, a willingness to help, teach and, be it said, a willingness to help, pay the taxes, or the fees (I do not now say which) by which alone large educational schemes can be financed. By this means only can we bring into the pale the 80 per cent. of children who are still outside education much as being done by the provision both of institutions and of technical scholarships, a full description of which can be found in the last quinquennial report on education in India—Command Paper 4365 of 1909. What is required there is, as I have said, to invite young men who have achieved a good primary education to choose these advantages rather than to crowd still further the entrance to the bar or the public service through the Universities. (*Hear, hear*).

Higher Standard of Living.

With education will come, I hope, a higher standard of living for the people and some reduction in the terrible wastage of human life. The present standard of living is deplorably low. Ignorance of sanitary or medical principles is practically universal. The birth-rate is extremely high, judged by the birth-rate of Western Europe. The death-rate, and notably the death-rate of children, is also, judged by European experience, appallingly high. The death-rate in the United Provinces and the Punjab in 1908, when malaria was very prevalent, exceeded fifty per thousand. The English death-rate is only 16 per thousand. The sickness, disease, and mortality which horrify students of Indian society are, from one point of view, the consequences of a very low standard of living, though from another point of view they are the rude restrictions placed by Nature on a population which continually multiplies up to the limit of bare subsistence.

Now at present only 10 per cent, of the Indian people live in towns. The effect of re-organisation of industry upon capitalistic lines will be to modify this. The concentration of people from the country side into large towns is bound to occur. The figures of the recent Census have not yet been published in sufficient detail to enable a definite judgment to be formed as to how far this process has already taken place, but the tendency is undoubted. The population of Calcutta, for instance, has increased by 10 per cent. in the last ten years, that of Bombay by 25 per cent., that of Karachi by 36 per cent., and that of Rangoon by 18 per cent.

SOCIAL AMELIORATION.

This will not be without its good effects. The consequent increase of wealth will provide meals wherewith to ameliorate the poverty which at present impedes the progress of India in so many directions. Again, the multiplication of industries will relieve the pressure on the land which now drives down the profits of agriculture, and will thus mitigate the severity of those recurring calamities which follow upon the failure of the harvest, for it has long been recognised that the encouragement of diversity of occupation is the only radical cure for famine. Moreover, in the concentrated population of the towns all those civilising and educational movements which are summarised in the word "progress" find their centre. Technical instruction in special trade and occupations is impossible in sparsely populated districts.

EVILS OF TOWN LIFE.

But, on the other hand, there is danger that all evils of town life—the overcrowding, the destitution, and all the squalid misery of main streets with which we are too familiar—should be reproduced in India, and be even harder to bear than here on account of the suffocating heat. Already we hear of overcrowding and insanitary tenements in the operative's quarters of Bombay. Mr. Dunn, late Chairman of the Bombay City Improvement Trust, in a paper of February 17, 1910, says :—" The rooms or ' chals', less than ten feet square are separated from one another by partitions of wood or split bamboos blastered with mud. There is no ceiling, only the sloping low roof, which is of rough round rafters and a single thickness of country tiles. The walls and roofs are black with smoke and durt of many years ; the rooms are filled with choking smoke from the wood fires and the naked lamps, and there is no exit from this except through the rough doors. The only opening are the doors leading from the rooms on to the narrow varandahs, no ventilation, darkness and a choking atmosphere, and a family of five or six persons, with perhaps a lodger or two. Refuse of all kinds is disposed of by the simple expedient of throwing it outside beyond the varandah, and the condition of the surroundings of the 'chal' may be left to the imagination." Of course a situation such as that demands activity from the Government. In Bombay a City Improvement Trust has been working for the last ten years with inadequate means. The Government of India have now given, as I have said, £333,000 to it, and proposals were being considered for providing the trust with a larger income from the local sources. A similar trust is now about to be created in Calcutta. In Rangoon again land reclamation on a large scale is being undertaken. Elsewhere much attention is being paid to the subject ; but the most urgent need is the education of the masses in the principles of hygiene. There is a limitless field indeed for private enterprises. Tolerable though archaic habits and practices may be in the open country, when transferred to the crowded town, they become insupportable. At the Bombay Medical Congress of 1909, a Parsi doctor read a painfully interesting paper on "Unhygienic Bombay". He said :—"A large portion of the insanitary condition prevailing in and outside the dwellings of the poorer classes is directly due to some peculiar and perverse habits of the people themselves through ingrained prejudice and stupidity, through want of personal cleanliness and through ignorance of personal hygiene. They form a painful picture of a stolid and unconscious ignorance, associated with great poverty such as can rarely be seen in the poorest civilised towns in the West." The picture is repeated with variations in all the great towns of India.

THE PLAGUE AND ITS REMEDIES.

If there were less ignorance and perversity, plague would never find in the country the lodgment that it has. It is an established fact that persons living under proper sanitary conditions are virtually exempt from the disease. Plague does not attack the gaol population, or the Native Army, it attacks the ordinary civil population because they live in houses which are not rat-proof because they treat the rat almost as a domestic animal, because large numbers of them refuse to trap or kill it and because they will not adopt the sanitary precautions which are pressed upon them. In plague we have examples from our own history. England has suffered many times, the most severe epidemic being that in the middle of the 14th century known as the "Black Death," which came from the Levant through Europe. A contemporary writer, quoted in Dr. Simpson's book on plague, says:—"At first it carried off almost all the inhabitants of the sea-ports in Dorset, and then those living inland, and from there it raged so dreadfully through Devon and Somerset so far as Bristol that the men of Gloucester refused those of Bristol entrance to their country, everyone thinking that the breath of those who lived amongst people who died of plague was infectious. But at last it attacked Gloucester—yea, and Oxford and London, and finally the whole of England, so violently that scarcely one in ten of either sex was left alive." Outbreaks of plague continued to occur occasionally throughout the next three centuries—notably in London in 1665, when nearly seventy thousand persons perished. Towards the end of the 17th century it rapidly disappeared from the whole of Western Europe.

Plague has now been present in India for 15 years and the appalling total of nearly 7,500,000 deaths from it has been recorded. Of this Punjab accounts for nearly 2½ millions deaths almost a third of the total. The tale of deaths in the last ten years represents 11 per cent. of the population of that province. When I think of the sensation that was caused in this country a short time ago by what it was by comparison, a minor outbreak in Manchuria, resulting in only 50,000 deaths, I fear that people in this country do not realise the awful ravages that this scourge is daily making among the Indian people. Scientific research has established that it is conveyed by rat fleas to human beings. The two effective remedies are inoculation and house evacuation. Professor Haffkne has discovered a vaccine by which comparative, though not absolute immunity can be temporarily secured. But by an unhappy accident, at Malkowal several villagers died of tetaneous after inoculation. Inoculation in India has never recovered from this disaster. It is hated by the people and avoided by them except when the disease is in their midst. House evacuation is easier in towns. Administrative arrangements by which plague is now fought include the provision of special plague medical officers and subordinates, and the district staff are on the look-out for the occurrence of plague, and when it occurs they visit the locality, offer inoculation, give assistance to persons to vacate their houses, advise rat destruction, and so on.

To the prevention there would seem to be no royal road. The case is one in which lavish expenditure of money is not called for and would be useless. But the Provincial Governments have spent, and are spending, a good deal. The United Provinces have expended some £600,000 up-to-date. The Punjab Government is spending about £40,000 a year. The improvement of the general sanitary conditions under which the population lives is more and more clearly seen to be essential, and to improve them the Local Governments are devoting all the money they can spare. They have been helped to do so by the grants for sanitation made by the Government of India. The scientific difficulties are enhanced by the difficulty of overcoming prejudice and ignorance, habit and apathy. In some districts there is actually religious objection to rat-killing and inoculation. No better work can be done for India than to offer example and instruction in principles of life that appear to us elementary and to strive to exercise the foes of progress—superstition and resistance to prophylactics.

LOCAL SELF-GOVERNMENT.

There are, I am glad to say, signs that the sanitary conscience is beginning to awake among the people. But it is not enough to point out evils to the Government, to urge the Government to do something, and to say that more money is required. Of course more money is required. More money is required for every item in India's programme of development, and we allocate to each item with as lavish a hand as we can consistently with the other requirements. It is no use to urge proposals requiring the immediate expenditure of money without any regard to ways and means, when there is so much to be done by private exhortation, by example, and by devotion to the problems of Local Self-Government. Municipal work in India, as elsewhere, is proving an admirable training ground in public affairs, and the better municipal Corporations, such as that of Bombay have carried through large drainage and water projects with the help and stimulus from the Government. What is now wanted is to obtain from the press and the community for municipal effort and a public opinion which can be relied upon to control and appreciate the responsibilities of municipal institutions.

THE INDUSTRIAL REVOLUTION.

I must mention one more danger that the industrial revolution involves. The developement of capitalization is sure to bring forward in India, as everywhere, certain men who, in the hurry to grow rich, will take advantage of the necessities of the poor and the want of organization among the Indian Labourers. These are the men, be it said, who would reap the advantage of a protectionist's tarriff. They would work their hands long hours for insufficient wages, exploit women's and children's labour, and reproduce, as far as the law will permit them, the horrors of the English factory system at the beginning of the last century. A factory Act was passed last year, after a long and exhaustive inquiry by a Committee and a Commission, giving increase to protection, to the worker and greater inspecting and controlling powers to the Government. But the Government cannot advance beyond that Indian public opinion, which, at the best, is only in its infancy. The leaders of Indian opinion must set their faces against the vigilant, because India's working classes, besides being themselves unorganised, are not directly represented on the Legislative Councils whose Indian members come almost exclusively from the landlord and capitalist classes. This is not due to any defect in the law, but to the condition of Indian society.

Labour long accustomed to silent drudgery, has not yet found a voice, and it will probably be long, before it makes itself heard in the Legislative Councils. All the greater reason that public-spirited Indians should take care that these unrepresented interests are carefully considered and the conditions of labour improved. India may derive one advantage from the fact that her industrial revolution has been so long delayed. She may profit by the abundant mistakes that we made in this country if she takes advantage of our experience, and, with a wise forethought, closes the door to industrial abuses before they have grown strong; and, in that case, she may look back upon her industrial revolution without the shame and regret with which we are forced to contemplate some of the features of our own. *(Hear, hear.)*

Caste Principles and Progress.

I have spoken of industrial and agricultural organisation and their subsidiary problems of education, sanitation, and a higher standard of living. There remains another subject on which I wish to touch in pointing out to Indians the objects towards which, as it seems to me, their activities should at present be directed. It is a subject of great delicacy; but I feel obliged to draw attention to it on account of its great importance and the intimate connection of one aspect of it, at any rate, with certain of the topics that I have been discussing. Nothing could be further from my attention than to say anything that might possibly be construed as offensive to the beliefs and usages of any religion. Every religion has forms and ceremonies which it is difficult for those outside its pale to appreciate and to understand. Even less would I have it thought that I desire to weaken the wonderful religious inspiration of the Indian peoples. But I wish to suggest to the leaders of Hindu thought that they might, if they thought fit, look carefully into certain of their institutions and consider whether they are compatible with modern social conditions and modern industrial progress. Of the 220,000,000, of the Hindu population, 53,000,000 form what are known as the depressed classes, who are regarded by the higher castes as untouchables.

There are 9,000,000 girl wives between the ages of one and 15, of whom 2,500,000 are under 11, and there are 400,000 girl widows forbidden to remarry. It is the first point that I wish to emphasise, because it is here in particular that I cannot help feeling that Hindu social conditions hamper to some extent modern development, both industrial and political. The way in which caste principles affect industrial development is this. English industrial history in all its branches shows how supremely important is the possibility of infusing fresh blood from the labouring classes into the ranks of the captains of industry. In India this is impossible under present conditions. Social distinctions are rigid and permanent; many occupations are still almost purely hereditary, and there is no fluidity. Even supposing—as I hope will be the case—that young men of education and capacity take to industrial careers and supposing that the shyness of Indian capital is at length overcome, still the conditions that I have mentioned must inevitably hamper and retard India's industrial progress. In the region of politics the matter came to prominence two years ago in rather a curious way. During consideration of the question of securing for Mahomedans adequate representation on the new councils, the point came up of the numerical proportion borne by the Hindus and Mahomedans in the community. The Mahomedans asserted that the Hindus have no right to count, as Hindus, persons whom no self-respecting Hindus would touch or come near. It is undoubtedly a difficult point, and there are now signs of a movement among leaders of Hinduism towards taking an interest in the conditions of these classes, and devising measures to bridge the gulf between them and the twice-born. It is this that has emboldened me to say what I have said on the subject. I would not have presumed to do so had it not been for the fact that there is evidently a growing feeling amongst prominent members of the community that all is not well with their social organisation. Let me quote to the House the words of the well-known leader, Mr. Gokhale. He said :— "If after 50 years of University education conducted on Western ideas, the essence of which is the equality and dignity of man, the condition of the depressed classes is practically the same as it was half a century ago, it is no reproach to them. There is no greater blot upon us to-day than the condition in which we have allowed 53,000,000 of our fellow-beings to continue."

NATIONAL FEELING IN INDIA.

One word more before I leave the subject. If the Hindu community think it possible and desirable—and it is for them alone to say—to effect the changes in these matters the movement must be effected by the community itself. Government may not—cannot help. I mention this, because in a recent debate on the subject in the Bombay Council there were signs of an inclination to turn to the Government for assistance. If the House will forgive me another quotation, I should like just to read the wise words with which Sir George Clarke concluded the debate :—" The fact is that the Government cannot force the pace in regard to social matters. We must leave them to the growing feeling among the Indian peoples themselves ; and if politics remain in abeyance for a time, it is possible, and, I think, probable, that social reforms will force themselves to the front. That we must leave to the people of India. I do feel that if a real sentiment of nationalism spreads throughout India, as I think it will, the time will come when the Mahars, in common with all other classes, will be treated as brothers." But brotherhood within the Hindu community is not enough. India needs more than that. Real national feeling cannot be produced while in the same Province, village, town, or street, you have Indians learning the national ideal and Indians denying their part or share in the history of the land in which they live. Provincial distinctions do not permanently matter. Racial distinctions do not offer a lasting obstacle to confederation and mutual share in the commonweal. But religious segregations which produce fierce, exclusive patriotism seem more obdurate and more hostile to amicable and united action. In India Hinduism teaches a fierce love of India itself, the motherland which is so wonderful as to be an example of love of country to the whole world, the love of country produced by worship of God. But Mahomedanism produces and teaches a sort of extra-territorial patriotism—if I may strain the words to describe it—love of a religion which seems almost to laugh at distance and material neighbourhood in breathing and praying mutual sympathy. How can one preach tolerance in this atmosphere ? How can one say to the Mahomedan :—"You need abandon no jot of your fervour if you add to it principles of less exalted and more Western desire to help and to share the destiny of the country in which you live ;" and how can one say to the Hindu :—"Your religious susceptibilities really should not be outraged by rites performed by people who do not share your religion, even if you would regard them as wrong if they were performed by Hindus." This trite advice is ineffectual. These are not mere denominations ; they are nations—the one bound together terrestrially and spiritually, the other spiritually only. Now, of course, it would be criminal to foster this difficult antagonism, but not to recognize its existence is to be blind to facts in a way which must enhance the evil. I cannot see how this state of affairs can do other than retard and indeed prevent the development of India in the way I have tentatively suggested,and I would appeal to all Indians—

and I include in these people of every inspiration, race creed and colour—to unite and join hands for this country's good. I need assure no intelligent critic that the Government would be the first to welcome and to help the co-operation which we all desire. (*Hear, hear.*)

I have now, I hope, made good my case. It is as good as I can make it if I forbear to produce, from considerations of time, all the evidence on which it rests. Let me now restate it. The opinion most familiarly, but not originally, stated by Mr. Kipling that the "East is East and the West is West and never the twain shall meet," is contradicted by the fact that India is now rapidly passing through with our aid, in a compressed form, our own social and industrial history, similar in its advantages and in its evils. She has, however, still a very long way to go if she desire to acquire as an outcome of certain conditions the same political institutions, and she cannot and ought not to acquire them in any other way.

PARLIAMENT AND INDIA.

Will the House forgive me if I now in conclusion address myself directly to members of this House? I hope I shall not be thought over-presumptuous if I try to explain what I conceive to be the functions of the British Parliament with regard to our Indian dependency. The importance of the subject cannot be overestimated. It affects us all, collectively and individually. India is woven as it were into the very fabric of our being. In a never-failing stream many of the best of our men and women give themselves and the best of their lives, ungrudgingly to the service of India. Their names are honoured and remembered whether by small groups of our fellow-subjects or by our whole Indian Empire and beyond. (*Hear, hear.*) These men are inspired by an Imperial patriotism, which I am thankful to say shows no sign of ailing, and which they will, I hope, infuse among the people whom they govern. This is no strange thing, this unceasing flow of workers drawn by the magnet of the East. However burdensome and unattractive Indian problems may seem from the outside, I can testify that even the shortest experience of them makes them lastingly absorbing in importance. I can well understand how it is that men who have fought on behalf of India until they are worn out put on their armour again and enter public controversy ; how they even go back to the country in which their life's work has been spent because of the intimate and lasting effect that India has upon their minds and thoughts. Thus it comes about that almost every street, mean or rich, has some one living in it who has worked himself, or whose relations have worked or are working in India. No better index of a nation's activity is to be found than the front sheet of a newspaper. Every birth, marriage, and obituary column has its item of Indian interest. India is part and parcel on the normal existence of our nation. Should not then the House of Commons ask itself what are its duties towards this question which affects so nearly the life of the nation and the lives of its people ? (*Hear, hear*).

I realise well that I shall probably read to-morrow that I have been guilty of the enormity of lecturing the House of Commons. But I cannot refrain from speaking out what I feel for I am convinced that Indian problems will become more important, more insistent, more vital, as the years go on, and I see so clearly the danger that we shall incur if they present themselves to the House of Commons inadequately equipped to graple with them. It is only a matter of time for questions of supreme importance, in connection with our Indian Empire, to come through the outer Lobby into the Lobby and knock irresistibly at the door of this Chamber. Are we prepared to meet them ? Have we the knowledge, the sympathy, the breadth of view, that they demand for a satisfactory and statesmanlike solution ? How many members of this House are able to say that they are in a position to discuss with knowledge and decide with wisdom the great problems of India—the problem of education both in India and in England, of commercial and industrial development, of military defence, of political concession, of the eradication of political crime ? On how many of these questions can Hon. members honestly say that they are fitted to form any views at all ? Indeed, when I think how this House is harrassed and overburdened by its innumerable domestic responsibilities, which I hope it will not always be persistently unwilling to delegate, I am bound to admit that there is lacking that first requisite for the efficient discharge of our Imperial duties—time for study and mature consideration. But, apart from this, when I ask myself the question, what is the present attitude of this House towards Indian questions, I am bound to answer frankly, that the salient characteristic of that attitude appears to me to be—speaking of the House as a whole—something approaching apathy. And, as regards those Hon. members who take most active interest in Indian affairs, may I say that I should be very sorry to see this interest represented by two parties, concerning themselves chiefly with points of administrative details, the one thinking it necessary to espouse the cause of the governed by attacking the Government, the other constituting itself the champion of the official. The tendency to assume an antagonism between the interests of the Indian and the interests of the official is one which I cannot too strongly deprecate—it is the negation of all we have done, or doing, and hope to do for India. We are there to co-operate with the peoples of the country in working out her destinies side by side with the same object, the same mission, the same goal. (*Hear, hear*).

PRESTIGE.

Time was, no doubt, when it was the most important function of this House to see that the theory of Government by prestige was not carried to excessive lengths in India. In the extreme form of Government by prestige those who administer the country are, I take it, answerable only to their official superiors, and no claim for redress by one of the ruled against one of the rulers can be admitted as a right. If, for instance, a member of the ruling race inflicts an injury upon a member of the governed race, no question will arise of punishing the former to redress the wrong of the latter; the only consideration will be whether prestige will be more impaired by punishing the offender, and so admitting imperfection in the governing caste or by not punishing him, and so condoning a failure of that protection of the governed which is essential to efficient Government. This illustrates, as I understand the matter, the prestige theory pressed to its logical conclusion, I do not say that it was ever so pressed in India. It has always been tempered by British character, British opinion, and the British Parliament. Whatever reliance upon prestige there was in, our Government of India is now giving place to reliance upon even-handed justice and strong, orderly, and equitable administration. But a great deal of nonsense is talked still, so it seems to me, about prestige. Call it if you will, a useful asset in our relations with the wild tribes of the frontier, but let us hear no more about it as a factor in the relations between the British Government and the educated Indian public. Do not misunderstand me—and this I say especially to those who may do me the honour of criticising outside these walls what I am now saying. I mean by "prestige" the theory of Government that I have just described; the theory that produces irresponsibility and arrogance. I do not, of course, mean that reputation for firm and dignified administration which no Government can afford to disregard. The reputation can only be acquired by deeds and temper, not by appeal to the blessed word "prestige," I think it necessary to make this explanation, for I have learned by experience how a single word carelessly used may be constructed by sedulous critics, as the enunciation of a new theory of Government.

DELEGATION OF RESPONSIBILITY.

It is, of course, a truism that Parliament acting through its servant, the Secretary of State, is vested with the supreme control over the Government of India. It is no less a truism that it is the duty of Parliament to control that Government in the interests of the governed just as it is the duty of Parliament to control the Government of the day at home in the interests of the people of these islands. This House in its relations to India has primarily to perform for that country the functions proper to an elected assembly in a self-governing country.

That I say, is its primary function. But that is not all. It is characteristic of British statesmanship that it has not been content with so narrow a view of Imperial responsibilities. The course of the relations between the House of Commons and the people of India has taken, and must take, the form of a gradual delegation, little by little, from itself to the people of India of the power to criticise and control the Government. You have given India that rule of law which is so peculiarly British and cherished by Britons; you have given elected Councils for deliberative and legislative purposes; you have admitted Indians to high administrative and judicial office. And, in so far as you do these things, you derogate from your own direct powers. You bestow upon the people of India a portion of your functions; you must, therefore, cease to try to exercise those functions, and devote yourselves solely to the exercise of the duties that you have definitely retained for your own. Permit me to say that I see signs that this most important point is not always sufficiently realised. The more you give to India the less you should exercise your own power; the less that India has the more you are called upon by virtue of your heritage to exercise your own control. The sum is constant; addition on the one side means subtraction from the other.

There are, then, these two problems always before this House. The one is how much of your powers of control to delegate to the people of India, the other is how most wisely to exercise the powers of control that you retain. It is not only that the powers that you have delegated are no use to those on whom you have bestowed them unless they are entrusted with them unhampered; it is not only that the more you have delegated powers of control the more important are such powers as you retain, demanding more and more study and thought. You must also remember the position of the British official in India. You cannot allow him to be crushed beneath a responsibility to Indian opinion, now becoming articulate and organized, to which he has now to justify himself in open debate added to an undiminished responsibility to British public opinion unwilling in fact to surrender the functions that it has professed, through its Parliament, to delegate. Let the Indian official work out his position in the new order of things, where justification by works and in Council must take the place of justification by reputation. I have every confidence in the result.

In conclusion, I accept the blame which I am fully conscious of deserving for the fact that I have wearied the House. I am painfully conscious that anybody who deals with this subject and makes it unattractive only does harm to the causes he espouses. My aim and object is this: I want people to think of India. There is enough to think of. I have spoken with a full sense of responsibility, knowing the fulness of the critics' wrath. There are those who hate the extinction of poetry, of lethargy, of the pictures of the bizarre, which they assert is inseparable from progress, from competition, from industrial development. There are the cynics who, forgetful of the history of their own country, would stop with their pens the revolution of the globe, and deny the opportunity to a world-force which is beginning to penetrate and stir in the country of which I speak. There are the pessimists who spend a useless life, mourning a past which can never return, and dreading a future which is bound to come. Then there are those who, filled with ante-diluvian imperialism, cannot see beyond domination and subjection, beyond governor and governed, who hate the word "progress" and will accuse me of encouraging unrest. I bow submissively in anticipation. I believe there is nothing dangerous in what I have said. I have pointed a long path, a path perhaps of centuries, for Englishmen and Indians to travel together. I ask the minority in India to bring along it—for there is room for all—by education in the widest sense, by organization, and by precept, all those who would be good citizens of their country. And when at intervals this well-ordered thought shows to us that they have made social and political advance to another stage, and demand from us, in the name of the responsibility we have accepted, that they should be allowed still further to share that responsibility with us, I hope we shall be ready to answer with knowledge and with prudence. In this labour all parties and all interested, wherever they may be, may rest assured of the sympathy and assistance of the Government. (*Cheers.*)

THE INDIAN BUDGET, 1912.

On the motion to go into Committee on the East Indian Revenue accounts, Mr. Montagu said :—

I am more than ordinarily impressed by the difficulty of diverting the attention of this House from important domestic concerns to the affairs of India, but I hope to be able to announce to the House a policy of such importance that I trust hon. members will pardon the large draft I shall have to make upon their patience. I do not intend to deal more than a minute upon foreign affairs because the House has kept itself informed of events on the North-West Frontier and in Tibet. The expeditions to the Abor, Mishmi and Mari countries have returned to India having successfully accomplished what they set out to do. If the geographic and scientific results of these expeditions have been somewhat disappointing, the incalculably adverse climatic conditions must be borne in mind. All that it is necessary for me to say about them is that the thanks of the House and all interested are due to General Bower and the other gallant officers and men who conducted the expeditions, and our sympathies will go out to those who lose their lives in the service of their country. (*Hear, hear.*)

THE KING'S VISIT.

Of course, the outstanding feature of the past year in India was the visit of His Majesty and the Queen-Empress. I do not propose to attempt what others have done adequately before me, to paint to this House the glowing success of their visit, and to try and describe the warmth of the welcome which awaited them from their Indian subjects. I ventured last year to prophesy the welcome which His Majesty would receive in these words. I said :

> His visit would receive a real and heartfelt welcome from all his peoples, not only because news of his popularity and devotion to his Imperial duties will have reached their shores, but because they will see in his visit an earnest that the passage of time and growing knowledge had increased the desire which has always animated the British people to help and serve their Indian fellow-subjects.

I quote these words because they describe the welcome which His Majesty received, a welcome enhanced by his own personality and the personality of Her Majesty, a welcome which was echoed from end to end of the Indian Empire.

THE SPIRIT OF NATIONALITY.

At the risk of incurring the anger of my critics, I would express once again my belief that there is a growing spirit of nationality in India, the direct product and construction of British rule. The Brahmin from Bombay speaks Mahratta, the Brahmin from Bengal speaks Bengali, and despite their community of religious belief they are separated by an incapacity to understand one another's language, but they come to discuss the affairs of the nation which is growing under British rule in the language of the British people. (*Hear, hear.*) There is growing up in India a caste of educated Indians which includes among its numbers members of all castes from all parts of India, discussing the affairs of the nation in English. It is small wonder that the educated people of India should welcome the British King as the representative of the unity which is Britain's gift to them. Above and beyond these there were the nine-tenths of the people of India who are still illiterate and uneducated, who welcomed our King because of the peace and tranquillity and the growing prosperity produced by those who govern India in his name. There is an old doctrine that we govern India by the sword. Without questioning the fundamental truth of this I want to assert that it is because we also govern India by the consent of those who know, and by the cheerful acquiescence of those who do not realise all that it means, that His Majesty's welcome was so wide and real as it was. (*Cheers.*)

THE REMOVAL OF THE CAPITAL.

I do not want to tread upon the more debatable ground of the results of His Majesty's visit. The House of Lords has had its say, and the House of Commons has also had its say. I have stated my case, the case for the removal of the Government of India from a provincial centre, and the case for what we conceive to be a more statesmanlike partition of Bengal; and although I fully recognise the importance of the grave misgivings felt by those interested in commerce in Calcutta, I am bound to adhere to the opinion that I have expressed in this House, that the changes are popular everywhere eles, that they have produced satisfaction and tranquillity, and that there is reason to hope and believe that the adverse and isolated, though important, misgivings of the commercial community at Calcutta will prove to be ill-founded.

THE FINANCIAL POSITION OF INDIA.

I pass to that part of my speech which no representative of the India Office, however careless of precedent, could afford to omit, what is, indeed, the real basis for this motion—a very short review, and I will make it as short as I can, of the financial position of the Empire. We have to consider two years—1911-12—in review, and, so far as we can, 1912-13 in prospect. The Estimates for 1911-12 were framed on the hypothesis of normal harvests, good steady progress in trade, and a satisfactory export season. The net revenue, Imperial and Provincial, was estimated at £52,141,700, and the net expenditure chargeable to the revenues of the year, after allowing for the amount estimated to be met from the balances of provincial Governments, was estimated at £51,322,500, which would have left a balance of £819,200. I think the House will agree that it is highly satisfactory to be able to report that the general economic conditions were far more favourable than was anticipated. Budget framers, taxpayers, politicians, and journalists all cast their eyes towards the monsoon, which is the vital element in Indian prosperity. I should like to give the history of this particular monsoon, because it may be taken to show the extreme difficulty of Budget making in India, and the caution with which deductions should be made from earlier rains. The monsoon began in June normally, but during July and August, rain practically ceased over the whole of India. The young crops sown during the first fallacious burst were destroyed by dry, westerly winds, fodder failed for the cattle, and the price of all grains rose rapidly to famine level. On August 25, the Punjab Government reported to the Government of India that the failure of the rains had up-to-date been greater than had ever been experienced in the history of that province ; everything portended as grave and as extensive a drought as any recorded in the history of India. We were, I am informed, within 24 hours of one of the greatest calamities we had ever known. Then in the last week of August, the monsoon currents freshened and copious rains fell in most parts of India and continued in unusual strength throughout September, but the north of the Bombay Presidency, and parts of the Native States of Baroda, Kathiawar and Central India were not reached by the later rains, and in those districts except where irrigation—which I think is the most beneficent triumph of British rule in India (*cheers*)—saved the situation, the autumn and winter crops failed and positively disappeared. Relief works were started in the famine districts, and in the later part of May of this year 100,000 people were employed on the relief works.

THE VOLUME OF TRADE.

These favourable conditions showed themselves in an expansion of the volume of trade. Imports and exports reached a record. I have some remarkable figures to read to the House. The imports of merchandise were of the value of £92,000,000, an increase of 7 per cent.; exports of merchandise were £151,000,000, an increase of 8 per cent.; and the net imports of treasure were £28,000,000, an increase of 32 per cent. To give a better idea of the general expansion of Indian trade the House will, if it compares the figures for 1911-12 with those of 1901-2, find an increase of imports of 70 per cent., an increase in exports of 83 per cent., and an increase in imports of treasure of 285 per cent. The favourable trade conditions were responsible for the fact that the financial results of the year were considerably more favourable than had been expected in the Budget estimate. Railways showed an increase in the gross receipts of £33,150,000, or an excess of £1,720,000 over the estimate. This was partly due to the great expansion of trade and partly due to the Durbar traffic in December. The net profit on the year's working was, therefore, the record sum of £3,204,000, an excess over the Budget estimate of £1,250,000. The local Governments, who are mainly reponsible for Excise administration, have lately raised their fees and duties in order to discourage the use of stimulants and of drugs, and therefore on this account the revenue of 1911-12 was expected to show only a very moderate increase, but good harvests and good trade led to an expansion, and the net revenue was £416,300 over the estimate. The Customs revenue benefited in a similar way. There was an increase of £308,000 in the Customs revenue as a whole, the only item showing a decrease being sugar and tobacco.

Under the heading of irrigation there was an increase of £320,000.

THE OPIUM TRADE.

The most important item which contributed to the surplus of the year was opium. The reduction of the exports has been proceeding at a very considerable pace since the agreement with China which came into force in 1908. In that year the total exports amounted to 61,900 chests, of which 48,000 went to China. In 1912 the exports to China were limited to 21,680 chests, and to the rest of the world 13,200 chests. Of course, this restriction of the exports affects the price and makes it very difficult to forecast from year to year the exact price which it will fetch in the market. Last year the situation was complicated by a new factor, because the Government of India had adopted a system of certificated chests for export to China in response to the wishes of the Chinese Government. It was impossible, therefore, to foretell the price of certificated or uncertificated opium. It is not surprising, therefore, to find that, owing to the poor yield of the season's crops, the expenditure was £444,000 less than the estimate and the receipts £1,624,000 more than the estimate, so that the net receipts were better than the estimate by rather more than £2,000,000. The most important decrease in the year was land revenue. Owing to the scarcity in the north of Bombay, and the lateness of the monsoon in the United Provinces and the Punjab, remissions and suspensions of the land revenue were granted, and there was a net decrease of

£696,000 in the land revenue as a whole. Thus the net revenue amounted to £56,209,000, a surplus over the estimate of a little more than four millions sterling.

EXPENDITURE AND SURPLUS.

When I turn to the net expenditure I find there was a decrease in the estimated expenditure of £780,000. There was, furthermore, a decrease in interest charges of £316,500. This was mainly accidental, and was owing to the fact that the large amounts received on loans granted from the Secretary of State's balances helped to decrease the amount payable for interest. I will draw the attention of the House to a decrease in the expenditure on education of a little over £250,000. It is not a real decrease, because £100,000 of the grant which was to have been spent on education was spent on educational buildings, and therefore appears under the head of "Civil Works" instead of that of "Education." There is also a certain decrease owing to the fact that the large grants which would have enabled the total outlay to exceed that of the previous year by £430,000 were not fully spent by the Department. If I add the excise revenue of £4,067,700 to the savings of £780,000 in Imperial and Provincial expenditure, it will be found that the Budget for the year showed a surplus of £4,848,000. Out of this sum the Provincial Governments receive automatically a certain proportion of the revenue raised in their provinces. £540,000 of the surplus went thus to the local Governments; £782,000 went to provide suitable opening balances for the new Provinces of Bengal, Behar and Orissa and Assam; £322,000 went to pay the two weeks' gratuity to the lower-paid provincial employees, which was promised as a Durbar grant. This reduced the surplus to £3,960,000. In dealing with this sum we have, of course, to remember the causes which contributed to the great excess over the Budget estimate. The opium revenue, so far as it is derived from exports to China, will probably in greater part disappear during the next five years. The railway revenue has yielded a very exceptional return, but must always be regarded as a fluctuating source of income. I think, therefore, that it is right to treat the surplus as the outcome of financial conditions which cannot be relied upon to recur, and to apply it to non-recurring purposes. £867,000 was given to the Provincial Governments for sanitation, research in hygiene, improvements in communications, and improvements in agriculture. The remainder of the surplus of a little over £3,000,000 went to the reduction of debt. At the close of the year there was in existence £11,166,300 of temporary debt—India bills, India bonds, and debenture bonds—for which the general liability was assumed by the Secretary of State when he purchased the railways or terminated the contracts of companies. Provision has been made to pay off during 1912-13 out of the large balances in hand, including the surplus I have just mentioned, the £4,500,000 worth of Indian bills outstanding and the £1,977,600 of bonds which mature during the year. So there will thus be left out of this large temporary debt only a little over £4,500,000. I do not think I need stop to labour the general theoretical advantages of reducing so large an amount of debt, but, of course, the more India can free herself in prosperous times from floating debt in London the better she is in a position to call on the London market in times of difficulty.

The Future.

Now I turn to the future. The Indian revenue for 1912-13 is estimated at £53,442,400. The net expenditure is estimated at £51,964,000, and the surplus is estimated therefore at £1,478,300. The latest telegram we have received from India concerning the monsoon gives a summary that the present conditions and prospects are almost universally good, but the House will not be surprised, after what I have said, to hear the warning that a continuance of such prospects depends very largely on favourable late rains. The receipts in the new Estimate under most of the chief heads of revenue, such as forests, salt, stamps, Excise and Customs, railways and irrigation, are taken at a somewhat higher figure than in the Budget of last year to allow for normal expansion. The estimate of the price of opium, having regard to the difficulty of forecasting the course of this exceptionally speculative commodity, is the same as in the budget for last year, with allowances made for a reduction in the quantity sold. Under the head of general administration there is a reduction compared with last year of £673,200, which was expended last year in the civil expenditure on the Royal visit to India, and there is a similar reduction in the military services of £307,000. The largest increase in next year's budget is that of £760,000 for education. *(Hear, hear.)* For 1911-12 the amount provided was £2,094,000. In 1912-13 the amount is £2,855,000. There is also an increase of £400,000 on medical services, £333,000 is allocated to waterworks and drainage schemes, and £80,000 for medical research, including the equipment of research laboratories and the establishment of a tropical school of medicine. Of course, the House will see that the surplus for which we have budgetted is abnormally large. In a normal year the natural course would be to use at least a part of the surplus for the reduction of taxation or, perhaps, for increasing administrative expenses. But, in this year, neither of those courses was possible. The revenue derived from the sale of opium to China will shortly disappear, both because it is a source of revenue which I think neither India nor Great Britain desires to continue to have—*(hear, hear)*—and partly because of our international agreements. The surplus, therefore, is going to be retained in order to reduce the amount to be borrowed on capital expenditure on railways, irrigation works, and the building of the new Delhi.

THE NEW DELHI.

I want now to make a short diversion and say something about the new city of Delhi. The site which has been recommended by the Expert Committee, which has returned to this country, lies to the south-west of the modern city of Delhi between the Kutab Road and the Aravelli Ridge. The area stands high, commands a wide prospect which includes the existing city of Delhi, and the ground is virgin soil because the man-worn sites of the early occupation lie, I understand, nearer the river and due south of Delhi. The drainage problem is simplified by the ample fall of the ground towards the river, and although no plan for the laying out of the city has as yet been finally decided upon, I think it is safe to say that the present intention is that a belt of park not less than a thousand yards in width should intervene between the walls of old Delhi and the new capital, and that this park will probably be extended to envelop the entire site at the eastern boundary, where will lie probably the bazaar and the quarters of the English and Indian Government servants. The distance from the new Government House to the Jama Musjid will be about three miles to the south-west, and between the two will lie the Government offices for the administration of the old and the new city of Delhi. The military cantonments will be to the west of the Aravelli Ridge, where I understand, there is much available and suitable land. I have only to add that at the earliest possible moment the report of the committee and the plans will be exhibited in the tea room. On the site I have described it is hoped there will grow up the heart of India, on the site of what I think may be described as its most ancient capital, at its most convenient railway centre, the enduring British seat of Government, firmly planted, I believe, in the affections of those for whom it labours.

THE QUESTION OF COST.

The estimated cost of the new capital is put at £4,000,000. The Government scheduled under the Land Acquisition Act a very large area round Delhi, so that they are able to acquire the land they want at the price it was worth before the Durbar announcement. The buildings which will be a public charge are the Viceroy's residence, the Government offices, a place of meeting for the Imperial Legislative Council, and offices for the municipal administration and the cantonments. If residences for other individuals are constructed in the first instance at the cost of public revenue, a rent will be charged to the occupants. The architects for the various Government enterprises have not yet been chosen, but efforts will be made by competition to obtain a wide field of selection. I am afraid I cannot give at present any revised estimate. Lord Hardinge, in his speech to the Council on March 25, expressed considerable confidence that the estimate would be found to be sufficient. I can only say this provisional estimate has been framed after considering the cost of lighting, road-making, drainage, and comparing it with the similar cost for places like Bombay, Calcutta and Madras, and making allowance for the fact that there will be little or no clearing. We do not intend to build streets of private dwellings and shops, but we intend to allow other people to build private dwellings and shops in harmony with the general plan; and, although, of course, nothing definite can be said, I really do not anticipate that this new

Delhi will, in the long run, prove to be a very serious burden upon the finances of the country.

FINDING THE MONEY.

How are we going to find this money? When Government offices and buildings are required in India the usual practice is to find them out of current revenue; but, in view of the magnitude of the Delhi scheme, it is proposed to adopt a different method of providing the money, and in this case to treat the outlay as capital expenditure and to meet it partly from loans and partly from revenue surpluses as they may arise. I think it is the same principle which is now adopted in this country, as a rule, whenever public buildings are to be built. If new taxation were going to be imposed for the purpose of producing a surplus for use in Delhi, or if a remission was going to be refused because we wanted to provide a surplus, or if money was going to be withheld from administrative needs because of this plan, there would be very much weight in the objection which has been raised in India. But there is no idea of creating a surplus in any of these ways. New taxation is not introduced in India except to meet a deficit or a prospective deficit in current revenue, and the fact that the expenditure on Delhi is to be treated as capital expenditure will prevent it from contributing towards a deficit in current revenue, and there is no intention or prospect that the building of Delhi will prevent a remission of taxation, because the probability is that it will be built in a time when revenue from Chinese opium is disappearing and when no prudent man in

India and no Government of India would ever recommend the remission of taxation which it would be certain to have to re-impose at the end of that time. Undoubtedly the expeuditure on Delhi, so far as it is met from surpluses, will lessen the amount available for objects which are paid for from revenue generally. But it is equally true, in view of the limited amount which can be borrowed in any given year, that, if we met it from loans entirely, it would lessen the amount which could be spent on equally important work in connection with such subjects as railways and irrigation. To meet the whole expenditure from loans would involve the possibility of so restricting the expenditure on these latter objects as to diminish India's prosperity in time of plenty and her security against suffering in bad seasons. Therefore, I contend the task before the Government, when once it had come to the conclusion that the change of capital was a measure of such importance as to justify the expenditure involved, was to survey the field of administration as a whole and adopt a financial scheme which seemed likely to be the least onerous to the interests concerned. We believe that the plan we have adopted of using a variety of resources, instead of relying upon one, is the plan best calculated to achieve this object. The vindication of the decision will have to be looked for in the way in which it is carried into effect year by year while the expenditure on the new buildings is in progress. The Government of India will have to submit each year to the criticism of the Legislative Council and of Parliament as to the way in which it co-ordinates the claims of Delhi with the other claims on its resources. I do not think that, having regard to its commitments and its pledges, it is likely to allow the claims of Delhi to obscure its other responsibilities or to impede their fulfilment.

A New Chapter in Indian History.

I want now to ask the House to listen to a few more general statements. Two years ago I discussed generally the political position of India and what I conceived to be the lines on which it could best be governed ; and last year I dealt at some length with the social conditions and development of the country, and tried to explain how political development must be contingent upon social development. The three contentions which I tried to establish last year and the year before were, first, that it is possible to distinguish and segregate legitimate aspirations for advancement from sedition ; secondly, that political institutions cannot be imported advantageously from one country to another unless they are the resultant of similar social organisations, and that it is towards improved social conditions rather than change of political institutions that our attention and the attention of Indians should be turned ; and, thirdly, that there are striking analogies in the history of India under British rule and the history of a European country, although this chapter of the history of India has been shorter, because it is governed and created by men who have inherited the results of European and British development. I want to resist the temptation of going over that ground again. I cannot help thinking that with the passage of the Reform Act of 1909 a chapter of Indian history was closed and a new chapter was opened. I do not believe that India has yet discovered what possibilities there are without alteration of statute, without any new political demand, in the great reforms which will be for ever associated in the history of India with the name of Lord Morley. (*Cheers.*)

THE INDIAN STUDENT IN LONDON.

I want this year to devote my attention to the one problem which I believe underlies all other problems in India, which I think is the keystone of progress and the keystone of the development of social conditions, and of, eventually, the improvement of political conditions—namely, education. It has two branches —education in this country and education in India. Those interested in India must never lose sight of the increasing army of those who come over to England and benefit by our educational facilities, and who present a very serious problem. The facilities which we offer here are often purchased at an exorbitant price, and I think it is difficult for Indians to estimate them at their real value. It may well be that the solution of some of the difficulties presented by them may be found by providing better facilities for education in India itself. If this were done—if the Indian doctor, the Indian barrister, the Indian aspirant to an unprejudiced share in the Government of his own country, were to obtain an adequate training in his own country, I venture to say that many a parent would be saved anxiety and worry, many an Indian would be saved bitterness and disappointment, and perhaps the financial disaster attendant upon a journey to England. But whilst they are over here, in search of what the heart of the Empire can give them, it is our duty and part of our responsibility for the good Government of India to welcome and to help our Indian fellow-subjects to the best of our ability.

THE ENGLISHMAN'S DUTY.

Let me say first of all how difficult it is to interest men and and women in this country in Indian problems. Is it too much to hope that when the problems come to their very door they will respond to the invitation which in all humility I make to them to show some hospitality to our Indian fellow-subjects? All men and women who show this hospitality to our Indian visitors are doing an Imperial work of the utmost value to the Empire. Nothing could be more valuable than for English men and women in particular, to afford opportunities to Indians of learning something of English homes. I do not want to go into details, but I want to assure the House that I have had ample and lasting proof of the serious consequences of allowing Indian students to believe that the majority of the women with whom they come most easily in contact in the lonely lives they lead in lodging-houses are typical of English womanhood. May I say a word to undergraduates in our great Universities? A responsibility of an exceptional kind falls upon them. Amongst those who go to our Universities, both Indian and British, are the future administrators of India, and if we allow our Indian visitors to be segregated, isolated or rudely treated, we are sowing seed which will sprout and fruit long after we have repented of the carelessness which helped its germination.

THE ORGANISATION AT THE INDIA OFFICE.

I want to say something more now of the efforts the India Office are making to ensure that those who come to this country are looked after. It is not the first time the House has been asked to consider this question. The Master of Elibank, who preceded me at the India Office, explained to the House in 1909 the measures which had been taken. The scheme has now been in existence for three and a half years. So great a measure of success has been achieved that the Secretary of State feels himself justified in making a considerable extension and development. I should like to give the House an idea of the work which Mr. Arnold, the head of the organisation, and his staff have been called upon to perform. In the first place, a bureau of information has been created which provides information upon educational matters to Indian parents and students, keeps for students a record of suitable lodging-houses and of families that are ready to receive them, furnishes them with references and certificates required by institutions which they wish to enter, serves as an intermediary between the Universities and other academic bodies in cases where their regulations impose unintentional hardship on students from India or do not harmonise with the system enforced in Indian Universities and colleges, issues a handbook of information relating to academic and technical education, the condition of life, the cost of living in different centres of the United Kingdom to which Indian parents may wish to send their sons, and finally assists Indian students in this country with advice on matters social, financial, and educational, and undertakes at the express wish of Indian parents the guardianship of their sons, sending to them from time to time periodical reports as to their progress and conduct. It is now calculated that this bureau is in contact with 1,062 Indian students, or about 62 per cent. of the total number in this country. As regards those of whom Mr. Arnold has undertaken the guardianship, let me give the figures :—In June, 1910, there were 27 ; in March, 1911, 91 ; and in February last, 137. Between April, 1909, and June, 1910, the amount of remittances received on behalf of these students was about £5,000 ; between July 1, 1910, and June 1, 1911, the amount was over £18,000. The educational adviser works in conjunction with the Board of Education in finding suitable courses of instruction for technical students, and in regard to engineering he is assisted by an expert adviser in Mr. Campion.

MR. MALLET'S APPOINTMENT.

I wish to say that the scheme inaugurated in 1909 has fully justified its institution, and, secondly, that it has grown far beyond the control of its original organisation. Mr. Arnold, to whose zeal, energy, and devotion I gladly take this opportunity of paying public tribute, has with his assistants worked nobly to grapple with an ever-increasing rush of work. That a reorganisation is necessary is, I think, a justification of their work, for it is only by tactful management and the taking of infinite pains that the natural repugnance of students to placing themselves under control could be overcome and that the number to be dealt with has therefore increased. The first step which we have taken is to increase substantially the very insufficient salary upon which Mr. Arnold and his assistants are doing their work. Then a secretary for Indian students has been appointed at the India Office at a salary of £1,000 a year. (Opposition cries of "Oh!") As the House knows, we have been fortunate enough to secure the services of Mr. Mallet.

Mr. PEEL: Is there a pension?

Mr. MONTAGU: There is a pension after ten years' service if he is invalided; and if he is not invalided when he retires at the age of 60 he gets a pension of one-eightieth of his salary for each year of service, together with a bonus of one-thirtieth of his salary for each year of service.

Mr. PEEL: Is there any examination?

Mr. MONTAGU: No; there is no examination of any sort or kind. The position is not an easy one to fill. What is required is largely a knowledge of the conduct of a public office. I have not the slightest hesitation in saying after the very short experience and opportunity we have had of judging Mr. Mallet's work that it shows us to the full how glad we should be to welcome him as a colleague in this new and difficult work he has undertaken.

Mr. PEEL: Is a knowledge of any Indian language required?

Mr. MONTAGU: No. Mr. Mallet is to be a link between the Secretary of State and the various organisations in India on the one hand, and in this country on the other hand, which have been formed and are being formed for this important work.

Mr. KEIR HARDIE: Was there no Indian available?

Mr. MONTAGU: No, for the very important reason that we desired to appoint one with knowledge of the working of an office. It was considered that the best appointment that could be made was from Great Britain and not from India.

Captain FABER: Has he any knowledge of India?

Mr. MONTAGU: So far as I am aware, not. Mr. Arnold will in future confine his attention to students in London. There are something like 800 of these at present, and the number will probably be increased. If he is to carry on the work with the same personal attention as he has done in the past, we want to limit his activities to the guardianship and care of Indian students in London. Mr. Mallet will organise and keep in touch with similar organisations to that in Cromwell Road and which are being founded with the same object and on the same lines as those which have been so successful in London. In no University town at present is there any real satisfactory organisation for looking after Indian students. We want at Oxford, Cambridge, the Scottish Universities, and the provincial centres, where Indians congregate for study, similar machinery to combat the sense of homelessness. Our hope is that each University which enrols Indian students may be willing to appoint an officer who will make it his duty to know and to help all the Indian students there, to give them information and assistance, and even to act as guardians. We believe that will be of great value to the University and of great value to the Empire. The Secretary of State is, of course, willing under the new scheme to assist financially such efforts. Mr. Mallet will be in close relation to those local advisers and will help them in every way to organise their work and to induce others to co-operate with them and to assist them in communication with India. Communications are being carried on with the General Medical Council for more satisfactory regulations for Indian students who wish to study for the medical profession. Mr. Mallet will play an important part in this scheme. I wish to take this opportunity of expressing publicly the thanks of the Secretary of State for the courtesy and consideration with which these bodies have met his suggestions. I may add that there is no intention of abolishing the position of Indian assistant at Cromwell Road which was formerly held by Dr. Ray and the selection of a successor to Dr. Ray is now under consideration. I come to another branch of this subject. Indian students in recent years have come over to this country for industrial and technical study. A few of them—about ten every year—come at the cost of the Indian Government. Others are sent by patriotic societies, and others come at their own expense. Some doubt was expressed as to the value of the training they get, and the Secretary of State has appointed a committee to enquire into the matter, under the chairmanship of Sir Theodore Morison. The committee has not yet reported, but I understand all the members are agreed as to the importance of practical training. The university or technological school can teach science and its application to industry, but it cannot make a man an engineer, a tanner, or a manufacturer. He can only learn the industry by practical experience in a business concern which is run for profit, and I am afraid that Indian students find some difficulty in getting the practical experience which they need in a concern run for profit as a complement to their theoretical knowledge. Our colleges and Universities are open to them on the same terms as to Englishmen, but in some industries at least they meet with great reluctance to admit them. This is a state of things which fills me with concern. India is going to develop great industries and her young men are going to learn how to direct them. It is not a development which we should want to prevent or could prevent if we wanted. If Indian students cannot learn from manufacturers here they will go to foreign countries for the purpose, and on their return to India they will send orders for machinery and equipment to those countries. That seems to me a matter of such great importance that I invite the attention to it of members of the House who are interested in great industrial concerns.

Mr. MACCALLUM SCOTT: Has the Government

considered the adoption of the practice of the Japanese Government when giving out contracts of stipulating for a certain number of apprentices being employed ?

Mr. MONTAGU : I do not think that I can say anything about that, beyond that I am sure that it is one of the things which the Committee will consider. They have not yet made their Report. Then the question intrudes itself : Why do so many Indian students come to this country ? And the explanation is largely to be found in the fact that we have not provided comparable facilities in their own country, and therefore compel them to come over, at whatever cost, to obtain the fullest opportunities for useful careers.

THE EDUCATIONAL PROBLEM.

And so I come to another important aspect of the question—the question of improved education in India. It is not an easy subject. In this country the bulk of the population is in large towns, where it is possible to equip schools which can always be supplied with a full contingent of pupils who can be trained with efficiency and economy of effort. But in India over 90 per cent. of the population live in villages, and most of them are very small villages indeed. It is almost impossible to select a figure in connection with this subject in India which is not almost startling. There are over 600,000 villages with less than 1,000 inhabitants, and these villages include more than half the total population. This distribution makes it enormously costly to bring educational facilities within the reach of every child of school-going age. In addition to this there is the distrust of parents, some of whom wish merely to train their children as retail petty traders, and consider that the primary school curriculum is superfluous. Some parents among the present population are unable to see that schooling does any good, while it certainly withdraws the children from helping to look after the cattle. The school committees who manage the public schools have been described in one province as "varying between enthusiasm, toleration, and hostility." Sometimes we have the Western idea that schooling will raise the village boy above his station or make him unwilling to accept the old rate of wages. Much of the education given up to the present has been of an unpractical nature. The boy was for a few hours a day taken mentally out of the world in which he passed his life and taught by rote what were to him utterly useless facts, such as the names of British possessions in Africa. If you do not know whether Africa is a hundred or a hundred thousand miles away from your village it is not of much interest to you to learn the exact political status of Sierra Leone. But, of course, it is much less troublesome to all parties concerned to teach a boy to learn by heart what a "cape" or a "bay" is than to go with him to the nearest stream or lake and show him in miniature exactly what the objects are. Then caste presents some difficulty. I do not want to overrate it, because I believe that among the castes and classes who can read freely caste prejudices bulk less largely than in the West. The description of a school in a Hindu village often reminds me of the description of a

Scottish village school in the eighteenth century where the sons of the laird and the ploughman sat side by side and thought no harm of it. But when we reach the gulf which separates the higher castes from the depressed castes, whose touch is regarded as pollution, we find ourselves in very deep waters indeed, and the question of the depressed classes constitutes one of the very serious difficulties in the way of universal primary education.

THE SCARCITY OF TEACHERS.

There are very great difficulties also in connection with the supply of properly trained teachers. The market value of a primary schoolmaster, if he is technically qualified, but untrained—that is, if he has certificates but has not passed through a normal school—may be as low as eight rupees per month. The average wage of a primary schoolmaster in 1907 was £6 13*s.* 4*d.* a year. The supply of qualified teachers for vernacular schools, even with increase of pay, is scanty at present. Any man who knows English is reluctant to become a purely vernacular teacher and prefers the Provincial Civil Service, which he finds far more lucrative than the Education Department. And when one reflects upon the enormous share taken by women teachers in this country and America in education in primary schools one realises the difficulty of getting sufficient teachers in a country where women teachers cannot be employed except for female education. Then, again, there is the question of inadequate buildings. We do not want elaborate buildings and furniture in schools in India, but in the case of schools under private management, which are three-fourths of the total number, it is the custom for classes to be held in verandahs lent for the purpose, or in the master's own dwelling house, or in any other place that can be obtained. I mention these difficulties only that the House may realise the magnitude of the task before us, but I do not think that the difficulties afford any excuse for apathy or indifference. On the contrary, they should only serve as an incentive to greater activity.

The Policy of the Government.

The only question we have to decide now is the direction this activity should take. The House will have heard of the proposals associated with the name of that eminent Indian educationist, Mr. Gokhale, who has introduced a Bill for what I may describe shortly as free compulsory primary education on a permissive basis. What I mean by that is that the education is to be free and compulsory where under certain conditions the local authority choose to apply it. He estimates that the cost of his proposal will ultimately be about 3½ million pounds. We are inclined to believe that that is a sanguine estimate. I hope Mr. Gokhale and those who sympathise with him will never misunderstand me when I urge a quality always irksome to self-sacrificing reformers like himself—the quality of patience. He thinks that primary education as it exists at present in India is sufficiently valuable to force it on the whole school-going population of India as early as possible. We do not. Universal and free education must come in India, as it has come in all other countries, but the time is not yet. I am confident that the Government of India has a policy dictated for the present by the same hopes and aims as the hopes and aims of Mr. Gokhale's Bill which will produce for the moment a better result. We have no hostility towards the principles which inspire his Bill. We and he together are working for the same end, the breaking down of illiteracy in India. No one who knows anything about the matter can deny that his energy and his speeches have helped us to create the public opinion, without which our activity would be useless, but we believe that the greatest expansion of education can be secured not by making it free or compulsory at the present moment, but by the improvement and the multiplication of the schools. In the Bomby Presidency it is roughly calculated that there are 100,000 children whose parents would willingly send them to school to-day if there were schools to send them to. And the same story is told about other provinces, where it has been demonstrated that the surest way of increasing the school attendance is to increase the number of schools. And with regard to compulsion, the case is even stronger. Compulsion really can only be worked where education is popular, and where, therefore, the need of putting compulsion into force would not show itself to the very large bulk of the population. There is not much use in applying it to resentful districts.

There is not much to be hoped from compulsion unless it is largely effective, and how much unrest and disturbance a really effective measure for making primary education compulsory would create it is not difficult to imagine. In the Native State of Baroda, where education has been made compulsory, the fines for non-attendance amount to 60,000 rupees per year. This figure gives an incidence per head of the population which is double the incidence of the fees charged in elementary schools in India. Yet what is the result? The percentage of literacy among the males in Baroda after five years of free and compulsory education is 17·5. In the adjacent British district of Broach, where education is neither free nor compulsory, the percentage of literacy is 27·4. I should like to read to the House the language of a leading Indian chief, the Raja of Rajpipla, a State in the Bombay Presidency. He is a progressive Chief, who takes a keen interest in his State, and has done much to advance education in it. He used only recently the following words:— "Make primary education as free as you choose; add as many further inducements as you can; but do not make it compulsory. In the case of the most advanced classes it is absolutely unnecessary, and would serve only to create irritation. In the case of the poor 'backward classes,' it would inflict harm where good was meant, would subject them to great harassment, would be positively cruel and unjust, and would be deeply though silently resented as such."

What is our alternative plan? We have already, I would point out, made a considerable step in the direction of free primary education. Primary schools for girls generally charge no fees. Primary education for boys is free in certain provinces. No fees are charged in the monastery schools of Burma. The sons of agriculturists in the Punjab and in certain districts of the United Provinces pay no fees. Primary education has been made free in the frontier provinces of Assam, Baluchistan and the North-West Frontier. There are arrangements in other provinces giving primary education without charge to backward sections of the community, with the result that from one-fifth to a third of the boys already receive free education. Let me tell the House something of the progress made in the last ten years. In 1901 Lord Curzon dealt with the subject with characteristic candour. He declared that "he could not be satisfied with a state of things in which four villages out of five are without a school, and three boys out of four grow up without education and one girl in forty only attended school." During the last ten years there has been an increase of 22 per cent. in the number of schools and 44 per cent. in the number of scholars, and to-day there are 4,500,000 boys and 866,000 girls receiving primary education in 120,000 schools. During the last four years there has been an increase of about 240,000 boys per annum attending school, but, while 15 per cent. of the population is of school-going age, of that population only 4 per cent. of the boys and 7 per cent. of the girls are at school. The educational grant of £330,000 a year announced at the Delhi Durbar is to be spent mainly on primary education, and is but a prelude to a much more extensive programme. The programme which we hope to work up in time is as follows :—We desire to increase the total number of primary schools by 90,000, or 75 per cent., and to double the school-going population. The cost of the new schools will be £25 each per year, and they will be placed in villages and other centres of population which are at present without schools. We are going to improve the existing schools, which now only cost about £10 a year ; the cost of these will probably have to be doubled.

Lord RONALDSHAY ; In what period ?

Mr. MONTAGU : I cannot give the period. As I am going on to say, it must take some considerable time. But this is the programme which we propose at once to set ourseleves to work on. We want to improve the teaching given in the schools, and make it practical, popular, and instructive, and for that purpose we have got to improve the teaching.

Sir J. D. REES : Up to what sort of grant would you work ?

Mr. MONTAGU : The additional expenditure this year is £750,000. I cannot give figures for a longer period.

Mr. WYNDHAM : Is the balance of £1,000,000 of increased expenditure for education going to higher education ?

Mr. MONTAGU : It includes both higher and primary education.

Mr. WYNDHAM : And that is comprised in the million ?

Mr. MONTAGU : No ; three-quarters of a million is the amount this year, both for higher education and primary education. As I said, we must make the education attractive, and therefore we want a larger supply of better-equipped teachers. We hope to lay down the rule that they shall have passed at least the upper primary school standard, that there shall be at least one teacher to every 50 scholars, that the pay shall begin at least with 12 rupees a month, and that there shall be better prospects for teachers by grading and instituting a provident fund or pension system. These two items of improvement and extension will involve a very large expenditure, and the recurring expense of these schools will be by no means the only charge on the Indian Treasury. There must be heavy initial expenditure for buildings and equipment. More serious and more costly will be the training of the teachers which the schools will absorb. I want to ask the House to remember that a considerable space of time must elapse before these hopes can be realised. The financial problems which these educational ideas involve are obvious to every one. What is not so clearly obvious is that, even if the money were now in hand, it could not immediately be spent. The Government of India is satisfied that, at the present moment, an increased salary would not bring forth any considerable increase of competent teachers. Trained men do not exist in sufficient numbers for the existing schools, and therefore the only way in which the problem can be dealt with is to call them into existence.

Higher Education.

Let us turn our attention for a moment to higher education. I want, if I may, to draw the attention of the House to the importance of this subject. May I venture on an analogy between the conditions of India to-day and of Europe in the Middle Ages? I do not want to press the parallel beyond this point, that we have a series of large countries, each with its own vernacular speech (or, perhaps, more than one vernacular), brought into an intellectual commonwealth by the use for purposes of higher education of a language which is not a native vernacular. Any Englishman, Frenchman, or German who proceeded to higher studies in the Middle Ages learnt to write and to speak Latin, the language of law, of science, and of politics. In India, to-day, the man who would serve the State in the higher departments of law, or science, or politics must learn English. Of course the parallel breaks down at this point, because English is not to India, as Latin was to Europe, the language of religion. It is, as Latin was not, the language of business and international commerce. Further, English is a living tongue, whereas Latin was not then a live one. Possibly my comparison may seem fanciful, but I make it for this reason. Very few of us, I think, stop to consider what it really means when we find Indian gentlemen taking high honours at their English University, passing competitive examinations in this country, or making admirable speeches in the Legislative Councils. I would like to ask how many Oxford or Cambridge graduates capable of turning English literature into the most excellent Latin prose, how many cultured Englishmen who can read German with ease, would be prepared to learn higher mathematics and write mathematical or scientific theses in German, or to sit down in an examination room and answer questions on Indian history in Latin ? How many of us would be prepared to conduct our debates in this Chamber in any foreign language which we were supposed to have learned when we left school ? That is precisely the achievement of many Indian gentlemen to-day. When we admit and deplore the manifest shortcomings of Indian secondary education, we forget that each of the pupils whom we so often hear of as being prepared by a process of cramming, has not only had to acquire the English language, which differs fundamentally from his own in structure, in spirit and in syntax, but has got to acquire all the other advanced knowledge through the medium of English. I think it is too often forgotten that this sort of thing is very typical in India, the sort of thing described by one member in a recent speech in the Viceroy's Council, a speech which, in point of form, might well serve as a model to many of us here, and in which he said : " That he received the elements of education sitting on the floor of the primary school, confronting a wooden board, covered with red powder, and with a piece of stick with which to write vernacular letters."

We propose in secondary education to extend our model schools where required, and not to replace private or aided schools, but to co-operate with them and set an example of standard. Only graduates will be employed as teachers. It is hoped to establish a graded service with salaries of from 40 to 400 rupees a month. We want to establish a school course complete in itself, with a curriculum comparable to a school course on the modern side of an English public school, giving manual training and science teaching. There is to be an increased grant to privately-managed schools, and we want to provide proper hostel accommodation.

I come now to the Universities. Mr. Balfour exposed the difficulty of the Indian University system with, if I may say so, admirable lucidity to the Congress of Universities. The words he used were these :—" How are you going to diminish the shock which the sudden invasion of a wholly alien learning must have on the cultured society of the East ? A catastrophic change in the environment of an organism is sure to inflict great injury upon the organism, perhaps destroy it altogether. In the East we are compelled to be catastrophic. It is impossible to graft by a gradual process in the East what we have got by a gradual process in the West." And so we have the complaint that our Indian University teaching has undermined religions, has weakened the restraint of ancient customs, and has destroyed that reverence for authority which was one of the attributes of Indian character. How can we combat these things ? We believe that the dangers of catastrophic change can be mitigated by adopting in India that part of the English system of education which has, so far as the Universities are concerned, proved most successful in moulding character. Character is not trained by lectures or taught by text-books. It forms but a small part of the work in the class-rooms. But it has arisen, as it were, accidentally, as a by-product of our residential schools and old Universities. Young men in their association together evolve certain rules of conduct which they impress on each other, and which we speak of as the tone or tradition of the school or college. There is evidence to show that in residential colleges in India traditions comparable to those in our own public schools spring into existence and stamp their indelible impression upon the young men who go there. The formative influence of the residential college can be stimulated by the presence of English masters and professors who have been trained in the same system in their own country, and who know how much can be done by example and how little by homily. It is this side of University education which we propose to develop in India. We have allotted large grants for building hostels and boarding houses attached to colleges. We are finding money for libraries in connection with the colleges; we desire to develop existing Universities by the creation of chairs in different branches of post-graduate research, and we propose to increase the aid to private colleges. The Universities of India have hitherto been of a federal or affiliating type. At their first inception they were little more than boards constituted for the purpose of holding examinations, and for these examinations students were prepared at a great number of institutions scattered over a wide area. As the Universities were only examining boards they could only recognise merit shown in the examinations. The training of character and other valuable by-products of collegiate life could not be recognised or encouraged.

Universities of this type came into existence in England in the last century, but after a short experience the type has been generally condemned, and the recent tendency has been for the federal University to be dissolved and for the constituent college to become independent Universities. It is upon such lines that the Government of India is directing the construction of the Indian Universities. The first step was taken in 1904, when the area within which each University could exercise the power of affiliation was demarcated. The next step will be to reduce the area over which each University exercises jurisdiction ; but where college is adequately staffed and equipped,and where it has shown a capacity to attract to itself students from a distance,that college will be elevated to the dignity of a University and will be given the power of conferring degrees upon the students who have been trained within its walls. Such Universities will be local and residential in the fullest sense of the term. They will, it is hoped, develop traditions of their own and become centres of learning. The Government of India have expressed a wish to create a University of this type in Dacca, and correspondence is passing between the Government of India and the Secretary of State upon giving a similar status to the college at Aligarh. It is probable that Universities of a similar type will shortly follow at Benares and Rangoon. *(Hear, hear.)*

THE DEVELOPMENT OF TECHNICAL EDUCATION.

Then, of course, there must be side by side with this extension of liberal University education an increase of technical education. Technical education is to be developed. A technicological institute at Cawnpore has been sanctioned in accordance with the recommendations of Sir John Hewett, who has done so much in the cause of technical education in India. I may say, generally, that technical education is to be advanced all over India. (*Hear, hear.*) This must serve as a summary of the educational efforts which the Government of India is making in all directions. I have attempted to show that we are extending our educational facilities in that country. We are making a courageous and sustained effort to break down illiteracy in primary education. We are leading the way towards the recognition of a higher standard of efficiency in secondary education by the establishment of model Government schools. We are spending large sums upon the provision of well-equipped hostels attached both to schools and to colleges and promoting the growth of a healthy residential system. We are trying to mitigate the evils of wholesale examination by the contraction of the area over which each University enjoys jurisdiction, and to establish a new type of University which may develop into a genuine home of learning. (*Hear, hear.*) At the same time, we are developing industrial and technological education. I say confidently that that is a record of which any Government may be proud and a programme to which the House can confidently look forward. (*Hear, hear.*) If the educational ideal which we have in mind is realised we will have laid the foundation of a national system of education by a network of really valuable schools, colleges, and Universities, so that facilities will be opened to Indians to qualify themselves in their own country for the highest positions in every walk in life.

OPPORTUNITIES FOR INDIANS.

The problem before us when we have educated Indians is to give them the fullest opportunity in the Government of their own country to exercise the advantages which they have acquired by training and by education. How are we going to remove avoidable disabilities under which Indians labour while promoting the efficiency of the public services generally? Those who desire reform in the Indian service will welcome the appointment by His Majesty of a Royal Commission of which the House has heard. There are many questions, a solution of which is confidently asserted by some to be as confidently refuted by others, and which will never be properly solved until we have an authoritative pronouncement on them. I want to justify the appointment of this Royal Commission, but I want most carefully, in what follows, to avoid the expression of any opinion lest it might be considered to be the opinion of the Government, upon whose behalf I speak this afternoon. Sir Charles Aitchison's Public Service Commission reported at the end of 1887, and final orders were published on its recommendation in 1891. Accepting, as I do, the supposition that those orders were the best possible orders that could have been passed at that time, he would be a bold man who would say, having regard to the development of India during the past twenty years, that there is now no necessity for any development of the system which owes its results to Sir Charles Aitchison's Commission. Many points remain, and some directly result from the orders which were based upon that Commissioner's report which have given rise (it is not an exaggeration to say) to grave discontent inside and outside the services concerned.

First of all, there is the Indian Civil Service. A competitive examination at the moment lays the way open for a choice between the home and the Indian Civil Service, and those who choose the Indian Civil Service have a year's probation at home before they go out to do the varied administrative, executive, and judicial work, the success of which is, I think, the marvel of the whole world, and a source of continued pride to the people of Great Britain. I do not think that I shall be accused of optimism when I express the confident belief that the innate power of well-ordered administration and prompt decisive action, which seems to me to be the characteristic of the British race and perhaps of no other, will never fail. Bur more than that is wanted,—humanity, capacity to deal with men, statesmanship, and, above all, that quality which is increasingly wanted as the keynote of British rule in India—sympathy. The Indians with whom the young Indian Civil servant comes into contact will be better educated, with a wider knowledge of other countries and of the world as the years go by. As we improve our system of education, and as we increase our capacity for the expression of popular opinion, and as Indians come over to this country, not only Government students, not only Indian princes, but zemindars and merchants, and travel in Europe, learning of England at its best and at its worst, it becomes all the more important that we should not risk any deterioration of our service, but that we should give to India, as we have undoubtedly done in the past, the very best material we can.

It is obvious that to open both the Home and Indian Civil Services to one examination gives us a wider choice, because it gives to the candidate a choice of profession when he passes the examination, but it will be for the Commission to consider how far nowadays it results in our getting only the "leavings" of the Home Civil Service, and how far further an examination, which can admittedly be passed by unaided cramming, is the best possible way of securing our Indian Civil servants. I do not know, and it would be improper for me to express an opinion, but this is for the Commission to consider, and there are many other questions which suggest themselves. Is the year's probation long enough ? Is it spent to the best possible advantage under our present system ? Do we get our young men at an age when they are too old to adapt themselves to the life they have to lead, or, on the contrary, are they too young for the responsibilities which they have to bear ? Ought not the training they receive to be supplemented by more intimate knowledge of our legal procedure in this country ? Might not certain difficulties of our

Indian judicial system be overcome by some such means as these ?

Sir J. D. REES : Will this Commission deal with the manner in which Barrister Judges are appointed to the public service ?

Mr. MONTAGU : After this attempt to justify the appointment of the Commission I intend to read to the House the terms of reference and the personnel of the Commission. Then again there is the position of the Indians in the Civil Service. The door to the Indian Civil Service is at present only to be found in this country, and this is one of the reasons why Indians come over here. It has been suggested that the examination for the Indian Civil Service should be held here and simultaneously in India, or, that if another process is adopted for selecting Civil servants that the same process should be gone through in India as is gone through here. It has been answered that it would be impossible under such a system to ensure the same status and the same standard in India as we require here. And when the service has been recruited is the door to promotion open as widely as possible to men of all races in the best possible way ? Are the rules of pay and of pensions suitable or incapable of improvement ? Is it right that Indians should not subscribe to the Family Fund ? There is then the Indian Medical Service which is only recruited in this country. Is the training which is possible for Indians in their own country of such value as to warrant us opening the door to Indians in their own country ? Does the existence of an Indian Medical Service prevent the growth of an independent medical profession? Would it be right to open the doors of the Indian Civil Service and of the Indian Medical Service to subjects of Fuedatory States? All these problems present themselves again and again to those who have to do with administration in India.

We come then to the other services. The House is familiar with the division into Provincial and Imperial Services. Roughly and generally the Imperial Service is recruited in England, and the Provincial Service is recruited in India. The Imperial Service has preserved for it the higher superior appointments, and the Provincial Service fills the higher subordinate appointments, while the lower appointments are filled partly from the Provincial Service and partly from the Imperial Service. The pay, leave, and pension rules in each service have been fixed by a consideration of what is necessary to secure Europeans to serve away from their own country and by what is necessary to secure Indians to serve in their own country. The result is that the branch which is essentially European has better pay, better prospects, and more responsibility than the branch which is essentially Indian. It does not necessarily by any means follow that these principles are wrong—that is for the Commission to decide. It is necessary to have a European element in most of the services. European officers must be given pay and prospects sufficient to induce them to join these services, and when good men have been trained and have been induced to join they must be placed in positions of responsibility adequate to their merits. It has been said, and again I express no opinion, that this has been achieved in a way which causes just discontent among Indians ; That it is not achieved in the most appropriate way, and that our present system excludes desirable men, and involves avoidable race distinction. In those services where the Imperial branch is recruited by nomination, although Indians are not in all of them declared to be ineligible, although in one, the Public Works Department, provision has been made for giving a certain proportion of the appointments every year to India, the result of the system is, in almost all the services Indians are shut out from the more important and highly-paid posts. In the Education Service, by recruiting the Imperial Service only in this country, only two Indians have been appointed in the last fifteen years. In the Public Works Department, Lord Morley deceided that 10 per cent. of the appointments should, if possible, be given to Indians each year. The result was that certain Indians were appointed to the Imperial Service who had failed to get into the Provincial Service.

So the system results in either keeping Indians out of the higher branches of the service, or appointing them with qualifications inferior to those required for the lower branch. And, if the principle of maintaining appointments in this country only for Europeans is abandoned, it imposes a course of education in England on Indians who wish to attain high office in their own country. In all these services there is the question of pay, pension, leave, the present conditions of which will be familiar to students of the subject, but which I dare not ask the House to listen to in detail now. Every service has its grievance. There is the Police, Forests, the Telegraphs, the Survey and the Educational Service, the examination of which is all the more necessary having regard to the development of education which is going on. I do not want to give an enumeration which might be held to be exhaustive, and I do not want to suggest to the House that the services can be dealt with piecemeal. It is a question of principle that we have to decide first. The principles must be adjusted before the details can be settled. The terms of reference to the Commission are as follows :—

"To examine and report upon the following matters in connection with the Indian Civil Service and other Civil Services, Imperial and Provincial :—

(1) The methods of recruitment and the systems of training and probation ;

(2) The conditions of service, salary, leave and pension ;

(3) Such limitations as still exist in the employment of non-Europeans and the working of the existing system of division of Services into Imperial and Provincial.

And generally to consider the requirements of the Public Service, and to recommend such changes as may seem expedient."

The members of the Commission are as follows :—

Lord Islington, the present Governor of New Zealand ;

The hon. Member for Hornsey (Earl of Ronaldshay) ;

Sir Murray Hammick, of the Indian Civil Service, at present acting Governor of Madras, pending the arrival of Lord Pentland ;

Sir Theodore Morison, Member of the Council of India ;

Sir Valentine Chirol ;

Mr. Frank George Sly, of the Indian Civil Service ; Commissioner of Berar ;

Mr. Chaubal, Member of the Governor of Bombay's Executive Council ;

Mr. Gokhale, Member of the Viceroy's Legislative Council ;

Mr. Madge, also a Member of the Viceroy's Legislative Council ;

Mr. Rahim, a Judge of the Madras High Court ;

The hon. Member for Leicester (Mr. James Ramsay Macdonald) ;

Mr. Herbert Albert Fisher, Fellow and Tutor of New College, Oxford.

It only remains for me in this connection to ask the House to wish these gentlemen, who have so patriotically devoted themselves to a very difficult, arduous, and lengthy investigation for the benefit of India, all good fortune in their labours. I am confident that the results of their deliberations must be of enormous importance to India, and that they will lead to an improvement in its Government. Perhaps the House will permit me to conclude with a few general words in which I will attempt to explain what I think is to be drawn from what is happening in India. I have often said before, and I say now, that I can see nothing alarming in the condition of India. Its revenue and its trade are expanding ; it is being better equipped year by year to withstand the calamities of weather and of disease; its people are better trained to play the part of citizens. We have given public opinion expression adequate to the present development of the nation. But, as I said last year and I repeat now, in what must be regarded more than ever as a progressive country, two warnings are necessary. The first is that you cannot now, even if you would, embark on a policy of re-action. The mighty mass in India is moving in response to our own stimulus, and to try and force it back into a condition of sleep, which would now be an unwilling sleep, and could only be achieved, if it could be achieved, by repression, would be a calamity-producing blunder. The second warning which, in all humility, I would give is that, seeing that India is never the same to-day as it was yesterday, and will never be the same to-morrow as it is to-day, the man who relies on out-of-date knowledge, the man who expresses a confident opinion about India, based on knowledge however intimate, or on work however admirable, but a few years out of date, who prefaces his every remark with the words *indicus olim* is a man whose advice must not be accepted without question.

If we are to do our duty by the enormous responsibilities which we have undertaken we must move forward, however cautiously, accepting the consequences of our own acts and inspirations, and keeping ourselves informed as intimately as we possibly can of the modern and changing aspects of the problem with which we have to deal. Nobody can possibly foretell what will be the eventual characteristic of the population we shall form in India ; the India which must be a heritage, not only of its Asiatic population alone, but also of that small handful of Europeans who have unified it, giving it its trend, brought to it its traditions and its ideals, and which must be reckoned in its destinies. There is a trite quotation so often made that I hardly like to quote it now, that "East is East and West is West." Nobody wants to deny it ; no living man whould have it otherwise. But as a great Bengali writer has laid it down, the East and West must meet "at the altar of humanity." And then they are meeting, not with clash or discord, but in harmony and amity. There need be no enmity and competition; the forces are not mutually destructive, they are mutually complimentary. Each learnt much and has much to learn.

THE INDIAN BUDGET, 1913.

The Under Secretary of State for India (Mr. Montagu) : I beg to move, " that Mr. Speaker do now leave the chair (for Committee on East India Accounts)."

This is the fourth time that it has fallen to my lot to move that you do leave the chair in order that the East India Revenue Accounts for the year may be reported to the House. I can assure the House that as the years go by I approach this task with more and more diffidence. I am afraid that the temper of the House with regard to Indian matters has not altered very materially since Mr. Gladstone, in 1834, wrote a letter to his father on a speech which he had made on the University Bill. He said :—

> " The House heard me with the utmost kindness, but they had been listening previously to an Indian discussion in which very few people took any interest, and the change of subject was no doubt felt as relief."

Since I last stood at this box for this purpose, I have had the advantage of a prolonged journey in India. I make no apology for that tour, though I do most sincerely apologise to the House for any inconvenience that my absence may have caused. After all, no one questions the wisdom of the first Lord of the Admiralty in journeying to see the ships under his charge, or of the Secretary of State for War in meeting and talking to soldiers, or of the President of the Local Government

Board in inspecting work-houses, or of the Home Secretary in going to look at the prisons. I am convinced that I did right, when I had been longer in my office than any of my predecessors, with the exception of three or four, in going to see something of the country and of the people with whose welfare I was concerned. I promised the House that I shall not weary them this afternoon with an account of the opinions which I formed in India. I am here only to express the views of the Government which I represent.

I have the opportunity from day to day in my office of bringing to bear upon my daily work the information given to me in India, and it was not for the purpose of making speeches, but for the purpose of helping me in my share of the administration that I went out. I can only say that it would be almost impossible for me to forget the cordial assistance given by British and Indian officials and non-officials alike in my eager desire to find out what we could do to help them, and I shall endeavour to prove my gratitude by helping to bring about, as time goes on, some the many schemes of reform which were advocated to me abroad. I am certain that the majority of those whom I had the honour and pleasure of meeting were glad, at all events, to get an opportunity of meeting face to face and talking to an inmate of that very vague and indefinite authority which so often is the instrument of alterations in the conditions under which they live—the India Office.

When I mention the India Office, I want to say a word to the House about the changes which we contemplate in the organisation of the Office. I need only say a very few words, because a week ago my Noble Friend explained in another place exactly what was in his mind. To lay certain possible anxieties to rest, I want to say at once that there is not now, nor, so far as I am aware, has there ever been, any intention to abolish the Council of India. It is not even proposed to curtail any of their powers. And in order to lay to rest another rumour that has been circulated, I want to say emphatically that whatever be the exact final shape of the scheme, one unalterable factor in it is the presence of two Indian members on the Council. The whole scheme is one of domestic reform such as might be accomplished by any other Minister by a stroke of the pen without consulting anybody. But in the case of the India Office the minutest detail of which is statutorily prescribed, it will be necessary to come to Parliament for a Statute. We have a dual aim : to speed up and to simplify the slow and complicated procedure of the office, and to make the expert advice which the Secretary of State derives from his Council more up to date.

Anybody who is sufficiently interested will have read my Noble Friend's speech in another place, and it will not be necessary for me to go into details, but I do not think that there is anybody familiar with the procedure of the India office who will deny—I cannot do better than use the words my Noble Friend quoted—that it is "intolerably cumbrous and dilatory." With regard to the other part of the scheme, it is possible, under existing Statute, that a member of the Council may by the end of this time have been twelve years out of India. We propose to reduce that period, so far as possible, to about seven years. This may not appear very important to people here, but it is very keenly awaited in India. When, at the end of my tour, I read, in one of the leading Indian newspapers an article commenting on my visit to India, an appeal to me to go home and do all I could to bear on the alteration of the Council, in order to bring about these results, so that the opinions it expressed and the advice it gave might be more up to date and more in accordance with recent developments, it gave me great satisfaction to think that we had been considering such schemes for two years, and that they were very nearly ripe for announcement.

Leaving the India Office and coming to India itself, I propose this year, with the permission of this House, to introduce an innovation which I cannot but think will be welcome to those Hon. Members who, by their presence this afternoon, show their interest in India. I do so with some trepidation, because I am fully aware of the years of unbroken precedents behind me, and I do so by way of experiment. As the House is well aware, the financial statement made by the Financial Member of the Government of India, together with the debates on it in the Viceroy's Legislative Council, has already been circulated to the House in the form of a Blue Book, and this Blue Book has been supplemented by a White Paper containing what is known as the Under Secretary of State's "Explanatory Memorandum." It has been usual for the Minister responsible for India in this House to superimpose upon this explanation a further explanation, amounting to nothing more than a copious analysis of the White Paper. This has occupied the first half of the Budget Speech of the year. The second part has been devoted to questions of general administration. When one considers that this Debate is, in ordinary circumstances, the only opportunity in the year for the discussion of Indian affairs, and that only one night is given to it, I really think that no apology will be needed from me if I rely on the Explanatory Memorandum and say very little about finance this year. I should like to devote that portion of the valuable time of the House which I desire to usurp to the discussion of matters of general public interest in the administration which have not before been discussed.

These are the salient features of the Budget. There was last year, due mainly to the very large railway receipts and the high prices obtained for opium, a surplus of not less than nearly £8,000,000 over the Budget Estimate. This surplus is to be spent mainly on Grants to provincial Governments for education and sanitation and, with the surplus estimated for in the Budget, on the reduction and avoidance of debt. For this year, 1913-14, it has been considered prudent to estimate the railway receipts at a slightly less sum than last year, but the remarkable feature of the year is that this is the first Budget in which no receipts can be expected from the Indo-Chinese opium traffic. May I remind the House of what I said two years ago on this subject—in 1911? My words then were :—

"We must now definitely face the total loss, sooner or later, of revenue derived from opium sold for export to China ... (but) the question whether the loss of opium revenue will involve fresh taxation is one which I hope no one will decide too hastily. The present financial strength of the Government of India, the growth of its resources and the growth of restriction of its expenditure, are all factors that have to be considered as the plans for each financial year are made."

My doubts whether the loss of the Chinese opium revenue would lead to the necessity for new taxation were, I believe, considered to be the index of a characterically too optimistic frame of mind, but in Indian matters, and on Indian finance especially, optimistic views have a way of being justified by the .event. In the present year the chief feature in the Budget Estimates is that, although the Estimate anticipated from the opium revenue is only £306,000 or £4,250,000 less than last year, yet without any increase of taxation without any abandonment of necessary or desirable, expenditure, and with, indeed, a very large provision for the two objects which the Government of India recognise as having a first claim on their resources, namely, the improvement of education and the spread of sanitation, we are estimating for a surplus of nearly £1,500,000

This position is mainly due to one factor—the improvement in the earnings of the railways. For the last two generations successive Secretaries of State and Governments of India have used the resources and the credit of India to build up a railway system which has always been closely associated with the State, and has become more closely associated with it during the last generation. They have met with difficulties and discouragements of varions kinds. In the early years there was a large annual loss which had to be made good from revenue. In later years, such has been the growth in the world of the demand for capital, there has been difficulty in obtaining the necessary capital, but they have persevered in spite of all, and the Budget of 1913-14, thanks to the growth of the railway revenue, enables them to make good a loss of £4,000,000 out of a total not revenue of less than £60,000, a rich reward for the work of many years. I think this story may be taken as a symptom of the marvellous possibilities of our Indian Empire, and as a lesson that bold Government enterprise in the direction of helping and exploiting her resources by developing her railways, or her irrigation works, or her wonderful forests, will lead to large national profit. I wish to say a word next about education, a subject which always interests Members of this House. At the Delhi Durbar, in December, 1911, it was announced that:—

> "The Government of India has resolved to acknowledge the predominant claim of educational advancement on the resources of the Indian Empire,"

and that it was

> "their firm intention to add to the Grant (made at the time of the Durbar) further Grants in future years on a generous scale."

In accordance with this declaration, last year and this year, a non-recurring Grant of £2,500,000 and a recurring Grant of £695,000 a year have been made for this purpose. The non-recurring Grant will be spent on capital requirements for schools (elementary and technical), colleges, and universities, including the new universities which it is hoped to establish at

Aligarh, Dacca, Patna, and Rangoon. The recurring Grant will be spent on such matters as scholarships and stipends, educational Grants to local bodies, and the strenthening and improving of the inspection and teaching staff. It is perhaps worth while, in order to show the progress of educational outlay by the Government of India and provincial Governments, to compare the provision this year with the outlay of the three preceding years :—

In 1910-11 the actual net outlay was £1,662,607.

In 1911-12 it was £1,815,579.

In 1912-13 it was £370,600.

In 1913-14 the provision is £3,847,200.

An increase in three years of about 130 per cent.

The service which has the next strongest claim after education on the resources of the Government is Sanitation. This year and last year recurring Grants of £261,000 and non-recurring Grants of nearly £1,500,000 have been made, some of which may be used for research, but the bulk of which are intended for schemes of urban sanitation. Anyone familiar with the horrible slums in such cities as Bombay, and the marvellous effect on health of such work as is carried out by the Bombay Improvement Trust, will welcome this additional expenditure. In order that the House may have comparable figures to those which I have given for education as regards sanitation, I may say that the Budget Estimate of expenditure for santitation under this head comes this year to nearly £2,000,000, showing an increase of 112 per cent. over the expenditure of three years ago. I am precluded from dealing with many things in the financial world, which I should like to say something about, because we are now engaged, with the assistance of a strongly manned Royal Commission, under the presidency of the right Hon. Gentleman the Member for East Worcestershire (Mr. Austen Chamberlain), in exploring the system of finance with a view to seeing if a system which has not been revised for many years, and which has been partly inherited from our predecessors, the old East India Trading Company, cannot be improved. Although it is one of the matters which is being investigated, there is one fact I wish to mention. From time to time proposals have been put forward, and have, I think, in theory, at any rate, found acceptance both here and in India for the establishment of a State bank. Such a bank would relieve the India Office of a very large amount of the commercial and financial work which it now does, and would, perhaps, find a solution of many of the difficulties which our critics have from time to time pointed out. The Secretary of State is of opinion that the time has now, come for the reconsideration of the proposals for the establishment of a bank which would act as custodian for a large part of the Government balances, manage the paper curreney, and take part in the sale of drafts on India for meeting the Secretary of State's requirements. The subject has been discussed in a Memorandum prepared by the Assistant Under Secretary of the India Office (Mr. Abrahams), and the Secretary of State, without committing himself in any way upon the subject, has directed that Mr. Abrahams should present his Memorandum for the consideration of the Royal Commission, and he will welcome the consideration of it by the Royal Commission, as he thinks it clearly comes within its terms of reference.

To leave finance and to come to the question of general administration, I should like to say one word about the Army, which is a subject which will play a part in the Budgets of the future. As the House is aware, a Committee has been sitting which has explored our military defences under the distinguished presidency of Field-Marshal Lord Nicholson. This Committee has reported to the Viceroy. I need hardly say that the report is a confidential document, comparable to the Reports on similar subjects drawn up by Sub-Committees of the Committee of Imperial Defence. It cannot be published, although I believe that this confidential document will lead to improvements in our Army of which the House may from time to time be interested to hear. But in order to dispose of hopes on the one hand and fears on the other, I want to state one general conclusion—that the expert Committee has proved that, although we may possibly get a better Army for the same money we are now spending, although we can possibly improve our defences without any extra expense, there is, I fear, no chance of any reduction in expenditure on either the British Army in India or the Indian Army. The most ineresting new feature in the Army expenditure for this year is the amount set aside for the formation of a Central Flying School. At first sight, one would be inclined to suppose that in a country where the conditions of wind and weather can, as a rule, be anticipated with certainty some time beforehand, the difficulties of flying would be much less than they are in this country. But I am informed by experts that the extremes of heat and cold, the variations of temperature, and the differences of radiation over cultivated and desert areas give rise to new difficulties. The type of machine best suited for India has yet to be ascertained, and, in order to avoid any unnecessary risks to our flying officers, we must discover to what extent heat and moisture, and especially the combination of the two, may affect the materials which have been found most useful in the manufacture of aeroplanes in this country. We, therefore, propose to start the Flying School on a very modest basis, and to confine the work in the first instance to experiments and not to include the tuition of beginners. It is intended to begin with four officers, all of whom are in possession of pilot certificates. They will be provided with six aeroplanes for experimental purposes. The school will be situated at Sitapur, in the United Provinces, where there is a large number of Government buildings, which are now unoccupied, which were formerly British Infantry barracks, but which, I am told, are very suitable for our purpose. The total Estimate for this year is about £20,000.

Turning to foreign affairs, I have very little to say. Last year was free from any serious disturbance on the North-West Frontier, though there was no intermission of minor raids, chiefly due to the presence of outlaws in the Afghan Border Districts of Khost. In March, 1912, the Mullah Powindah made a deliberate and almost successful attempt to embroil the Mahsuds against the Government, and for some time it looked as if drastic military action would be necessary. Fortunately, a demonstration of force was sufficient to rally the friendly tribes to our side, fines were levied and paid, and order restored. Save for a disturbance this year in the Tochi, which might have been serious but fortunately remained isolated, these were the only two incidents on the North-West Frontier. The rapidity with which they were dealt with is proof that Sir George Keppel and his officers have not only been successful in keeping the troubled borderland tranquil, but in making great educational progress on the North-West Frontier. On the Nort-East Frontier complete peace has reigned. Various survey parties which visited the tribal country were very well received, and arrangements are being made for the tribes to visit the plains for commercial purposes and to do so unhindered. As regards Tibet, I need not say anything here this afternoon, because my Noble Friend Lord Morley made a statement upon the subject last week in another place. At the present moment the Government of India have invited the Tibetan and Chinese Government to send representatives to Simla to confer on the subject of Tibet's future relations to China. At this conference the protagonists will be the Chinese and Tibetan delegates, for we desire, if possible, that they should settle their differences between themselves. His Majesty's Government have no interest whatever in the internal affairs of Tibet. All that we desire is to preserve peaceful relations between neighbouring States and to see that order is maintained on the Indian Frontier from Kashmir to Burma. These are very important interests, and His Majesty's Government cannot permit them to be endangered, directly or indirectly, by the Chinese. They are, therefore, not only concerned in bringing about a settlement between China and Tibet, but are bound to see that that settlement secures that there will be no repetition of the events of the last five years. I may mention that the Russian Government have been fully apprised of the action and intentions of His Majesty's Government, and have expressed their goodwill.

The only other foreign matter with which I need deal is to say that the Central Indian Horse, which went in 1911 to Shiraz, has been withdrawn. The Secretary of State for Foreign Affairs has instructed the Consul-General at Bushire to convey to Colonel Douglas and the regiment under his command his sincere congratulations that their most arduous duties in Persia have been brought to a conclusion. The tact and self-restraint which has been displayed by all ranks under trying conditions for the past one and a half years have been highly appreciated. I am sure the House would wish to endorse this tribute to men who have worked for some time in very trying circumstances. The Foreign Department of the Government of India not only deals with Foreign Affairs, such as those to which I have referred, but, what I think is nowadays an anomaly, with the affairs of Native States. We are not often concerned in this House with the affairs of Native States, though the territories which are described under that name and their rulers loom large in Indian affairs to-day, and will loom larger as time goes on. They are not merely places to be visited by tourists who wish to see interesting places and old buildings, to study ancient customs, or to indulge in sport. Those who visit them can gain many an opportunity of political speculation and instruction by observing their widely diverging political racial and social conditions. However marked is the influence of Western education in India generally, nowhere is it more markedly to be seen than in the Native States, where the rulers of the present generation vie with one another in improving the condition of their administraton and their reputation for efficient Government. Consequently, in the last twenty years, there has been a great development in all the affairs of the States—in finance and administration, in railways, irrigation, and education—and this advance brings with it the necessity for modernising our methods of dealing with the affairs of the Native States, where we are concerned with them. I need hardly say that in the majority of cases in their internal affairs we do not interfere.

At the present time the links in the official chain between the Native States and the Viceroy are the Resident or political Agent—in Rajputana and Central India, the Agent to the Governor-General ; then the Deputy-Secretary in the Foreign Department, who deals with internal affairs, then the Foreign Secretary and then the Viceroy. The Foreign Secretary is already overburdened with work. He has to deal with an increasingly delicate sphere of operations all along the Indian borders. It is quite impossible for any one man at the same time to cope satisfactorily with the affairs of the Native States. The Government of India have, therefore, now proposed, and their proposal is being considered by the Secretary of State, that a separate Secretary should be appointed for the affairs of Native States. He will bear the title of political Secretary ; he will have all the rights and privileges of a Secretary to the Government of India, and he will have in his Department a branch of the present Foreign Office to deal with internal affairs. The change can be brought about at very little cost and will, I am quite sure, be acceptable to the Chiefs, as tending to the quicker discharge of business and to a more thorough and more personal representation of their problems to the Viceroy. In addition, too, the Conferences which are to be held from time to time at Delhi or Simla, to which ruling princes will be invited will give them opportunities of meeting one another and of discussing alterations of custom, of practice, or of rule. That will be a very valuable procedure. There was a Conference held at Delhi this year on education in the Native States, and the success which attended that Conference augurs well for the future.

Coming to British India, I know that is very difficult to make a choice of the subjects which those Hon. Members who are interested in India will agree with me are ripening, but I have tried, without any attempt to avoid anything of difficulty to choose the three things which I think are most pressing. I need only say that if the House will be good enough to allow me to reply at the end of the discussion, I shall be only too glad to give any information on any other subjects that I can. The first subject with which I wish to deal is that concerned with the relations between the religions and races of India. The second, is the problem connected with the maintenance of law and order, and, third, those service questions with which the Public Services Commission is now dealing. I said something about the relations between the Mussulman and Hindu some years ago. I think, it is possible to say something more to-day, because it is difficult for Indian national ideals to take any intelligible or any satisfactory form so long as the great Mussulman community stands apart from the rest of the Indian population. I am confident of the future. I believe that the Indian peoples of all races know full well to-day that the desire and the intention of the Government, communicated to all its officers and understood by them, is that there should be complete harmony between all the races there. The maxim *divide et impera*—one of the most dangerous maxims—has no place in our text-book of statesmanship. I can state emphatically that if the leaders of the Mussulman and Hindu communities could meet and settle amongst themselves some of the questions which from time to time arise out of and foster differences of opinion and of tradition they would find ready co-operation from the Government. I found in India that one of the outstanding causes of trouble between the Mussulmans and the Hindus was the problem of special representation for the Mussulmans on legislative and municipal bodies. Another was the difficulty of obtaining for the relatively backward Mussulman youth a full share of Government employment. On the first question, I believe, it is recognised by all parties that the Government is committed to the principle of special representation. If the Hindu community who understand this and the Mahomedans were to accede to the request of the Hindus for special representation too, I believe, by agreement between the parties, we could arrive at a basis for the modification of the present rules to suit them both, but the Government has to await that agreement before any move can be made. However, the divergence between these two people is very marked. Hinduism is self-contained, and so far as events outside India attract their attention at all, it is due to an ordinary interest in the politics of the world, consequent upon the spread of education and the improvement in means of communication. So while the mutual relations of Europe and Asia are interesting to the Hindu generally, the Indian Mussulmans, members of a religious community which for generations have exercised a marked effect upon the politics of the three Continents, are naturally interested in the welfare and importance of Islam as a whole, and, despite the neutrality of this country, despite our refusal to take part in these affairs, I think this House will sympathise with the fact that the Mussulmans of India have been and must be deeply stirred by the misfortunes which have come to their co-religionists in Persia, in North Africa, and in the Balkans.

Amid these misfortunes educated Mussulmans are, I

think, keenly conscious that there was a time when Islam was not only abreast of the general culture of the rest of Europe, but, through its scholars and men of science, took a leading part in the development and learning in Europe. They contrast the conditions of Morocco to-day with the history of the Moors in Spain. They remember that under Akbar and his immediate successors they were not only prominent in politics, but led the Eastern world for a brilliant period in arms, in letters, in art, and in architecture. I think the Indian Mussulmans realise that they have, as a whole, too long neglected the educational opportunities that the British Government wish to offer as freely to them as to the Hindus, with the result that in those spheres of public employment, the doors of which are opened by Western education, they have not attained a position proportional either to their achievements in the past or to the numbers at present. They see some of their eminent men in high places. There is a Mussulman who is a member of the Judicial Committee of the Privy Council; another sits upon the Council of the Secretary of State for India; a third is legal member of the Viceroy's Council, and many of them occupy important judicial and administrative positions. These examples are indications, if indications were needed, that there is no sort or kind of discrimination against their creed or their race. The Mussulmans themselves have only to utilise the opportunities that already exist, and there has been considerable progress in the last ten years. During that time the number of Mussulmans at the elementary schools has increased by 50 per cent., and during the last few years the number of Mahomedan students in higher institutions has increased by 80 per cent. The scheme for raising the Mussulman Anglo-Oriental College at Aligarh to the status of an independent university has been delayed, among other reasons, by the generous contributions which have been given to the Red Crescent fund in Turkey. The Government of India has recently called the attention of the local Governments to the necessity for increased facilities for Mahomedan education in more modest ways. A community that has once lagged behind in education has more difficulty than in almost any other sphere in making up leeway. All educated Indians must recognise that it would be disastrous to India if divisions of the population, due to religious or historical causes, were to coincide permanently with a difference of intellectual level, and if 57,000,000 of people who include the rulers of great States, land-holders, merchants some of the most vigorous and martial elements in the Indian Empire, were to remain outside the forces which are moulding the India of the future. I think we may be sure that such arrangements as local Governments can make for the encouragement of the Mussulman pupils by scholarships and by special courses, will be welcomed by the best elements in all the other communities.

As regards higher education, I should like to call attention to the scheme for the proposed new University at Dacca, which has been framed by a Committee. We have not yet received any definite proposals from the Government of India. There are certain points which require consideration, but the presentment of this scheme opens a new chapter in higher education in India. Existing Indian Universities have been formed on the model of the London University, although the Indian Universities Act of 1904 has, in a measure, modified this conception. The Universities of Calcutta and Bombay are, it is true, now developing post graduate teaching; but the old Indian University is an examining body affiliating remote colleges which they control to a certain extent, but do not teach. The new University at Dacca will have eleven constituent colleges, all at Dacca, all residential, and it will be somewhat similar to the Old Universities of Oxford and Cambridge in this country. That is the novel and important point of the scheme. It is to serve as a model for Indian Universities in the future. The University at Aligarh and the University at Dacca will consist of one or more colleges, all local, in which the pupils will reside, and in which it is hoped that we shall obtain something like the best features of English University life. I mention Dacca in connection with Mahomedan education not because it is to be a Mahomedan University, but because it is situated in the centre of a rather backward Mahomedan community, and therefore will offer to the Mussulmans the best opportunity of university education that they have yet had.

I should like to say a word about the other education progress of the Government. They have issued this year a resolution which declares their policy and makes announcements something on the lines of those which

I was privileged to make this time last year. It clears up some misconceptions. We intend to rely, as we have relied in the past, on private enterprise for secondary education. It is difficult to exaggerate the debt that we owe to private enterprise in teaching in India. One can see on all hands the marvellous work done by the missionaries. I am not now talking about any efforts at conversion. I am talking of the real educational work which they achieve in virtue of the inspiration which they derive from their religion. Mr. Tyndall Biscœ's school in Srinagar has done marvellous work for Kashmir. The Anglo-Vedic Arya-Samaj School at Lahore is another example of private enterprise and in a sense the Brahmo Samaj is a missionary body. The Christian College at Madras, the Oxford and Cambridge Hostel at Allahabad, St. Xaviers College at Bombay, and the Salvation Army work among the criminal tribes—all this private education is of a kind which, assisted by Government inspection, recognition and control, by the very energy and influence of their teachers, has accomplished wonderful work in the development of India, and everything in India, but particularly education, depends upon the personality and human influence in enlivening and interesting the peoples. I think we are alive, too, to the importance of making education in India something different from the process merely of teaching Indians enough English to enable them to obtain, or fail to obtain, a B.A. degree. The Resolution which I am referring to draws attention to three matters in which education in the past has been imperfect, the formation of character, sound hygiene in the schools and colleges, and the improvement of the teaching and study of Oriental languages. The first Grant of the old East India Trading Company of 1813 was chiefly for the encouragement of literature. I am afraid we have lagged rather behind since then, but the project for establishing a central Oriental Institution in India and an Oriental College here in London, will remove from us the reproach that we have lagged behind Germany and France in our treatment of Oriental learning. The Resolution concluded with an appeal for the co-operation of the Indian people. We cannot have education in the true sense from without. Millions of apt pupils engrossed in codes and schemes drawn up by Europeans will not suffice of themselves to make an educated people.

I come to the second of my subjects, the question of law and order. I think it may generally be said that peace reigns in India. The Legislative Councils with their opportunities for discussion, the great progress that has been made during the last few years, the evidence that we are considering all outstanding questions, these have their effect, but I cannot paint a rosy picture without saying a word about certain disquieting features. I am bound to express the view that all is not well with Bengal. The elaborate rules and the diverging procedure in all the provinces which have for their object the fixing of rent or revenue due by land-holders to the Government or from tenants to the Zamindars or land-lords, are absorbingly interesting to any student of Indian agriculture. I am not sure that they are not in some cases perhaps over-elaborate and over-irsksome, but no one can study them without being impressed by the fact of the relentless efforts with which land records, unequalled in the world, are kept, and by the help of these records justice and equity between the States and the land-holder on the one hand, and between thel and-holder and his tenants on the other are meted out. This elaborate system of rent and revenue administration has incidental advantages in bringing together the rulers and the ruled. It gives infinite opportunity for knowledge of the condition of the peasant, and occasion upon which to foster village life and agricultural co-operation—which, as I have described before to the House, is making such wonderful strides in India—and for understanding and appreciating the character and the habits of the people.

In Bengal, the permanent land settlement and the absence of continuous land records have together resulted incidentally in one tremendous disadvantage, that these opportunities for close relationship between the people and the administration have been limited, with the result of estrangement and a reliance, not on the revenue officer, but on the police, for the link between the people and the Executive. The problem in Bengal is, then, to devise some remedy for this state of affairs by perfecting the machinery of local Government, and on the other hand, improving the police. All these matters are engaging the attention of the Government, and I have only stated them because it will enable the House of Commons to realise the sort of problem with which we have to deal. The House hears from time to time about dacoity in Bengal. In the year 1912 there were fourteen cases of dacoity, or attempted dacoity, by armed gangs in Eastern Bengal in the quest of money or of weapons, and in December a large quantity of arms and ammunition was discovered in a house in Dacca, in which also were found many articles of jewellery looted on some of these occasions. The peculiar feature about these crimes is that they have nearly always been brought home to a class which, outside Bengal, is very law-abiding—the young men of the more or less educated middle class, sons of respectable parents. There are not many of them—an infinitesimally small number when thinking of the population of India, but gangs of a dozen or fifteen young men of respectable parents cannot engage in these exercises without attracting the notice of their neighbours. A head constable was murdered in the streets of Dacca last December by three young men armed with revolvers who were seen by many passers-by. We must rely in our effort to correct these things upon the co-operation of the people. But it must be remembered that in Eastern Bengal the communications consist almost entirely of waterways, and crimes of violence are difficult to guard against and hard to detect. An enormous area of country, full of small isolated villages, intersected with rivers and courses must always offer an easy field to daring criminals and present great obstacles to the police.

There was a remarkable case in 1908, when about thirty young Bengalis were able to travel for many miles with the loot obtained by robbery in broad day-light, meeting no police and encountering little resistance from villagers, though they murdered four men, and that led to an investigation of the position. It was then found that the average of police stations, excluding out-posts, was one to every 400 square miles. It is all very well to talk about the co-operation of the people, but you cannot expect villagers to travel great distances, leaving their agricultural pursuits and leaving their homes and women unprotected, in order to go and help the police. The situation is being faced, the police are being strengthened and reorganised, and a system of river patrols is being established. The first step is necessarily to cope with existing crime. The larger problem is to prevent the recruiting of criminals in the future. So far as prevention goes, the Bengal Government are engaged in a comprehensive and carefully devised scheme,including, besides the measures I have described a reorganisation of the village chaukidars and police. But the permanent problem is the cure of the conditions which made these crimes possible, and here we are face to face with economic and educational problems of great complexity. The development of the industrial resources of the province, the improvement of education on lines which will enable young men to earn a living in practical pursuits, instead of turning out educational failures who find themselves divorced from the humble callings which their fathers followed, endowed with just enough book learning to make them bad politicians, yet far too little to enable them to live by any liberal profession—these are the real problems of the future in Bengal, and their solution must be at best, slow.

In the meantime it is plainly the duty of the State to protect the law-abiding, to give confidence to the timid, and to deal so energetically with crimes of violence that public confidence may be restored in the ability of the Government to give protection to a population which has no natural sympathy with crime, but which has too often found that the dacoit can strike harder and quicker than the Government. One necessary steps is to improve the police. The attention of the House is from time to time called, quite justifiably, to cases in which Indian constables have abused their powers. I only want to pause for a moment before saying a word on this well-worn theme, to regret that no members of that force, except its few bad characters, are ever heard of by the public in this country, and I should like to draw attention to the splendid material we have in the English officers and those under their charge. I have been looking at the most recent rewards and I wish to tell the House of some of them. I find that three recipients of the King's Police Medal risked their lives to save helpless people from drowning, while five awards were made to two superior officers and three constables on the occasion of a fire and explosion in the laboratory of the Delhi Fort. Twenty-five live shells were known to be in the burning building when a superintendent and three constables mounted an adjoining wall, and for two hours played the hose on the fire, until their comrades succeeded in getting into the building and removing the shells. I find that a

Calcutta constable, unarmed, captured an armed burglar after he had just killed another constable. A Punjab constable, who had saved two women from drowning at the risk of his life, came to the rescue of a comrade felled to the ground by four criminals. Two constables in the United Provinces attacked a band of twenty armed robbers, wounding and capturing one, and putting the rest to fight. A sub-inspector in Madras, unarmed saved a magistrate from an angry mob during a religious disturbance. A European inspector in Behar saved two Indian women from a burning house at the risk of his life. I have taken these from different provinces, and all from the one year's record, because I wish the House to realise what good material we have in the Indian police. I hope that the recital of such cases may raise a desire on the part of some of my fellow Members, who are laudably anxious to eradicate torture and practices of that kind from the Indian police, to encourage merit by seeking information also as to the other side of the shield.

In Bengal, within three years, no less than five Indian police officers have been murdered by political assassins, and one has been severely wounded. We punish severely any constable whom we can detect in abuse of his power. Facts are notified by way of warning to all members of the force. We must to complete the process, say a word of recognition and sympathy for the members of the force who have lost their lives in the fearless performance of their duty, and amid difficulties which I think are not always sufficiently appreciated by the House. May I add that, although we propose to relax no effort in improving the condition of the police and their character, we cannot see our way to doing what some Members of this House would have us to do—abolishing a record of confessions prior to trial. We have two duties, one is to avoid and to prevent torture, as I believe we are increasingly successful in doing, but we are not justified in hampering ourselves against the other side of our duty—the punishment of crime and the protection of law-abiding citizens—by action which, as the House will see when the papers are published, is opposed by all the local Governments, and nearly every Court of law throughout the country. I have said before, and I say again, that the prohibition of confessions would not prevent the risk of ill-treatment of accused persons by constables. It would not prevent the ill-treatment of witnesses in hopes of discovering clues of stolen property. However, we can, I think, perfect our precautions to ensure that confessions are really voluntary and carefully recorded.

I should like to read to the House some of the measures which the Government of India propose to adopt. These proposals are still under the consideration of the Secretary of State, and I am able to say that he will be only too glad of the co-operation of any Hon. Member of this House in suggesting further reforms for consideration by the Government of India. The police are to be forbidden to interrogate accused, if remanded, without the permission of the Magistrate. Instructions will be given that a remand of a confessing prisoner to police custody should only be granted if the police could show good and satisfactory grounds, and only by magistrates who have first-class or second-class powers under the Criminal Procedure Code. Where the object of the remand is verification of prisoner's statement, he is to be remanded to the charge of the magistrate, and the remand should be as short as possible. When a prisoner has been produced to make a confession, and has declined to do so, he is in no circumstances to be remanded to police custody. The recording of confessions is to be limited to special divisional magistrates and magistrates of the first-class, or, if especially empowered, of the second-class. An effort will be made not to record a confession without the orders of the District Superintendent of Police, or until the accused has had some hours out of police custody. The police are not to be present when confession is recorded, and ordinarily a confession shall be recorded in open Court, and during Court hours, and a magistrate recording a confession shall endeavour to ascertain the exact circumstances in which confession was made, and shall record on the Record the statement of the grounds on which he believes the confession genuine, and the precautions taken to remove accused from the custody of the police.

MR. MACCALLUM SCOTT: The Hon. Gentleman used some words which I do not quite understand. Will he kindly explain what is meant by the words "remanded to make a confession."

MR. MONTAGU: I am very sorry if I did not make the statement quite clear. I did not say, "remanded to make a confession." What I said was: "When a prisoner has been produced to make a confession, and has declined to do so, he is in no circumstances to be remanded to police custody."

MR. MACCALLUM Scott: May I ask what is meant by "produced to make confession?"

MR. MONTAGU: When he is produced in Court for the purpose of making a confession, and he declines to do it, he is not to go back to the custody of the police who produced him.

I wish to say one word about the Delhi outrage. A bomb was thrown in daylight, the Viceroy was severely wounded, and two men were killed. The assassin got clear away and has not yet been caught. That is the story, and I want to say how it was possible for such a plot to be matured without any inkling of it reaching the authorities, why the actual attempt was not frustrated, and how it is that the criminals have not been detected. If there is an active organization, however small in number, however abhorrent to the general sense of the people, an organization including men competent to manufacture effective bombs, and men willing to take the risk of throwing them, and if that organization is in the hands of men who can keep their secrets and confine their knowledge of particular plots to a very narrow circle, then carefully thought-out plans could be prepared and no Government in the world can guard against them, except by such a network of surveillance and of espionage as would be absolutely intolerable. Even so, history has not shown that Governments who were ready to subordinate their main business to a policy of intense suspicion have thereby succeeded in preventing political murder, and State occasions which draw immense crowds may draw, too, persons secretly armed with explosives and ready to use them. There are certain precautions which are not only possible, but which it is the clear duty of the police or authorities to take. They include careful arrangements for the regulations of traffic, the presence of troops and police, a knowledge of the occupants of houses along the route; and the ascertaining whether strangers of known bad character have come to the place. The judgment of the Government of India, after the most careful inquiry, is that there was no failure on the part of the local authorities or the police to carry out these duties. There was no reason whatever to suspect that such a crime would occur, or that the arrangements made to guard against crime were not thoroughly adequate. Lord Hardinge said in the moving speech with which, while still suffering from his wounds, he opened the first Session of the Legislative Council in Delhi, one of the most moving occasions at which I was ever privileged to be present.

"In my desire for kindly intercourse with the people and accessibility to them, I have always discouraged excessive precautions, aud I trust myself and Lady Hardinge more to the care of the people than to that of the police."

I think we owe to this fact, and to the splendid courage with which the Viceroy and Lady Hardinge acted throughout (*cheers*), the magnificent display of sympathy with them and the abhorrence with which the crime was treated throughout India. (*Hear, hear.*) Had His Excellency desired, further precautions would have been taken. When a procession moves through a city of flat-topped houses, it is possible by posting men practically to garrison the roofs, but this would not prevent the throwing of a bomb. There are assassins who will kill even with the certain knowledge that they cannot escape. The building from which the bomb was thrown is really a collection of houses built round a courtyard, a warren of passages and staircases with over a dozen means of access to the adjoining buildings and streets, and so the assassin got clear away. The fact that the assassin got away does not mean that the police have been idle and that there is no hope of ultimately bringing him to justice.

Indian Abhorrence of the Crime.

But this crime is not an outcome of a wide national movement. The fact that a lot of irreconcilables, enemies of authority, can effect political murder is not confined to India. There have been times and countries in which the deliberate opinion of the people was opposed to the Government and in which political murder is the extreme manifestation of a sentiment which in its milder form the mass of the people shares. In such cases as the detection of a political crime is, as a rule, not difficult, for the existence of conspiracies is no secret to the people at large. In those circumstances a particular crime can be detected and punished without affecting the general situation. A situation of this kind differs radically from the present situation in India. A spontaneous expression of horror came from all classes and all creeds from one end of India to the other, wholly apart from any difference of political opinion. The splendid thanksgivings for the recovery of the Viceroy constitute one of the most striking things in the history of our Indian Empire.

A closer association of leading Indians in the Government of the country has precluded all possibility that an attempt on the life of the Viceroy, the President of that enlarged Legislative Council, in which speeches of sympathy and dismay of such striking eloquence and sincerity were made, can be the act of a politician-nationalist.

India abhors the crime, and I think Indians have reflected sadly that its occurrence casts an unmerited stain upon the reputation of their country. Lord Hardinge declared at once that he would pursue unfalteringly the policy which he had followed hitherto. There is no question of withdrawing from innocent millions the measure which we have thought it right to take, merely because in India, as in a dozen other countries, terrorists have committed a crime which could by no possible means have brought one single national aspiration nearer fulfilment. (*Cheers.*) The good name of India has suffered very unjustly, and the position of our Indian fellow-subjects in other parts of the Empire, difficult enough already in many ways, has not been made easier by the Delhi bomb. The outrage provoked a genuine outburst of indignation from severe critics of our Government as well as from those who are more generally in sympathy with us. I want to draw attention to the words of one Indian member of the Council who said in a recent debate :—"I fully share the feeling of shame, but I ask myself, 'Have I been able to help the Government or those responsible for the administration of the country to get rid of these people? Though these outrages are committed against my own countrymen, my kith and kin, what have I done? That is the real thing." This question, I think, shows a feeling of personal responsibility which is new, behind a feeling of loyalty which is not new and this feeling of responsibility is one of the greatest needs, as it is one of the most hopeful signs, in the India of to-day. (*Hear, hear.*)

I come to my last subject, the Royal Commission which is now sitting. I think that I can describe the year of which I have been speaking as the year of deliberation. It has marked out, as it were, a halt after a period of advance. The last March, the march of the Morley-Minto Report, covered a vast tract of unconquered and valuable territory, and we are now halting to consolidate our recent conquest while reconnoitring parties are being sent out to spy out the land that lies before us. To two of our pioneers I have already referred, the Royal Commission presided over by the right Hon. Gentleman, the Member for East Worcestershire, and the Military Committee which has sat under Field Marshal Lord Nicholson. The third is the Public Services Commission, Lord Islington's Commission, now sitting in London, and soon to go back again to India, where it has already sat during the last cold weather. The Commission has conducted its inquiry under conditions of great difficulty. It has been subjected to misunderstanding, based on imperfect reports of its proceeding and often to slander. I want to say that the Government appreciates the determination and assiduity with which it is pursuing its labour, and the Government is confident that when its Report issues we shall have the basis of many desirable alterations in our system, the material for another march forward. I do not want to say one word which would prejudge its conclusions, but I do want to say that we cannot go on governing India with a dissatisfied public service, and there is evidence that the recruiting sergeant is hampered by the evil reports which are brought home from India at this moment.

At the risk of once again stating a platitude I will say that unless you can get the best men, selected by the most suitable tests, animated by the highest traditions, proceeding—this is the important point—to India confident of their choice of a permanent career and of the goodwill of and fair treatment by the British people in whose name they are going to administer, you will lose, and you will deserve to lose, the hold of the British people upon the affection of the Indian people. In saying that, I am not referring for one moment to those few, very few, Civil servants who regeret the good old days when they were sent out to govern the people, who were content to be governed, and lament the fact that they have now to co-operate with the people and the Government of India. With all respect and all recognition for their services in the past, we do not want those men in India. After all, what did we go to India for ? If the people of India have not made any progress under British rule, if the problems of the Government are still to-day what they were a hundred years ago, or in the days of Lord Clive, then I think we have failed in our justification. Nor do we want to listen for one moment to those men who tell us that they do not like the educated Indian, and that the educated Indian does not like us. If the educated Indian has faults or shortcomings, different from or greater than the faults of the educated Englishman, these faults are the faults of the education which we have given them.

Even if it can be said against us that there are some educated Indians who do not like us, do not sympathise with us, do not believe in our motives, I think that there is no necessity to be dismayed. Our part, difficult and worthy, is to bring the educated Indian on to our side, and to go on helping him in order that he may help us, or to ask him to help us in order that we may go on helping him. The problem of India is not a problem of material advance of increasing prosperity. It is not a problem of new schools and university buildings. It is not a problem of new hospitals and Government Houses. It is a problem of Government and of co-operation, of giving to the Indian increasing opportunity in the country which is his own, and increasing assistance in the development of his capacity for local government and administration. No, the grievances, as I understand, in the Indian Civil Service, to which I desire to call attention are three : The first is want of pay. The Indian Civil Service claim that their pay has not been revised as has the pay of people in private employment, to keep the pace with the enormous increase in the cost of living in India. The standard of life, the slowness of promotion, and the lateness of life at which they are recruited are all questions of the utmost importance, and if an underpaid service is an unsatisfactory service, the Royal Commission have got a worthy task to perform in a thorough investigation of this grievance in order that they may recommend pay which shall be adequate to the altered conditions, and pensions proportionate to the services rendered.

SIR J. D. REES: Is the Hon. Gentleman referring to any general complaint by Indian Civil servants or a complaint by the Punjab, the United Provinces, and the Central Provinces? Is he referring to something specific and local?

MR. MONTAGU; Of course, I know that there is a particular grievance from the Punjab and the United Province owing to the block in promotion, and we have taken some steps, not wholly satisfactory perhaps, but which will not—if I may use the expression—queer the pitch of the Royal Commission, for temporarily dealing with these places. But I was taking a general view that the cost of living had increased, and that the pay had not. The next grievance of the Indian Civil Service is the growing complexity of the system under which they live. Half the faults which are found from time to time with the Indian Civil Service are mainly attributable to their overwork. Every year sees an increase in the inflexible rules laid down for the guidance of all grades of officers. Every year, therefore, decreases the responsibility of officers which makes their task less agreeable, and who devote more of their time to reports. I have heard of an officer who said that when he joined the Service a small volume of rules was sufficient to guide him when he went into camp ; now he has to pack a portmanteau with codes and regulations. At the risk of repeating what I have said before in this House, I cannot pass by this subject without saying that one of the cures for this is devolution. We must seek to find indigenous voluntary agencies to conduct a large amount of our detailed work. We are always inclined to thrust upon India, in the light of our own experience in this country, laws and regulations comparable to those which have been found satisfactory to us. In this country, when laws are passed, we hand them over in the main to our voluntary agencies—our county councils, our municipal councils, and our rural district councils—to carry out ; but in India every such enactment and every such resolution must at present mean work for the officials. Even if there be some loss of efficiency, even if a district board be worse run, a municipal body be less capable, we ought to find the indigenous agency in India which will alone ensure our progress being real and complete.

How can this be done ? I hope the House will forgive me for saying that there is this problem : How can a district officer entrust details of his work to voluntary assistance if the local Government is always asking him detailed questions on matters for which he ought to be responsible ? How can the local Government forbear worrying each district officer if the Imperial Government at Delhi is for ever interfering and worrying the local Government for reports ? How can the Imperial Government at Delhi refuse to interfere with its local Government if it is always being worried for reports or details by the Secretary of State, and how can the Secretary of State forbear to worry the Imperial Government at Delhi if the House of Commons and the House of Lords are always asking for information? The tightness of control of each step in the machine is an excuse for the step below. I hope the House will forgive me. Honourable Members are entitled to know anything and everything they want to know, but if you devolve on other people duties which you cannot or will not perform yourself, you must leave them with trust, to do the things that you have asked them to do for you. Let them do confidingly the things that you have asked them. I know I shall be told, indignantly, by Honourable Members that were it not for their interpolation of questions as to Indian affairs, there would be no opportunity of any public and recognised criticism of the Indian Government. All these things are a matter of degree, and, as time goes on and you take steps in India to bring the Government more and more face to face with the people, every step you take in India in that direction ought to lessen control here. But I should like to remind the House that devolution in this respect was accomplished by recent reforms, and that in the Legislative, Councils, now enlarged, elective and representative questions are asked and answered, and resolutions moved and discussed, on questions of every variety of importance concerning every branch of administration. It is only necessary to glance at the proceedings of one of those councils to realise that a very genuine interest in administration is taken by the leaders of Indian opinion, and that there is very little danger that any real or apparent grievance, or any Government action of any kind which appears to require explanation, will pass unchallenged.

Then there is a third grievance, the last grievance of the Indian Civil Service, and this applies to all the Services in India, British and Indian. They are sensitive of your opinion and dependent on your support, and, believe me, I speak from the bottom of my heart when I say they are in every way worthy both of your support and of your good opinion. The isolation, the courage, the indefatigable work of exiled men and women, often in lonely stations, in the Forest Service of the Indian Civil Service, in Salt, in education and other services, to name only a few, ought to call for the admiration of every Member in this House. What I ask in their name and what they ask silently, is an appreciation of their difficulties and a belief in their undoubted singleness of purpose. It too often happens that they are discouraged in their work, because the criticisms of them from this country, are so very vocal, whereas praise and appreciation is so often silent, because men have not time to attend to Indian subjects. So much for that side of the public services inquiry. But there is the other side of the public services inquiry which opens up the whole vast territory of the share of Indians in the administration of the country. What our attitude is in regard to this I have already indicated. The old era of a hard and a fast division between Government and the governed on racial lines has long ago disappeared. The watchword of the future is co-operation. We are pledged to advance, and we mean to advance, but it must be steadily and prudently. The very appointment of the Commission is a good earnest of our sincerity, and, as their share, we ask from the progressive section of the Indian community, patience. The Commission will advise us as to what changes, what reforms are necessary to take us as far forward on this new road as we are now justified in going.

All I take leave to do now is to make this one comment on the subject. It is not only a question of new regulations, of carefully balanced proportions between the two races, it is not only a question of words and of figures, it is, above all, and beyond all, a question of real determination on both sides to act up to the spirit of the underlying principle. Mere lip-service to a formula is worthless. I wish to appeal to British and to Indians alike, to make this co-operation a real thing by inspiring it with the vital elements of tact, sympathy, and sincerity—the instruments of success in India.

Finally, I want to remind the House that there is another side of the question which the Commission probably will not touch, but which is as important, as serious, and as deserving of our most earnest consideration. There are in India millions, tens of millions, I might almost say hundreds of millions, who do not, cannot, and probably never will aspire to a share in the Government of their country, who live the life of an

Oriental, unstirred by the Western life we have imported. We measure their lands, we administer justice to them, we teach them to keep themselves, their houses and their village clean; we show them how plague may be avoided, and we bring to bear on their material improvement all the resources of Western science and civilisation. But all this is to them but as a phase passing in a maze and murmur of words, in the Eternal Scheme of things. (*Cheers.*) The principle on which we act is right. It is our bounden duty to give of the best that we have to the betterment, according to the best of our ideas, of the people under our rule. We must do these things, and we must do them by rule and by code, and through the agency of officials who speak the language and use the practices of officials. But let there be added to the rules and codes, and to the official book, a note of explanation, a gentleness of application and an endeavour to interpret. (*Hear, hear*). The Indian of whom I now speak has a view of life which is not our view. His ways are not our ways; our books, our medicine, our sanitation, are as mysterious to him as the rites of Shiva or of Vishnu to the average middle-class Londoner. The language of officialism booms in his ears and stupefies him; he is entangled and trapped and terrified in the coils and meshes of official codes. He is, in spite of all our Western importations, the same man as he was 15 centuries ago. That is one of our difficulties that we find in India—living side-by-side the 20th century and the fifth, and the same machinery to deal with both of them. I do not ask for separate machinery, but what

I do ask is that, where the machinery, with all its complications and intricacies, suited to the 20th century comes in contact with the fifth century, let every effort be made to simplify, adjust, and explain. (*Cheers.*) Understanding is what is wanted. Understanding is impossible unless the officer who meets the people in direct contact has the time to see and talk to them face to face, and the liberty, the freedom, to adjust and to lighten their difficulties, and to ease their condition by the intervention of his personal agency and sympathy. And so my last word is a plea for devolution, not necessarily by a redistribution of duties and powers, but by the liberty to exercise a wise discretion in the use of duties and powers as they now are. If we make co-operation and devolution our guiding principle, I am convinced that we shall be on the right lines, and if anything we have done during this year, or if anything I have said this afternoon, helps towards securing for the one section of the Indian community another instalment of their just and proper ambition, for the other and largest section of the Indian community a more personal, a more elastic, a more understanding rule, and for our public servants some due recognition of their loyal and unsparing service by the removal of any existing or potential cause of discontent, then I shall feel that, though I have taxed the patience of this House, I shall not have wasted its time. (*Cheers.*)

IRRIGATION AND RAILWAYS.

On the motion "that the East India Loans (Railways and Irrigation) Bill, be now read a second time." Mr. Montagu said in the House of Commons on 17th March 1910 :—

The Secretary of State for India possesses no power to raise money by loan in this country except with the consent of the Houses of Parliament, and so from time to time he comes down to the House of Commons with a Bill of this kind and asks for power to raise a limited sum of money. There were Loans Bills passed into Loans Acts, comparable to this, in 1893, 1898, 1901, 1905 and 1908. There are two kinds of these Bills. Sometimes power is sought to raise money for general purposes. Sometimes it is sought only for specified purposes. The Bill which is now under discussion is of the latter kind, and only seeks to raise money for the specified purposes of irrigation and railways.

General borrowing powers are only used to meet great emergencies, such as war or famine, and it is a matter of great rejoicing that since the Bill of 1908 no such emergency has arisen ; and the Secretary of State still possesses unexhausted the whole of the borrowing power for general purposes granted by this House in 1908 together with an unexhausted portion of the borrowing powers granted by the Act of 1898, to the extent of sums amounting altogether to £6,371,699, so that it is absolutely unnecessary to ask for power in this

Bill to borrow money for general purposes. The Government asks the House for power to raise £25,000,000 sterling for railways and irrigation. I may say that these powers are not to be exercised at once, but only during the years 1911, 1912 and 1913, and subsequent years, and they will only be exercised with due regard both to the necessity of the services involved and the conditions of the money market at the time. I may also say, having regard to the discussion in the previous Debate, that in the undertaking contemplated there is nothing military or strategic. All the work contemplated has to do with the development of the commercial prosperity of India. The subject of irrigation is only included in this Bill so as not to limit unduly the powers of the Secretary of State. But, as a matter of fact, the money required for irrigation is nearly always raised in India, and probably the money raised under this Act will be used entirely for railway purposes.

Irrigation Grants.

I will deal shortly with the subject of irrigation first. There can be no doubt as to the value of irrigation, and the success of expenditure under this head is one of the outstanding features of the recent development of India. It was in 1864, that the principle was accepted of constructing works of irrigation out of funds supplied by loans, and since that date various systems have been steadily pursued of supplying water to country previously arid or exposed to the danger of famine in seasons of occasional drought. The policy now governing this work is based on the approved report presented by Sir Colin Scott Moncrieff's Commission in 1903. The sum of £32,143,278 had been invested in major irrigation by the end of 1908-9, and £4,028,294 in minor works, irrigating together the enormous area of 16,435,527 acres. This showed increase over the preceding year of £1,628,541 capital expenditure, of £126,761 gross receipts, of £22,041 working expenses, of £104,720 net receipts, and of 358,639 acres irrigated. These figures are only the departmental index of the general increase in the productivity of land and the effective production of districts previously liable to famine in times of drought and in some cases the settling on land previously uncultivated of large and prosperous populations. The major works only are constructed from borrowed money. The net receipts from these have increased from £1,711,000 in 1900-1 to an estimated net capital liability at the same time has increased from £23,475,332 to £33,643,278, so that the percentage of net receipts to capital liability has remained practically constant throughout the ten years. We can therefore face the consideration of increased expenditure on irrigation with a confidence that the money spent is not only of immense profit to the population of India, but is spent on sound commercial undertakings, eminently satisfactorily to the revenues of the Government of India.

RAILWAYS IN INDIA.

Turning to railways, we are again occupied with work, the advantages of which are undoubted. The building of railways in India, dating from 1853, has been the foundation of the growing prosperity of its people, the basis of any war against the famine, the fundamental support of law and order, the root of all progress. Thanks to railways, food can be supplied to distressed districts, and good harvests do not entail the waste of crops. Railways have equalised prices and distributed food and produce; they have colonised new districts and led, so far as is possible, to establishing a greater community of interest among the various peoples of India. Turning to the more material question of profit to the Government of India, again, we see a story of satisfactory investment. About 24,000 miles out of the 31,485 opened for traffic are now the remunerative property of the Government of India, yielding in 1909-10, which has not been a particularly favourable year, 4·41 per cent. of the money invested in them, which now amounts to about £300,000,000. The railway service gives employment to 525,000 persons, of whom 508,000 are Indians. The number of passengers rose from 161,000,000 in 1899 to 321,000,000 in 1908, and during the same period there had been an average increase of 790 miles opened per year. Loans raised under Bills such as we are now discussing are spent, first in fulfilment of the railway programme for the year; and, secondly, in the discharge of capital liabilities. The railway programme for the year is decided by the Railway Board, which, subject to the approval of the Government of India and the Secretary of State, manages Indian railways. A portion of the money spent goes to improve the equipment of existing lines ; increasing trade makes increasing demand on the lines built to meet the more modest requirements of earlier years. A great increase of goods carried necessitates the provision of more rolling-stock and heavier waggons. This means new bridge girders, strengthening the permanent way, and new goods yards. By far the larger part of the money raised for capital expenditure is used for such purposes. Of the £20,900,000 included in the programme of capital outlay for this year 1909-10 and the coming year, £8,800,000 goes to open line works, £7,600,000 to rolling-stock, and £4,500,000 to new lines and lines in progress. I may add that the Railway Board and the Indian Railway Companies themselves pay particular attention to the proper distribution of the charges for improved equipment between revenue and capital, and only such work as can properly be said to improve the revenue is charged to capital.

Continued representations were received from India some time ago as to the insufficiency of railway development to keep pace with the development of India to supply the needs of its trade and to enable the railways to be worked to the best possible advantage. A Committee was appointed as a consequence of these representations, which was presided over by Sir James Mackay, and reported in 1908. The report recommends that a capital expenditure of £12,500,000 should be incurred annually on railways, on which £4,000,000 should be provided in India and the remainder in England. It is with a view to meeting the recommendations of this Committee that expenditure has been increased, and this accounts for the shortness of the interval between this and the last Loan Bill. The full expenditure recommended, however, has not yet been attained, and may not be attained for some time to come. The resources of India in the near future may fall short of the £4,000,000 contemplated by the Committee which was to be contributed from such sources as the Revenue Surplus, Rupee Loans, and Coinage Profits. It is probable, therefore, that about £8,000,000 a year must be raised in this country for the purposes of the programme. Some part of this sum will be raised in the form of Capital Stock or Debentures of Guaranteed Railway Companies, for the creation of which the authority of Parliament is not required. It is not possible to give any accurate estimate, but, based on past experience, it may be suggested that about £6,000,000 a year will be raised for programme purposes by the Secretary of State. The amount raised for programme purposes under the Bill of 1908 has been £13,307,273.

RAILWAY CONTRACTS.

As regards liabilities for the discharge of capital, most of the railways belonging to the State in India are worked by companies, guaranteed by the State, under contract. Termination of a contract with any company means of payment of capital contributed by them; this, together with the repayment of terminable bonds, must be met by borrowed money. Under the Loans Act of 1908, £997,300 has been spent on the discharge of debentures; before the end of this year, when the contract between the Secretary of State in Council and Indian Midland Railway Company comes to an end, it will be necessary to repay to that company £2,250,000; possibly, also, though I hope this will not be the case, £1,510,000 may be required for repaying capital and certain debenture bonds to the South Indian Railway Company. The loans for these purposes will be raised under—and, I may add, go far to exhaust—the borrowing powers of the Act of 1908. In 1911-12 £1,776,200 worth of bonds originally issued by the Madras and Indian Midland Companies will have to be discharged, and in 1912-13, £1,477,600 worth of similar bonds, and in 1913-14, £1,281,200. Accepting, therefore, the estimate of six millions as the amount to be raised annually under present Bill for the railway programme, the House will see that it is possible to estimate the requirements of the Secretary of State in each of the next three years at about seven and a half millions and that the powers asked for under this Act will have to be renewed at the end of 1913-14.

There are only two other points which I should mention, rather by way of anticipating criticism, and they are not wholly unconnected. I have shown that railway undertakings have in recent years nearly always meant a considerable profit. This amounted to £9,770,000 during the last ten years, supplementing the revenue raised by taxation for meeting general administrative expenditure; but in 1908-9 there was a loss of £1,242,000. This was due to a decrease in gross earnings consequent on unfavourable agricultural and trade conditions, and an exceptionally high rate of working expenses, resulting partly from the necessity of giving special allowances to compensate for the high prices of food while the effects of famine were still felt, and partly from the large outlay on renewals. This brings me to say a word on the matter raised on discussion of the last Bill as to the passenger facilities of the railways, the improvement of which was responsible to some extent for the increase of working expenses in 1908. The Railway Board in 1905 issued a circular to the several railway administrations urging the necessity for providing (1) facilities for passengers to obtain their tickets a longer time before the departure of the trains ; (2) facilities for examining tickets of third-class passengers so as to enable passengers to have proper access to the platform ; and (3) proper accommodation for the third-class passengers to prevent overcrowding. There is every evidence that ample response has been made to this circular. Continuous booking at the principal stations, and the opening of town offices for the taking of tickets, deals with the first evil. As regards the second, the railway administrations are rearranging their waiting-halls and platforms. The only way of dealing with the third evil is to increase the supply of coaching stock. New third-class carriages of a modern type are being provided with every possible speed.

RAILWAYS : A COMPARISON.

Finally, if there be any Member who thinks that we are proceeding too rapidly, I would remind him that, if we compare India with any of the advanced countries of the world, there is room and need for a great development of railways. To compare it with the United Kingdom, with one-fourteenth of the area and one-sixth of the population, you find that the United Kingdom has three times the mileage of railways. I would also point out that the productive debt of India makes up by far the larger portion of her debt. The total permanent debt on 31st March, 1909, amounted (in round figures) to £251,000,000. Of this total £182,000,000 represented railway debt, producing more than 4 per cent. interest; £31,000,000, irrigation debt, producing 8 per cent. interest; and £38,000,000, ordinary or unproductive debt. Few countries can show so favourable a record.

Railway Profits.

I wish it to be clearly borne in mind that it is for this remunerative debt, not for the unproductive debt, that I now ask for powers to raise money. Profitable as the expenditure of capital on railways is now, it will be more profitable in future. In the first place, the purchase of railways by the State has in the majority of cases been made by means of terminable annuities. When these are paid off, the railways in the possession of the Government of India will become an unburdened commercial property of enormous value. In the second place, a considerable number of railways have been built, not for immediate profit, but for the development of certain areas, and these will become remunerative in proportion as they achieve their object. Nor do the peoples of India have to pay highly for the inestimable benefit conferred upon them by railway development.

Although during the four years ending 1907-8 the net annual gain to the State from this source was approximately £2,000,000, the rates charged for passengers are only one-fifth of a penny per mile and for goods half a penny per ton per mile. I think now I have laid before the House sufficient evidence of the necessity for this Bill, and the purposes for which it is required. This was granted to the Secretary of State in 1908 borrowing powers for railway and irrigation purposes, which have now been nearly exhausted on new construction, better equipment, and repayment of capital. I ask it with confidence to renew this power in order to give further assistance to the Government in providing for the continued improvement of the first necessity of the modern development of commerce, agriculture, and general prosperity—improved means of communication.

INDIAN HIGH COURTS BILL.

In moving " that the Bill be now read a second time" in the House of Commons on Friday, 21st July 1911, Mr. Montagu said :—

In asking the House to agree to the second reading of this measure, I do not think it will be necessary to occupy much time, because so far as the House is concerned it is a very unimportant measure indeed. But I want to explain it as fully as I can, because, as at present advised, I propose, if the House gives it a Second Reading, to move that it be retained on the floor of the House, and I will ask the House to be so good as to pass the subsequent stages of the Bill without discussion, which is not in any way necessary. The reason for introducing the measure at all is the great congestion of legal affairs in India at present. The House will agree with me that if you have great arrears in the Law Courts the delay of justice very frequently amounts to a denial of justice. I have only to read to the House some figures concerning the Calcutta High Court to show what I mean. In 1908 the cases in arrear on the appellate side of this Court were 5,245. At the end of June, 1911, the number of civil appeal cases pending was no less than 8,389. The Courts work as hard as any Courts could possibly work. Every kind of rearrangement has been attempted, but it has now become obvious, not only to every judge of the High Court, but to the Government of Bengal and the Government of India, that the time has come to ask for the raising of the maximum number of judges in the Courts. At the same time, because I think it is desirable in these matters to be prescient, a similar increase of the maximum of possible judges in India is asked for. There is no fear that the Government of India will abuse the power for which it asks. The Courts of Madras and Bombay, which have a maximum of fifteen now, have got eight judges, so that it is for future and not for immediate application that the first clause of this Bill includes them. I should like, before I dismiss this clause, to remind the House that there is no excess of judges in India at the present moment. The maximum number of judges of the High Court in Bengal and Eastern Bengal is now fifteen.

There are 86,000,000 people there. In England and Wales the population is 33,000,000, and there are thirty-three judges of the High Court.

Now I come to the second clause, which is highly technical, and only, I think, of technical importance. There is no immediate desire to establish a new High Court anywhere in India, but the Government of England desire to be able to cope with circumstances which may arise by a less clumsy method than having to wait for an opportunity to pass an Act of Parliament while justice is being delayed. It is possible for the Government of India at present to immediately establish a new Chief Court anywhere. Anyone familiar with the Indian Courts will appreciate the difference between a Chief Court and a High Court, and I venture to suggest that it will not be wise to drive the Government of India for the sake of expediency and the saving of time to the establishment of a Chief Court, having regard to the circumstance that in prestige, dignity, and confidence the High Court is the better alternative. In the Act of 1861 it was enacted that a High Court might be established by letters patent in any area where no existing High Court has jurisdiction. At that time the well-known appreciation of the advantages of litigation, which is a characteristic of the Indian people, had not yet developed so far as it has at the present moment. It was not contemplated that it would be necessary at any time, I think, to establish new Chief Courts or new High Courts in areas in which existing High Courts affected by that Act already had jurisdiction, and I submit that if it should become necessary in the future to establish a High Court or a Chief Court, Parliament should adopt the same procedure with regard to this as was adopted by our predecessors under the Act of 1861.

There is only one other clause in the Bill of any importance which is clause 3. It deals with the appointment of temporary judges. There is no intention at any time that the number of judges, temporary or permanent, in any Court in India, should exceed the maximum number prescribed by this Act. If a judge is away on leave or if a judge is ill, at present it is possible for the Lieutenant-Governor of a Province to appoint a temporary judge on his behalf, but even if there is not the maximum number of judges at the time occupying seats on the bench, if there is a lesser number than the maximum number of possible judges, which is fifteen, and there are only fourteen, and there are great arrears which the Government of India is anxious to wipe off, they have no power to appoint a temporary judge. The only possible way in which it can be done is to appoint a new permanent judge, raising the number to the maximum of fifteen and leaving no vacancy. That is a very cumbrous method, and it may lead to overstocking the bench, and these powers allowing the Government generally to appoint temporary judges up to the maximum number with a view to clearing off arrears are, I think, necessitated in the interests of economy and of speed in dealing with legal matters. We are only asking for power to appoint temporary judges. The House will agree with me, I think, that this measure does not require any elaborate Debate, and I think that all classes in India will welcome its speedy passage for the improvement of the legal machinery in the Provinces of India.

THE GOVERNMENT OF INDIA BILL.

Mr. Montagu, in moving the second reading of this Bill in the House of Commons on April 22, 1912, said :—

The Bill which I ask the House of Commons to read for the second time to-day is a Machinery Bill necessary to carry out the policy which was announced at the Imperial Durbar at Delhi last December. The House of Commons is proceeding to discuss it at a moment when it is safe to say that the policy has been acclaimed by the vast majority of all classes and all races concerned until its out-and-out opponents have come to occupy a position of pathetic, if splendid, isolation. The Bill begins with a preamble which recites acts which have already been performed, and since every act recited in the preamble is an act for which there is ample Parliamentary authority, the method proposed for carrying out these changes is strictly constitutional, and is, in fact, the only method that the Government could have adopted. It has been said that we are relying upon antiquated or even obsolete practice, but they are only obsolete in the sense that they are unfamiliar to members. They are perfectly well-known to those who have to administer India. Acting under those powers, in a strictly constitutional way, the Governor-General of India ir

Council fixed by proclamation the limits of the Presidency of Fort William in Bengal and constituted a new Province of Behar and Orissa on March 22, 1912. On March 21, 1912, His Majesty appointed by Royal Warrant Lord Carmichael as Governor of Bengal, under Section 29 of the Government of India Act, 1858. On the same date, under Section 58 of the Government of India Act, 1869, His Majesty appointed three Councillors to be Executive Members of the Council of the Governor of Bengal. I have quoted these sections as the evidence on which I base the claim that we have acted strictly in accordance with the powers given by Parliament in past years and that we have proceeded in the proper way to carry out the changes as recited in the preamble of the Bill, which I ask the House to read a second time.

THE PROVISIONS OF THE BILL.

The first clause of the Bill gives to the new Governor of Bengal exactly the same powers as are now possessed by the Governors of Madras and Bombay. The Act of 1853 extended to the Governor of the new Presidency that might be formed all the powers of the Governors of Madras and Bombay at that date. It is now only necessary, by Section 1 of the Bill, to extend to the Governor of this new Presidency the powers given to the Governors of Madras and Bombay since the passing of the Act of 1853—such powers as were granted, for instance, under the Councils Act of 1861, through the Governors of Madras and Bombay, to make rules for the conduct of business in the Legislative Council, and so on. The House will see, in Clause 1, that there are two provisoes added. The first reserves to the Governor-General, who now ceases to be Governor of Bengal, certain powers that have been exercised by the Governor-General in the past. The powers specialy referred to are powers granted to the Governor-General under the High Courts Act of 1860 and 1911, which gives the power to appoint temporary and acting Judges of the High Court. At present the jurisdiction of the High Court sitting at Calcutta will extend beyond the limits of the Presidency of Fort William and Bengal as testified by the proclamation. It will extend to the Province of Behar and Orissa, and it seems right to leave the Governor-General the power of appointing Judges. The second proviso obviates the necessity of appointing the Advocate-General of Bengal as a member of the Legislative Council of Bengal. The reason is that the Advocate-General is a law officer who has to give advice by the terms of his appointment both to the Government of Bengal and to the Government of India. Sub-section 2 of Clause 1 merely transfers from the Governor-General the power to alter the limits of the town of Calcutta, which was conferred upon him by Section 1 of the Indian Presidency Towns Act of 1815 and which is now obviously under the Government of Bengal. Clause 2 of the Bill gives power to establish an Executive Council for the new Province of Behar and Orissa. Behar and Orissa will have a Legislative as well as an Executive Council, and it is necessary to put in a provision for that in the Bill because, under the Indian

Councils Act of 1909, it is possible to appoint an Executive Council for the Lieutenant-Governor. Clause 3 gives power to the Governor-General to appoint a Legislative Council for a province which is governed by a Chief Commissioner. The Governor-General has power to take under his own Government, and therefore technically to appoint a Chief Commissioner to govern a territory in India under Section 3 of the Act of 1854, just as Lord Curzon, when Viceroy, made the North-Western Frontier a Chief Commissionership.

COUNCILS FOR CHIEF COMMISSIONERSHIPS.

If the Government obtain the powers now sought it proposes to exercise them at once in two provinces under a Chief Commissioner. The first is Assam. I do not think the House will deny that the case of granting a Legislative Council to Assam is a good one. Lord Curzon, in the speech which he made in the House of Lords, made a complaint against the scheme that it would detract from the position of Assam by removing it from conjunction with the Government of Eastern Bengal. Assam has been under a Legislative Council, and by giving it a Legislative Council through this Bill we shall enable the province to go on with the same representative Government as it has had in the past. The other provinces—the Central Provinces—to whom the Government of India propose to give a Legislative Council include the territory of Berar, with a population of 14 millions and extending over an area of 100,000 square miles. I think that those who have some experience of that part of the British Empire will agree that in education, in enthusiasm for progress, the claim of the Central Provinces to have the same legislative system as exists in the neighbouring provinces is a good one, and it is, at any rate, a move strictly in accordance with the principle of the Liberal Imperial policy of devolution and the granting of representative Government in response to the demands of the majority of those people in the country who have expressed an opinion. Clause 4, read with the Schedule, repeals and amends certain enactments which now either require alteration to harmonise with the new condition of affairs or require repeal. The only one I need mention is the repeal of Section 57 of the East India Act of 1793, which dates from the time when the Civil Service of each Presidency was a separate Civil Service, and which prevents us from appointing civil servants from one Presidency to act in another. Now that the whole of the Indian Civil Service is an Imperial Service it seems to the Government of India that that provision is unnecessary. The repeal of Section 71 is consequential, and the other provisions are merely slight verbal alterations. Perhaps I may make special mention of Section 50 of the India Councils Act of 1861, the amendment of which makes it possible for the Governor of Bengal to act as Governor-General in the absence of the Viceroy. The Bill, it will be seen, consists merely of alterations in machinery to carry out a policy which has been generally accepted and which, I believe the House will agree, contains elements of lasting advantage and the germs of improved Government for the great Empire of India. *(Cheers.)*

[*Replying to criticisms in the House on the Government of India Bill, Mr. Montagu said* :—]

I have not the right to address the House again, but perhaps I may be allowed to reply to some of the questions which have been put to me. Sir John Jardine asked whether the repeal or alteration of certain sections of the Act of 1793 will affect the position of the Indian Civil Service. The answer is emphatically in the negative. This Bill only repeals parts of the Statute which were not repealed when the rest of the statute was repealed in 1865. Colonel Yate put three specific points. The first was as to the defence of Delhi. I want to assure him that, I think, the authorities are agreed that the strategical position of Delhi as the central point of the railway system of India is a very good one, but the weighty words which he addressed to the House will, of course, be noted by those who are concerned with these affairs.

THE MAHOMEDANS OF EASTERN BENGAL.

We come to a much more substantial point when we consider the position of the Mahomedans in Eastern Bengal. Much has been said in various places and in various newspapers on this point. It would be a mistake to talk of the Mahomedan people of India as though they were a homogeneous people of one nationality. The Mahomedans of Eastern Bengal are the descendants of Hindu converts, or are Hindu converts themselves, and have little or no relation except that of religion with three-fifths of the Mahomedan population of India outside the limits of Bengal, but also belonging to the native races of the north. So far as the Mahomedan population outside Bengal is concerned, they have no objection to the restoration of Delhi, which they have always regarded as the capital of historic India. They have shown good will and have gratefully acknowledged and accepted the change. Their position is very carefully safeguarded under the Bill. They are perhaps the most backward part, or one of the most backward parts, of the population of the old Presidency of Bengal, and they are keenly and eagerly desirous of new educational facilities. They are to have a new university which will be largely used for the benefit of Mahomedans, and that is one of the most valuable consequences connected with the new arrangements. They will form in the Presidency of Bengal rather more than half of the population. I could give the House statistics to prove that there will be more Mahomedans than Hindus in the new Governorship, but, roughly speaking, they are about equally divided. In the Executive Council which has been appointed by His Majesty the King for the Presidency, the Indian Member is a well-known Mahomedan. Again, it is the avowed and declared intention of the Government that the new Governor of Bengal must spend a substantial part of each year in Dacca in the Government Building. It is not to be a statutory provision, but the Mahomedans of Eastern Bengal are perfectly entitled to rest assured that that will be part of the settled policy. It has never been the policy of the British Government in India to interfere with and construct artificial regions, territories, and provinces for the benefit of one race or one religion. They have always tried to hold impartially the balance between different races and religions.

LORD CURZON'S POLICY.

If it be claimed that the policy of parting Bengal in 1905 was a policy intended to set up a Mahomedan province, then I say emphatically that that departure from British policy for which Lord Curzon will stand revealed to have been guilty was a far greater blunder than his worst critics have accused him of committing. But Lord Curzon will be the first to admit that there was no such policy. Sir J. D. Rees, who was welcomed back to the House in surroundings which will be more congenial to his ultra-Conservative views, talked about this new policy as a reversal of the old policy. I do not mean it disrespectfully of one of the greatest Viceroys we have ever had when I say that Lord Curzon in this matter had no policy of any sort or kind. He was a great administrator. He produced efficiency which is one of the most cherished possessions of the Indian Government at the present moment. But his concern was with an unwieldy province. He found it too big, and determined to divide it. He moved nationalities about and he moved individuals about as though they were automatons.

MR. MALCOLM: The Hon. Gentleman is speaking now by leave of the House, and I wish to know whether he can enter into this controversial matter, to which none of us can have the opportunity of replying.

MR. MONTAGU: I apologise to the Hon. Member if he thinks that I am doing something I ought not to do. I quite appreciate that it is only by the courtesy of the House that I can speak now. But Sir J. D. Rees charged us with reversing the old policy.

SIR J. D. REES: We did not discuss it. I would have done so if I had been at liberty to do it.

MR. MONTAGU: The Hon. Member made the charge that we were reversing Lord Curzon's policy, and I am defending the Government against that charge. I wish to point out that much of the criticism made by Hon. Members opposite this afternoon against this measure would have been more appropriate if it had been directed against a reversal of policy which is going to happen. Sir Gilbert Parker and Mr. Malcolm based their speeches upon the great constitutional outrage which had been perpetrated by the Executive Government, which is increasingly aggregating to itself powers, and which is bringing about these changes before the consent of Parliament has been obtained. Mr. Malcolm is not quite accurate in his facts. He talked of two opportunities which the House of Lords had no opportunity of discussing the matter before it was a settled fact. They took the opportunity of discussion on two occasions after it had become a settled fact. In this Session of Parliament Hon. Members opposite could have had similar opportunities by raising the subject on the Debate on the Address, or they could have asked a day for the discussion of it afterwards. They deliberately did not do so. Neither of these opportunities have been taken.

MR. MALCOLM : The Speaker has already ruled that it is out of order.

MR. MONTAGU : I do not understand that the Hon. Member is in a better position than myself to decide points of order. The Bill concerns the whole of the re-partition of Bengal, the creation of the new provinces of Behar and Orissa, the segregation of Assam under a new Chief Commissionership, and these matters and nine-tenths of the Durbar policy could have been discussed under this Bill, and in so far as the removal of the capital was incidental to the changes in Bengal that was equally in order. That has not been done by Hon. Members. They claim great patriotism in refusing to discuss the matter. The fact of the matter is that there are some acts which this House, or the great majority of its members, have never claimed, and rightly never claimed, to criticise. I suggest with regard to policy in India that the practice of this House never has been to claim to criticise in detail the administrations in India before certain acts have been accomplished. I base myself upon the speech made by Mr. Gladstone on the Indian Councils Act Amendment Bill in this House on March 20, 1892 :—"It is not our business to devise machinery for the purposes of Indian Government. It is our business to give to those who represent Her Majesty in India ample information as to what we believe to be sound principles of Government, and of course it is the function of this House to comment upon any cases in which we may think that they have failed to give due effect to those principles." When Bengal was divided in 1905, there was no discussion in this House of Commons at all and no information or opportunity was given to the House of expressing any opinion until after the proposals of the Government of India had been accepted by Mr. Brodrick, who was then Secretary. The fact is that these changes, in which so many interests are involved of grave Imperial concern and result, have always been dealt with by administrative action, and afterwards the House of Commons has had its opportunity of expressing its opinion upon them.

THE "AGITATION" AGAINST THE PARTITION.

Sir J. D. Rees has thought fit to revive the old charge that we are altering the partition of Bengal in response to an agitation. All the information at the disposal of the Government of India is to the effect that he is totally misinformed. Lord Curzon, in making precisely the same allegation in the House of Lords, relied on and quoted the authority of two gentlemen. One was an Indian gentleman who had long been absent from Bengal altogether, and another an English writer who never wrote the words which Lord Curzon quoted. I venture to suggest that the root of the Hon. Gentleman's objection is this, that there are in India, as has often been said in this House, two kinds of agitation. One is the agitation which is the genuine expression of a genuine grievance, or what the people believe to be one ; a grievance against an outraged nationality ; an agitation which is the genuine desire for redress of something which is wrong. Then there are those agitators often of the anti-British purpose who take advantage of the existence of that grievance who are almost a parasitic growth upon the legitimate unrest. That kind of agitation is almost dead. It was wisely handled and severely repressed during Lord Morley's Secretaryship of State, when Lord Morley and Lord Minto used exceptional measures for dealing with that sort of agitation, which was not genuine and could not be permitted to continue. But the real, deep, bitter resentment against the line which Lord Curzon drew right across the Bengali-speaking district, the sentimental grievance, the grievance of unfair and disproportionate representation, remained as deep after that long interval as it did when the new state of affairs was first created. That kind of agitation was at the root of everything that was threateningly wrong in India. I conceive it to be the wisest kind of statesmanship to investigate this grievance to see how well-founded it was to remove the grievance and to settle a national wrong. So no one can say that we have responded to illegitimate clamour or have done more than merely redress a grievance which would remain as great as long as it lasted.

SIR J. D. REES : Does the Hon. Gentleman include the compounding of a felony by the Government of India among these wise measures ?

MR. MONTAGU : The Hon. Member is bringing a new charge which I will be happy in a general Debate to prove to be as unfounded as any of the other charges which he has brought. But it would be trespassing too far on the matter before the House at present to deal with it now.

THE QUESTION OF FINANCE.

Mr. Malcolm asked me a question about the finance in connection with the establishment of the new capital. The estimate with regard to Delhi remains to-day what it was. It is not possible yet to submit the revised estimate. The Hon. Member is at liberty to suggest twelve millions. He has opportunities doubtless of arriving at a more accurate figure than the Government of India. But the estimate given was put forward by the Government of India and accepted by the Secretary of State with due regard to the existing difficulties. There are all sorts of offsets to be made. New buildings would have been necessary if the seat of Government had remained unchanged, and there is a certain amount of profit to set off against outlay, appreciation in the Government lands and the sale of certain lands and buildings. It is a rough general guess. The site is now being surveyed by an expert Committee, and as soon as the revised estimates are available they will, of course, be presented to the House. But it is as fair to assume that the expenditure would be approximately four million pounds as to assume that it would be approximately eight million pounds.

THE PROMISE OF "FEDERATION."

Mr. Bonar Law, with other members, referred to the change of policy which was obtaining as the result of this measure. He quoted the words of Lord Crewe and words of my own in Cambridge, and he suggested that there was a discrepancy between them. The despatch and the answer to the despatch have been published in the White Paper, and the words of paragraph 3 are definite and unmistakable, and I should have thought would have admitted of no possible doubt. If a microscopic examination can detect any difference of meaning in the words that I used at Cambridge and the words which my chief used in the House of Lords, I will ask the House to attribute the difference to the obvious difference of atmosphere between the other place and the platform in my own constituency. There is to be no immediate step, no resulting step as a consequence of the changes which the House this afternoon is passing, but surely, when every moving section of the people of India has got a policy, when there are preachers and teachers all over the country advocating this and that course of action, and some are advocating policies which are hostile to British interests, it was not out of place, I conceive, to show to the people of India, as Lord Hardinge did in paragraph 3 of this despatch, that there was a direction in which the British occupation was tending, that there was some definite aim and object in which, in the opinion of the Government in India, all these changes might be co-related, that we were there, not merely to administer, but to develop India on a plan which had been brought out by those who had been advising the Secretary of State. That is, as I understand, the meaning of paragraph 3, and as such I regard it as one of the most important parts of that historic despatch.

THE POLICY OF THE OPPOSITION.

If there is one other matter which I might respectfully venture to put forward, it is that I feel a deep regret that even those who confined their remarks entirely to the way in which these changes have been brought about took an opportunity by some side phrases to express their doubts of and their disagreement with the policy and the Bill which carries it out.

SIR GILBERT PARKER: I expressly said that I would forbear from making a single remark about change of policy, and I did not make any such remark.

MR. MONTAGU: And then you added that there were large numbers of people in India who had grave doubts as to its efficacy. What I mean to say is that I should have thought it was quite clear to the people of India that what they believed to be a great step forward in the process of governing that country was the gift offered by His Majesty at the Durbar on the advice of his responsible Ministers from the people of Great Britain in respect of party. And it is a matter, I think, for regret that Lord Curzon, who has spoken most on the subject, adopted an attitude of complete hostility, and so far as in this debate any expression of opinion has come from those benches at all it has been either like that of Mr. Malcolm or like the assertion of Mr. Bonar Law. Why was it wrong for His Majesty most graciously to make this announcement himself at the Durbar? Is it that Mr. Bonar Law objects to the policy of Durbar boons altogether, or is it simply that people feel that there is a peculiar sanctity about a policy recommended by His Majesty the King on the advice of his Ministers which does not touch the ordinary policy recommended by the Viceroy on behalf of His Majesty the King, and with the sanction of the Ministers? If that is the criticism, then it is based upon the partition of Bengal, and very much of what has been said falls to the ground. The same sanctity, in our opinion, would have attached to the Proclamation had it been made by the Viceroy as attached, and I think rightly attached, to it when it was made by His Majesty the King.

SIR J. D. REES: The Opposition have not had an opportunity of discussing what was done under the cover of His Majesty's prerogative, and the Opposition and those who oppose this policy are really deprived of the opportunity of stating their objections.

MR. MONTAGU: I am merely suggesting that there has been no difference in the treatment of the question from the announcement having been made by His Majesty instead of by the Viceroy. It was announced in His Majesty's gracious speech from the Throne at Delhi, instead of by Lord Curzon, as in the partition of Bengal, by Viceregal Proclamations. In spite of the criticisms which have been made, and notwithstanding some small questions of boundary readjustment which remain, I am profoundly convinced that this policy has been welcomed by the overwhelming majority of all races and all creeds, and that it will open, as Colonel Yate has said, a new era of peace, contentment and progress in India. There is every sign upon the horizon which gives those who are proud of the achievement of the Government in India of great hope of increasing contentment, increasing prosperity, and increasing consent of the Government to be governed by those whose policy shows sympathy with their legitimate aspirations.

Replying to the criticisms in the House of Commons on June 10, 1912, on the Third reading of the Government of India Bill, Mr. Montagu said :—

He would leave the discussion of the finances of Delhi to the Debate on the Indian Budget. All he would say now was that Delhi was being financed out of windfalls which were due to exceptional circumstances which did not render them available for the reduction of taxation. It did not very much matter whether debts were paid off with surpluses such as these, and fresh loans contracted, or whether these surpluses were used directly for purposes for which they were bound to borrow.

The scheme in the Bill provided for the removal of the seat of the Government of India from Calcutta to Delhi. Calcutta was the seat of the Government of Bengal, and the difficulty of disentangling the Government of India from that of Bengal was so great that it would be far better for both the Government of India and the Government of Bengal if they removed the seat of the Government of India to Delhi, which was not the centre of any provincial Government. The word " provincial" was used in this sense, that it merely referred to the fact that the Government, whilst at Calcutta, was the centre of the Government of one of the provinces of India. It was provincial in the sense that Calcutta was the provincial centre of Bengal, and, therefore, the Imperial Government of India was in the provincial centre of Bengal. He asserted without fear of contradiction that students of the Government of India for generations past had been impressed with the growing difficulty which was presented by the two sets of government in the same place, interlaced and intertwined, so that those who were affected by the decisions of one or the other had difficulty in disentangling the responsibility. The Government of India was now going to Delhi, which was not the centre of a provincial Government, because it was strictly the enclave of India, as Washington was the enclave of the United States of America. Sir J. D. Rees so far as his position was based on the statement that we were going from one province to another, was misrepresenting the true state of the facts to the House. The same object might have been achieved possibly by making Calcutta the enclave, and transferring the Government of Bengal out of Calcutta. But, as the Hon. Member would be the first to admit, Calcutta was far too large and important a commercial centre to be adapted to the purposes of the Imperial Government.

SIR J. D. REES : In what respect are the Government of India and the Government of Bengal interlaced and intertwined ? Their functions are quite distinct.

MR. MONTAGU said that he would send the Hon. Gentleman papers which would instruct him. Delhi was the historic centre of India, and it was also the railway centre. It was from many points of view the most acceptable part of the great Empire to which to remove the seat of the Government of India, for it was far nearer to Bombay and the whole of the East of India than Calcutta was. It was also a considerable manufcturing town already. He could not enter into the dispute between the Hon. Member for Nottingham and the Government of India as to the reverence felt for Delhi by the various peoples of India. He would only say that his description of Delhi did not carry conviction to him when he read such words as these which appear in paragraph 6 of the White Paper:— "Throughout India, as far south as the Mahomedan conquest extended, every walled town has its 'Delhi gate,' and among the masses of the people it is still revered as the seat of the former Empire."

THE FUNDAMENTAL ERROR OF THE CRITICS.

So much for the removal of the Government to Delhi. The fundamental error made by critics of the policy of the Government of India was the suggestion that there had been a reversal of the Partition of Bengal. He had been accused of speaking in derogatory terms of Lord Curzon, when he suggested that Lord Curzon in these matters had no policy at all. It was merely a well-known fact. Lord Curzon was as great an administrator as India had ever had. He had found a great province of 98,000,000 people—(An Hon. Member: "Eighty-five millions")—and had become acquainted (as he had said) with the scandalous maladministration which was going on in the eastern parts of Bengal. He had found that, owing to its vast size, it was quite impossible to administer the province according to modern ideas. So Lord Curzon decided to divide it, but he did not divide it with the idea of making a Mahomedan State, or with a view to redress alleged Mahomedan grievances. There was no policy underlying it; it was merely an administrative reform to produce efficiency. He could quote from Lord Curzon's own words :—"What was the particular line to be drawn was a matter not for the Viceroy. The line was settled by consultation and discussion between the Local Governments and the officials." Lord Curzon was not concerned to find where the line was drawn at all. He wanted to split up an unwieldy province and make two parts of it which would be more wieldy. Bitter experience had taught that even in the sacred cause of efficiency we could not move masses of the population about and destroy their national ideals without regard to their thoughts and opinions.

The EARL of RONALDSHAY : What am I to understand by the Hon. Gentleman's statement as to moving masses of population about? Nobody has ever suggested moving the population.

MR. MONTAGU explained that he meant moving them from one Government to another. You could not order the man to cease to be a subject of the Government of Bengal and put him into Eastern Bengal, without very serious consequences, even in the cause of efficiency. It did require investigation as to whether the line—

SIR J. D. REES : The man remains where he is.

MR. MONTAGU : The Hon. Gentleman is perfectly

right in saying that the man remains where he is, but he is no longer in Bengal.

Sir J. D. REES : He is subject to the same class of administration.

MR. MONTAGU, continuing, said that the Government had therefore, because the unrest produced militated against the efficiency which Lord Curzon desired, done over again in the light of experience Lord Curzon's work.

A BETTER PARTITION.

There was now a partition of Bengal, not into two pieces, but into three pieces, and all they claimed was that, having regard to the fact that they had kept the national boundaries, their partition was a better one than Lord Curzon's, and likely to produce greater efficiency, because it was more acceptable to the population. Lord Ronaldshay might say that, whatever the motives of Lord Curzon were, a Mahomedan State came into existence, and the Mahomedans had a right to expect that that state of affairs should remain for ever, and that the Government had in that sense broken their pledge to the Mahomedans of Eastern Bengal. These were serious charges. Nobody knew better than the member for East Nottingham how what was said in these Debates found its way to India. Nobody had been more vehement in criticising members below the gangway on this ground, and he hoped the Hon. Member would have serious misgivings about his own utterances that afternoon, when he had brought accusations of breach of faith and of pledges, not only against Lord Crew and the Government here, but against the whole fabric of the Government in India, who were jointly responsible for these great changes. The Hon. Member regretted, and the noble lord regretted, that there should be any idea in India that we had broken our pledges. But how much had the Hon. Member not done to encourage that idea by words carelessly thrown out which were without a shadow of foundation ?

SIR J. D. REES said he only pointed out the facts.

MR. MONTAGU said the Hon. Gentleman's alleged facts were not facts. The words which had been continually quoted against the Government in that Debate were the words of Lord Morley, "The partition is a settled fact." He would ask the noble lord to be good enough to read Lord Morley's own speech on this subject in the House of Lords. Lord Morley was a member of the Government responsible for this Bill, as he was when he used the famous words, "The partition is a settled fact." What Lord Morley meant was that the great improvement of administration which was to result from the sub-division of Bengal could never again be sacrificed, and that the partition of Bengal could never be reversed. There had been no reversal. What was to be the meaning of the words "settled fact" in politics ? Were they to mean that a thing once done should never be modified in the light of experience ? However badly it had been done, were they all to sit and admire it for generation after generation without having the courage to alter it ? That was a theory of crystallised conservatism which he believed to be the worst that could be applied to a quickly changing and developing country like India.

THE MAHOMEDANS OF EASTERN BENGAL.

The Mahomedans of Eastern Bengal had lost nothing by this change. At the commencement Eastern Bengal was not the overwhelming Mahomedan State some critics seemed to think it was. At the commencement of last year the Legislative Council in Eastern Bengal included ten Hindus. What had the Mahomedans got now? They had got their new university. One of the seats of Government of the new Presidency of Bengal was at Dacca. They were governed under Lord Curzon's scheme from Dacca by a Lieutenant-Governor—the Lieutenant-Governor of Eastern Bengal, who had no Executive Council. Sir J. D. Rees poured scorn on the difference between a Lieutenant-Governor and a Governor. Surely he forgot that the Lieutenant-Governor of Eastern Bengal had no Executive Council. The Governor of Eastern Bengal has an Executive Council.

SIR J. D. REES: And the Lieutenant-Governor of Bengal had an Executive.

MR. MONTAGU: The Hon. Member is wrong in his facts. The Lieutenant-Governor of Eastern Bengal had no Executive.

SIR J. D. REES: Bengal, I said.

MR. MONTAGU was afraid the Hon. Member was now getting excited. (*Laughter.*) He was referring to the Mahomedans of Eastern Bengal. The Mahomedans were in form governed under Lord Curzon from Dacca by a Lieutenant-Governor, who had no Executive Council to assist him. Under the new scheme they were governed still from Dacca for certain portions of the year by the Governor of Bengal, who would be assisted by an Executive Council, and they would, therefore, have a more modern and up-to-date system of Government. Further than that, when the Partition of Bengal was brought about, Eastern Bengal had no representative Legislative Council, because the Reform Bill of Lord Morley and Lord Minto was in 1909. The form of Government Mahomedans would enjoy now would be better and more efficient than the old Government. When the partition was brought about, the Mahomedans of Eastern Bengal were 30 per cent. of a population of over 80 millions. Now they would be about 50 per cent. of a population of 50 millions. Under the partition they were about 35 per cent. of the old population of Eastern Bengal. In numbers, in form of Government, in position, the Mahomedans of Eastern Bengal had lost absolutely nothing by the modification of the partition. In addition, though it was only a side question, the present Indian Member of the Executive Council of the Governor of Bengal was a Mahomedan from Eastern Bengal.

THE CLAIM OF CALCUTTA.

He desired, in conclusion, to deal with two criticisms made by Sir J. D. Rees. The Hon. Member had referred to the position of the member for Commerce and

Industry. He said he had been asked to voice the opinion of the Chambers of Commerce, and then showed that he meant the Chamber of Commerce in Bengal. He would be the last to detract from the great importance of that representative Chamber of the greatest commercial community in India. But it was only that Chamber which was anxious to have its objections to this policy represented. Naturally, what Calcutta lost, Bombay and Karachi gained. If the Hon. Member would come to the India Office and read the files of the newspapers in India, which he had carefully collected ever since this reform scheme came into being, he would be struck by the remarkable way in which the serious alarm of the Chamber of Commerce in Calcutta had been isolated and ignored by the rest of European opinion from one end of the country to the other. He thought that alarm was probably based on a misapprehension ; and he believed that when the scheme was seen at work the fears of the commercial community in Calcutta would be allayed, and that they would share in what was the enthusiastic welcome of this scheme from the vast majority of the people of all classes and races in the great Empire of India.

THE CHARGE OF SURRENDER TO AGITATION.

There was one further matter he felt bound to refer to. The Government had been accused of giving way to agitation and irresponsible clamour. The House would have noticed a very curious inconsistency in the way in which this charge was brought. It was levelled with great vehemence by Sir J. D. Rees, who immediately afterwards quoted from Lord Minto an assurance that there was no agitation and no clamour to which to give way. He could not have it both ways; he could not say that there was no agitation to which to give way, and immediately afterwards award blame for having given way to an agitation that never existed. The fact of the matter was that in Bengal, as in so many other countries, the large, overwhelming, and almost universal number of the inhabitants were peaceful, law-abiding, and loyal citizens. There was a small—very small and insignificant—minority of irresponsible agitators. He challenged the House to say, looking back over history since 1906, that the Government which he was there to represent had been supine in putting down the agitation, which was the work of that insignificant, disloyal, and rebellious minority. Lord Minto himself brought back from India, as one of the greatest triumphs of his rule, the way in which he and Lord Morley put down and, as he believed, stamped out what was known as the seditious movement in India. But there were two ways of stamping out sedition, and neither was complete without the other. They had not only to punish the seditious, but they had to remove the just causes of complaint which brought recruits to the ranks of the seditious, and which, therefore, prevented repressive legislation from having the effect they desired, whilst there was the slightest suspicion to make honest men's minds uneasy that those responsible for the Government of the country were not quick to redress legitimate grievances. The Government of India believed that the real feeling—spreading far beyond the miserable confines of the seditious, disloyal, and rebellious—of wounded nationality, of wounded race susceptibilities, of unfair treatment, which had resulted from the Partition, was as strong on Durbar Day as it ever was when the irresponsible agitation existed.

He hoped Lord Ronaldshay would not think he was making any accusation against him, but no greater disservice could be done to the Government of India than carelessly to lump together in speech an agitation such as the presentation of a petition against the University at Dacca, and, let them say, the agitation that was punished by deportation. The one was a legitimate Western method of gaining access to those who were in authority, and in a country like India the responsibility of those who governed to listen to grievances when they were represented was even more vital than in a country where votes were the armoury of those who were governed. If in any part of his speech he had shown irritation with anything that had fallen from Hon. Members opposite, he could only plead as an excuse that a charge of broken pledges against a Government, annoying and irritating and wounding as it might be in domestic affairs, could not be ignored and must be met by a Government which had the overwhelming responsibility of the good Government of India to answer for. It was because he believed he had answered a charge which he wished had never been made on a subject in which party politics played no part that he ventured confidently to commend this

Bill to the House, a Bill which, he believed, would lead to the improved Government and the greater peace of a country which benefited to a greater degree every day by the fact that the British people were responsible for its government. (*Hear, hear.*)

LIBERALISM AND INDIA.

The Hon. E. S. Montagu, M. P., Under-Secretary of State for India, visited Cambridge on Wednesday February 28, 1912 *and in his capacity as President of the Cambridge and County Liberal Club, addressed a large meeting at the Guildhall. The chair was taken by Dr. Apthorpe Webb, and among those upon the platform were Mr. A. C. Beck, M. P., Sir J. J. Briscoe,* Bart., *Dr. Sims Woodhead (Professor of Pathology), Dr. J. S. Reid (Professor of Ancient History), and Dr. Searle, F.R.S.*

Mr. Montagu, after devoting the opening portion of his speech to domestic questions continued :—

TRUE EMPIRE-BUILDING.

I want, also, to invite your attention to the other branch of the justification of our Imperial organisation —our oversea activities—and I am going to contend, and, I think, prove, that the Empire, as we know it, and the ideal which it fulfils, is the production of the Liberal Party. Englishmen have a conception of Empire different from that of their predecessors or forefathers, and different from that of other countries, an ideal which alone justifies the existence of an Empire. It is not enough for this thinking generation to wave a flag or shout a song or do a turkey strut in pompous celebration of the number of square miles over which the British flag flies ; or the population which owes its allegiance to His Majesty the King. Land has been won by conquest often under Conservative rule, not by Conservative statesmen, but by British, Scotch—and I would remind you in this important juncture—by Irish soldiers on behalf of an Imperial ideal which should know no party. (*Applause*). But it is not a question of land, but of hearts. It is not a question of domination and of subjugation, but of alliance, co-operation, and perfect freedom between the component parts. Empires have died or been destroyed either from deterioration at home, which the legislation of the last six years is designed to combat, or through the denial of justice or arrogant misrule which makes the yoke galling to the younger parts. We should use our administration and our legislation at home as an example to those sister nations who are linked with us, and we should make our Imperial ideal one of spreading throughout the Empire free institutions and all that is meant by the wonderful word "Justice." If this be true, then, if you will bear with me while I go into history, I think I can show that the freedom of the Empire has been the gift of Liberalism, which has ensured its permanency in the teeth of a short-sighted, stubborn Conservatism.

Canada and South Africa.

The keystone of Canadian loyalty is the freedom of the Canadian people. Yet Lord Stanley, speaking in the House of Commons in 1839, voiced the opinions of the Conservative Party when he said: "What would be the consequence of granting the Canadian demand? The establishment of a Republic. The concession would remove the only check to the tyrannical power of the dominant majority, a majority in numbers only, while in wealth, education, and enterprise they are greatly inferior to the minority." Translated into Carsonian English they could imagine how it would sound: "Ontario will fight, and Ontario will be right." (*Laughter and applause.*) And then you had the Duke of Wellington in the House of Lords: and "Local responsible Government and the sovereignty of Great Britain are completely incompatible." Well, Canada has not moved a step towards separation nor Republican institutions, yet Canada is divided only by an imaginary line from the greatest and most progressive Republic in the world, and the tie of free association within the Empire has held in face of the strongest natural and political attractions. From that the Conservatives ought to have learnt a lesson in Empire-building, but they learnt nothing. When more than fifty years had passed, when Canada was becoming increasingly loyal and prosperous, we came to South Africa. Had the Conservatives learnt anything in Empire-building. The Lyttelton Constitution, rejected by the Dutch, fraught with friction and irritation at every step, was their best performance! When, fortunately, and by the mercy of heaven, the end of their reign came, and Sir Henry Campbell-Bannerman, by his application to South Africa of the liberal principles of freedom, laid the foundations of the South African Union, of another Canada in Africa, which in my opinion justified the policy of the British Empire in the eyes of the world, yet the then leader of the Conservative Party, Mr. Balfour, called our policy "the most reckless experiment of modern times," and declined to take any responsibility for this experiment in principle and civilisation, and there once again we have the Conservatives objecting to a Liberal institution, which I think is the only principle of modern Empire-building.

THE TURN OF INDIA.

Well, then, when these principles of self-government had been applied in their most extreme form, came the turn of India, when Lord Morley introduced his Indian Councils Act in 1909. Here was no far-reaching scheme, here was no reckless experiment, merely a cautious attempt to associate the governed with the governor and to give expression to popular opinion in India. And we had the late Lord Percy in the House of Commons saying, "Therefore, although it is our duty to warn the Government of the dangers which in our opinion attend many of the steps which we are recommending, the responsibility of acting upon or neglecting the warning must rest with the Government themselves." And we had the usual carping criticism of Lord Curzon. Well, nobody can doubt the success of the Indian Councils Act, but still the Conservatives have learnt no better. The latest efforts in Imperial workmanship were the far-reaching reforms announced the other day at Delhi as the central feature of His Majesty's successful visit to his Indian dominions. It would be improper for me to discuss these reforms without prefacing my remarks with a word of my own personal belief that the great outstanding triumph of that Indian tour was the personality of King George himself. The good results of his gracious voyage to India will long outlive the pleasure afforded the Indian people by the opportunity of demonstrating their overwhelming loyalty to the British Throne. But what of our policy, what of the new provinces and Delhi? You have invited a Departmental Minister to occupy the office of President, and you have so brought it upon your heads that I should take, as I am bound to take this, an opportunity which does not assort ill with the theme of our discussion, of answering the critics of that scheme.

THE DURBAR ANNOUNCEMENTS.

In the House of Commons Mr. Bonar Law dismissed it with two criticisms: firstly, that it would cost money; and, secondly, that the reversal of the partition of Bengal, as he called it, was a damaging blow to our prestige. I would say in passing that the complaint about expense as the first objection to a great Imperial measure is typical of modern Conservatism. To them, ideals, poetry, liberty, imagination are unknown; they reduce Empire to a profit and loss account; their ideal is one of a cash nexus, and a million or two is to them far more important than the fact that the transfer of capital provides India with a new city, in a historic place, amid the enthusiastic welcome of the whole of a tradition-loving people. And as for prestige—

'O India, how much happier would have been your history if that word had been left out of the English vocabulary! But there you have Conservative Imperialism at its worst: we are not there, mark you, to repair evil, to amend injustice, to profit by experience —we must abide by our mistakes, continue to outrage popular opinion simply for the sake of being able to say, "I have said what I have said." I have in other places and at other times expressed my opinion freely on prestige. We do not hold India by invoking this well-mouthed word; we must hold it by just institutions, and more and more as time goes on by the consent of the governed. That consent must be based on the respect which we shall teach them for the progressive justice of the Government in responding to their legitimate demands. But Mr. Bonar Law knows nothing of India, as he will be the first to admit, and it is to the House of Lords that we must turn for a more exhaustive criticism of our proposals.

LORD CURZON'S ATTITUDE.

And here we come face to face with the great Lord Curzon himself. Now, sir, no one who has held my office for two years would be absurd enough to speak on a public platform upon this topic without paying a tribute to the great work Lord Curzon has done for India. His indomitable energy, his conspicuous courage, his almost unrivalled self-confidence have placed India under a lasting debt to him. But I would venture, with all respect, to ask how has he spent his time since? Admiring what he has done, not looking and saying, "We have done this," but saying, "This is my work." In the lengthy speech which he delivered last week in the House of Lords he did lip-service to Parliamentary control, but notwithstanding the fact that Lord Midleton was sitting next him, notwithstanding the fact that it was Mr. Brodrick, as he then was, not Lord Curzon, who was technically responsible for a large part of the Curzonian administration, he never mentioned the Secretary of State in the whole course of his speech, nor did Lord Midleton speak himself. Lord Curzon has chosen as a point of survey for the work of which he is so proud a point in which he is in his own light, and his shadow is over everything that he has done. It is not "Hands off India" that he preaches: it is "Leave Curzonian India as Lord Curzon left it." To alter anything that Lord Curzon did would be damaging to our prestige. I want to ask you in all seriousness what would be the first criticism which a man wholly ignorant of India—the man-in-the-street—would make to Lord Curzon's speech? I think he would say: "We read of the welcome given in India and in England to this scheme by statesmen, soldiers, civil servants, by speech and by Press of all parties, and we know, therefore, that it is not wholly bad." Therefore, am I not justified in discounting the whole of Lord Curzon's speech by the fact that, although he went into exhaustive details, although he knew the sensitive nature of Indian opinion, the way in which his words would be telegraphed throughout India, although he did not hesitate to bolster up his case with a gossiping story which, as he told it, was obviously untrue and for which he could not state his authority in public, he had no word of praise of any sort or kind either for the conception of our policy or for any detail by which it was carried out—(*applause*)—although he spoke even longer than I am speaking to-night; he curses it from beginning to end; he curses it for what it did and for how it was done; he curses it because we did it without consulting him—oh, horror of horrors!—and because it ended something which he had done; he cursed it because His Majesty the King was graciously pleased himself to announce it to his people assembled at the Durbar at Delhi. I say again that these are not the grave and weighty criticisms of a statesman: they are the impetuous, angry fault findings of a man thinking primarily of himself.

THE STORY OF 1905.

May I take his criticisms in a little more detail? He objected to His Majesty making the announcement because, he said, that made it irrevocable. Well, educated India reads with full knowledge the words of His Majesty's proclamation: "I make this change on the advice of my Ministers," and knows what is meant by a constitutional monarch; and that blame, if there be blame, and credit, if there be credit, must be laid at the door of His Majesty's advisers. Lord Curzon complains that what the King has said is irrevocable; so I hope it may be, but if it had been made by the Viceroy, Lord Curzon would have said it is irrevocable, and surely what is said by the Viceroy on the King's behalf is as irrevocable as what the King said. In fact, as the Prime Minister said, "What Lord Curzon might do in Lord Curzon's opinion His Majesty the King ought not to do." (*Laughter and applause.*) Then he asks why Parliament was not consulted. It is a little curious that he should blame us in this regard, for he objects to our having reversed, as he says, a policy of his. Lord Curzon's partition of Bengal was an accomplished fact before any discussion in the House of Commons had taken place. Mr. Herbert Roberts asked Mr. Brodrick on July 5, 1905, a question, and was told : "The proposals of the Government of India on his subject reached me on February 18, and I have already communicated to them the decision of the Secretary of State in Council accepting the proposals." But the proposals themselves were not divulged. Mr. Roberts, having moved the adjournment of the House on the question of the partition, withdrew his motion on Mr. Brodrick's promising to lay further papers. The recess intervened, during which the proclamation, which finally constitued the new provinces, was issued, and when Mr. Roberts protested against this treatment he received from Mr. Brodrick a letter from which I quote the following passage: "You will remember that when the discussion took place in the House of Commons the scheme put forward by the Viceroy had already received the assent of the Home Government, and the resolution of the Government of embodying the scheme has been published and presented to Parliament." Again, Lord

Curzon says that the decision in the case of his partition was announced after a Blue-book full of information had been for months in the possession of Parliament. What are the facts? After despatches had been passed between the Government of India and the Secretary of State, the decision was announced in a resolution of the Government of India, dated July 19, 1905. The resolution was presented to Parliament in the form of a White-paper on August 7, and a Blue-book, containing further papers, was presented on October 12—*i.e.*, almost three months after, not months before, the announcement of the decision.

THE REAL RESPONSIBILITY.

The fact of the matter is, the Secretary of State is responsible to the House of Commons, and the House of Commons can censure him or the Cabinet just as much as it could have done if the Viceroy had made the announcement. The House of Commons has never claimed more than a general control over the Government of India. Therefore announcements such as the partition of Bengal, and new administrative changes which must be made suddenly and by proclamation, conflicting interests, conflicting claims having to be balanced and adjusted, public discussions would make them difficult, if not impossible, of accomplishment; and that is why the British and the Indian Constitution retain the Royal Proclamation as a method of bringing about such changes as this in India or the self-government of the Transvaal.

WHY THE PARTITION WAS REVERVED.

Next, Lord Curzon stated that our policy involved a reversal of his policy. I trust Lord Curzon will forgive me for saying that he never had a policy at all. (*Laughter and applause.*) He was a mere administrator, an industrious, fervid, and efficient administrator. He was, in a word, a chauffeur who spent his time polishing up the machinery, screwing every nut and bolt of his car ready to make it go, but he never drove it; he did not know where to drive it to. (*Applause.*) He merely marked time and waited until a reforming Government gave marching orders. If he were to claim that the partition of Bengal was more than an administrative measure, designed as a part of a policy, then I say that it was even a worse mistake than I thought it, for the making of a Mahomedan State was a departure from accepted British policy which was bound to result in the antithesising and antagonising of Hindu and Mahomedan opinion. I had always hoped that this was the unforeseen result, and not a deliberate achievement, of Lord Curzon's blunder. It has always been the proud boast of English rule in India that we have not interfered between the different races, religions, and creeds which we found in the country. That he himself regarded the partition as not more than a mere matter of local administrative convenience may be gathered from the passage in his speech in which he says that, owing to the size of the old Province of Bengal, it had become necessary to draw a line dividing it into two; and he goes on to say, "what was the particular line to be drawn was a matter not for the Viceroy." The creation of a vast new province, the meddling with the lives of millions of people, with all the possibility of offending religious and racial susceptibilities, not a matter for the Viceroy! He looked no further than the necessity for instituting two small provinces where previously there had been one, and thought it not a matter for his concern what line the division should take. So far from being a reversal of Lord Curzon's policy, if policy it can be called, are the changes announced on December 12 last, that we maintained the necessity for the division of the province, but have made three where he made two divisions.

THE NEW POLICY.

Where the difference lies is in this: that we have endeavoured to look ahead, to co-ordinate our changes in Bengal with the general lines of our future policy in India, which is stated now for the first time in the Government of India's despatch that has been published as a Parliamentary Paper. That statement shows the goal, the aim towards which we propose to work—not immediately, not in a hurry, but gradually. Perhaps you will allow me to quote the sentence in the despatch which contains the pith of the statement: "The only possible solution would appear to be gradually to give the provinces a larger measure of self-government until at last India would consist of a number of administrations autonomous in all provincial affairs with the Government of India above them all, and possessing power to interfere in cases of misgovernment, but ordinarily restricting their functions to matters of

Imperial concern." We cannot drift on for ever without stating a policy. A new generation, a new school of thought, fostered by our education and new European learning, has grown up, and it asks: "What are you going to do with us?" The Extremist politicians, who form the outside fringe of this school, have made up their minds as to what they want. One of their leaders, Mr. Bepin Chandra Pal, has drawn up and published a full, frank, detailed, logical exposition of the exact form of "swaraj," or, as may be roughly translated, "Colonial self-government," that they want. The Moderates look to us to say what lines our future policy is to take. We have never answered that, and we have put off answering them for too long. At last, and not too soon, a Viceroy has had the courage to state the trend of British policy in India and the lines on which we propose to advance.

The Transfer of the Capital.

As for the transfer of the capital from Calcutta to Delhi, Lord Curzon objects, as far as I can understand, because the Duke of Wellington thought Delhi was a bad military centre. The Duke of Wellington was not one of our greatest contemporary soldiers. His interference in military matters dates from a time when there were no railways in India, and to mention even one detail, when artillery had not reached its present perfection. The battle of Waterloo is a long way removed from present problems; we have taken our stand and placed our King's Government in the historic capital of India. He talks of Calcutta, the capital of

India of 150 years ; Delhi, the scene of a King's Durbar —and, yes, of Lord Curzon's Durbar—has been the capital of India for dynasty after dynasty, for family of rulers after family of rulers, right back into the dim and distant epochs of Indian history, and it is reverenced from one end of India to the other. I venture to say that we have chosen a spot not only the centre of India from every point of view, not only the most convenient for the carrying out of administration, effectively, but also one which would appeal to Indian opinion of all classes and all kinds from one end of India to the other. Lord Curzon goes on to say that if you put the capital at Delhi you will have a capital remote from public opinion. I say it will be remote from Calcutta opinion, and that the Government will survey India from the real centre of India, from an eminence in the midst of India, and not from a depression in the corner. It will no longer have its vision of the wood obscured by the obstruction of one single and very large tree.

INDIAN LAND POLICY.

[*At a dinner at the Liberal Colonial Club, London, on February* 19, 1914, *Mr. Montagu delivered this interesting speech on the Agrarian Policy of India.*]

I am painfully aware that I ought to begin by saying, first, that India is a very large land, or rather sub-continent, sheltering some 317,000,000 souls of every language, race, and creed; secondly, that the problems of its administration are a sealed book to all but the experts and that the experts learn by long experience that nothing is to be learned about India; thirdly, that of all administrative problems that of the land is the one which is sealed with seventy times seven seals. Yet I am tempted to leave out for once in a way the time-honoured warning. There are of course great and essential differences between the land systems in India and those to which we are accustomed; and we can best clear the ground by fixing them in our minds at the outset. When once the ground is cleared, we shall be ready, I hope, to see what are the positive lessons which India has to teach us.

In India you find the state inheriting the immemorial claim of the ruler to a part of the proceeds of land cultivation. The Moghul Emperors to whom we succeeded interpreted their claim in a spirit of Eastern magnificence; they fixed one-third of the gross produce as a fair share for the ruler to take. It is hardly necessary to say that the British Government has been a great deal more modest; but it has accepted the principle, and continues to hold the position of premier partner in the land; that is to say, in by far the greatest and most permanent source of livelihood in the country. It is impossible to define this feature of Oriental sovereignty in the precise terms of Western economics. Perhaps it will be enough to say, very generally, that the land revenue taken by the State in India is something more than a tax, because the revenue-collecting authorities undertake at the same time a number of paternal duties more or less like those of a beneficent lord of the manor; and it is something less than a rent, because the State has recognised or even created individual proprietorships in land, while reserving its right to revenue from the areas so assigned. It will not at any rate, I think, interfere with the plan of this paper if I am allowed, like Dr. Johnson when he was pressed for exact details concerning the life hereafter, to "leave the subject in obscurity." The practical points to remember are that the claim to land revenue is readily accepted by the people whose traditions it follows: that it provides, with a minimum chance for oppression on the one hand or for evasion on the other, a stable contribution amounting usually to no less than two-fifths, (20,000,000*l* sterling) of the net revenues of Government; and that it is practically the only impost of any importance that is paid by the agricultural classes which form something like two-thirds of the entire population of India, and whose income, so far as it comes from agriculture, is exempt from any form of income-tax.

DOMINANT POWER.

My first point, then, is that the State in India is a dominant power in land administration, with powers of control that so far we have hardly dared to contemplate in this country. My second point is that underneath the State, with its functions of superior landlord, the grouping of the agricultural classes, as we shall see, is peculiar. Where there are landlords below the State, competition for the land in India, as in Ireland, has squeezed the tenant a good deal more than it has in England ; there is no distinct labouring class underneath, as we know it to form an economic back-ground on which the pressure can be conveniently, if perhaps immorally, worked off. The Indian tenant or cultivator is a small man holding we might say a five-acre plot. We can return to this point later in discussing tenant law and practice in India. In the meantime it will be useful to begin with a description of the way in which the claim to land revenue is enforced, in order to form an idea of the basis on which the land system is worked.

In assessing and collecting the land revenue, the Government has to deal with a number of classes of landholders. To avoid the complication of using Indian names, I will try to define the members of the hierarchy in my own terms, always on the understanding that definition in English phraseology is an elusive matter. At the head is the State as superior landlord, levying revenue which, if paid to a private individual, would be called rent. Below the State there are two main divisions of landholders. In the one you find landlords, who may either be individuals, representing for the most part the successors of the great contractors to whom revenues were framed out in pre-British days, or landlord communities letting their common holding. They differ of course from British landlords as we know them in that their right to the possession of the soil is qualified by the revenue claims of Government. Below these are tenants, paying rent to their landlords but not directly to the State. The second main division consists of petty occupants or peasant proprietors, who hold their lands under the State without an intermediary in the shape of a landlord, and consequently pay revenue direct to the State. Although many of them are practically established as landowners, they are allowed as a class the right of escaping the whole or any part of the revenue liability by relinquishing the whole or any part of their holdings, in fact, they are to the State as the average tenant is to the average landlord in England. I propose to refer to the two divisions as 'landlords' and 'cultivators' respectively. In the one division the tenants, and in the other the cultivators, usually till the soil themselves, though occasionally with the aid of labourers whose wages are paid in kind.

The general principle of revenue assessment in the landlord areas is that the State is entitled to a share of the 'net assets' of the landlords, which are taken to represent the rents received *plus* the rental value of the lands occupied of the landlords themselves. The basis of assessment is naturally the rent-roll, supplemented or checked where necessary by direct valuation of the output of the soil. The proportion of the net assets claimed by Government usually varies somewhere between 45 and 55 per cent. ; in fact, a share of one-half may be taken as a fair index, though not by any means as a positive rule. I would like to quote at this point two principles laid down in a comprehensive statement of the Government's land revenue policy issued in 1902. They are as follows :—

(1) 'That in areas where the State receives its land revenue from landlords, progressive moderation is the key-note of the policy of Government, and that the standard of 50 per cent. of the assets is one which is almost uniformly observed in practice, and is more often departed from on the side of deficiency than of excess.'

(2) 'That in the same areas the State has not objected, and does not hesitate, to interfere by legislation to protect the interests of the tenants against oppression at the hands of the landlords.'

The first of these allows free scope for elastic treatment where it is called for ; the second shows that the Government rejects the shortsighted policy of acquiescing in a high scale of rents merely for the sake of the extra revenue that could be assessed thereon. To turn to the cultivated areas, the State takes a varying proportion—usually a good deal less than one-half—of what is known as the 'net produce' of the land ; that is to say, gross profits, *minus* the cost of cultivation. It will be noticed that revenue is assessed on the actual cultivator's own profits where the States deal direct with the cultivators, and on rental profits alone where the State deals with the landlord. This is explained by the fact that in the cultivated areas the State itself stands in the relation of landlord to the cultivator, so that the revenue in this case corresponds more directly to rent. I may mention by the way that in the great cultivated tracts of Bombay, the system is peculiar in that revenue is assessed on a system of classifying the fields according to their probable fertility, and not one of valuation of the net produce of the land.

REVISION OF ASSESSMENT.

Continual re-assessment on these lines from year-to-year would of course be a hopelessly cumbrous and harassing procedure. In nearly every province there is a periodical revision of the revenue demand, known as a 'settlement,' which is undertaken once in a cycle varying from 20 to 30 years, and the amount then assessed holds good for the term of the settlement, subject to such minor adjustments or remissions as special circumstances in each year may make advisable. There is, however, a very important exception to the system of recurring assessment, or 'temporary settlement,' as it is known, which is not a little instructive in its working. In the last quarter of the eighteenth century, at a time when administrators were under the conviction that the best way of securing prosperity on the land was to free the hands of the landlords as far as possible, the revenue payable in certain landlords' areas was declared to be permanently settled, and Government definitely abrogated from that date any claim to share in the increased profits that were sure to come with the rise in the value of the properties. Consequently, in the greater part of Bengal, in some of the districts of Benares to the west and in parts of the Madras Presidency to the south, there has been no revision of assessment for something like a century, while the value of the land has risen greatly in direct consequence of State activity in maintaining security and providing trade facilities by the construction of railways and other means of communication. The result is that the land revenue received by the State over the whole province of permanently settled Bengal is somewhat less than one-fourth of the lands. It is, I think, generally recognised that the conviction on which the system of permanent settlement was based was over-sanguine. The general level of prosperity in these areas is no higher than in the temporarily settled tracts ; the tenants are by no means under-rented nor are the estates better run ; indeed, the main result seems to have been a process of sub-letting carried almost *ad infinitum*, with its train of monopoly, profits, absentee land-lordism and inefficient or exacting management. The Government of India have profited by their experience. They have intervened in the permanently settled areas, so far as is compatible with their pledges, to safeguard the rights of tenants ; and they have retained throughout the greater part of India their controlling authority by the simple means of revising their revenue demand periodically, with all the activities which accompany the process, as we shall see. But the permanent settlement may help us, I think, to realise the disadvantages of landlord endowment on an extensive scale. We can leave out of account the loss of the unearned increment which the State has established the right to share in other parts of India. That, no doubt, is a peculiar feature of the Indian land system. But apart from this, the facts have shown that you cannot increase prosperity on the land by giving permanent relief to any one class unless you extend the relief to those who work below the privileged class. We hear a good deal just now of the panacea of State-aided land-purchase for the tenant. So long as the tenant stands at the bottom of the scale of cultivators, the road is safe; but it is safe only so long as you work upwards from the lowest class to the highest. In England the foundation of agriculture is the labourer; and if the foundation is neglected it only over-weights the structure and then you have only to strengthen the joists. It is a noteworthy fact that when the Government in India has had to deal with properties that have come into its direct possession—properties that often lay within permanently settled areas—it has departed from the earlier policy of disposing of them to private landlords, and has put them into the hands of men of the 'cultivator' class, for the reason that the agriculturists could be better protected. The principle of working upwards from the foundation is one that we shall meet again in Indian land administration.

SYSTEM IN VILLAGES.

The work of assessment in the temporarily settled areas is of course a very intricate affair, with wide diffierences of practice in the several provinces. Our chief interest to-night, I think, will naturally be with the landlord areas of Northern India ; and we might perhaps look at the work as it is done in a single province by way of illustration, and correct one-sided impressions so far as we can by reference to other provinces with different methods. I would like to begin with the Punjab, a province for the most part under the ownership of joint village landlords or proprietor communities. These may be called, if you like, yeoman farmers. The method of assessment may, of course, vary in details almost from district to district within the province ; but a summary of a few typical features may help to give a working idea of the process on which land administration ultimately rests. The unit dealt with is the village, that is, the communal group with the area covered by its holdings. Each village has its 'patwari,' or village accountant to act as intermediary between the people and the representatives of Government. An exact record is kept in his charge, and continually corrected up-to-date, giving the entire history of each plot of land in the area, with not only the full terms of ownership and tenancy, but a complete account of its crop possibilities and the particular advantages or drawbacks under which it is worked. To ensure accuracy, the patwari, accompanied by the tenant or owner, who is bound under penalty to go with him on his rounds, inspects each field twice a year, and records the condition of the spring and autumn crops, whether the field is used for fallow-land, pasture, fodder, millet, wheat, sugar-cane, and so forth.

The account is based on a more or less scientific system of survey, and the result is the building up of a record which for accuracy and minuteness ought to satisfy the most hardened administrator. It is not easy to draw a picture vivid enough to make an impression in England of all that this annual verification of agricultural records means. The accuracy of the village maps is tested again and again: indeed, I was told very early in my connection with India that a man who thoroughly understood and appreciated the patwaris maps and books understood India, and nothing I have seen so convinced me of the paternity of Indian Government and the confidence of Indian people as the testing by an Assistant Collector of these records.

Flat, and of course hedgeless, fields, separated usually only by the little mud dams which coax the irrigation water in the most desirable direction; the sharply-defined, glaring, baked mud walls of the village; the crowd of patient, interested cultivators; the hordes of little children, and the heavy manures dumped on the field. And then, all the machinery of the survey: the rough cross stick—for ready surveying the only instrument; the books in which are recorded the owners, the tenants, the mortgages, the sales, the leases and the condition and nature of crops on each field in the village; the patwari, the kanungo, the tahsildar, the Assistant Collector—all eager to see that measurements are true, that records are accurate, and all taking the opportunity of discovering—for the opportunity is unique—the daily life, the calamities, the good fortunes, of the people concerned. Here is a system, which does not permit any ignorance of the owner of the land nor does it allow profit to escape just taxation, or hardship to fail of beneficent easement. Remove it, and it seems to me that you leave tenant at the mercy of landlord, labourer at the mercy ot tenant, the governing classes as uninterested and inquisitorial busy-bodies, and the police the only source of information between villager and the man in charge.

The next step in assessment is that a number of villages, under similar conditions as regards soil, water-supply, trade facilities, and so on, is grouped into a larger division known as a circle, for the purpose of broadening the basis on which the calculations are made; and the average of landlords' rents are taken for a period of 20 to 30 years, corresponding to the term of the settlement, so as to cover any changes in the conditions of tenure during the period. If, as is generally the case in the Punjab, the land is held by the proprietors themselves as co-sharers in the proprietary body, or if the rents are paid, as often happens, in produce, arrival at the revenue estimate is naturally a complicated process. The average yield of each crop is found by experimental cutting and threshing, and the value of the yield by reference to the published market prices. From the result is deduced a cash equivalent for the rents paid in the circle, and this in turn gives a theoretical estimate, on the 50 per cent. basis, of the total revenue that is due to Government. In the same way, the ratios are determined in which different kinds of land ought to pay according to their relative advantages of soil and position; for instance, if it is found that the value of the output on land irrigated from a canal is twice that of the output on land which is watered by a tank or well; the assessment on the former will be two to one, as compared with that on the latter. With all the varieties of land roughly classified in the village records, it becomes a fairly easy matter to adjust the circle rate of assessment to the different village areas, so that an estimate—still of a theoretical kind—is reached of the amount of revenue due from each village. Where the rents are paid in cash and not in produce the work of assessment is of course a good deal simpler, although even here recourse may be had to the method of direct valuation in order to check the result.

TEST OF REVENUE OFFICER.

But, in a sense, the real work of assessment begins instead of ending at this point. It is now the business of the Settlement Officer who is usually a member of the Indian Civil Service in the charge of the operations, to see that the theoretical rates do not in effect fall too heavily, or it may be too lightly, on the areas under his supervision. In dealing with each village, he has to take into account all the factors, such as the level of prosperity, means of communication, mortality rates, whether the inhabitants are by nature good or bad cultivators, everything in fact which calls for elasticity in making the actual revenue demand; and the final result is usually reached after full and probably prolonged discussion with the village representatives. It is in the right appraisement of these governing details that the man in charge of the work proves himself to be a capable revenue officer. There are two points I might bring forward at this stage as possible subjects of interest for discussion. One is whether the risk of duplication of work in assessment—the double valuation first of natural or artificial advantages and then of the actual output—might not be more completely avoided by some system standardising the valuation rates of assessment, and thereafter varying the revenue demand according to changes in local circumstances, such as the rise in food prices, the improvement of communications, and so on. Such a system is already used to some degree in Madras, and might perhaps be extended with advantage elsewhere. The second point, I think, is one of rather more general interest. You will notice that each individual liable for revenue has to pay the proportion demanded in his locality according to the nature of his holding ; if this should happen to amount, say, to one-fifth of the net profits of cultivation, the big man pays 20 rupees out of 100, and the small man pays one rupee out of five. We are getting accustomed to recognise that the hardship in the latter case is a good deal greater than in the former. Allowances are made, it is true, for the small man in India, not it is done at the discretion of the revenue officers, and not on any uniform principle : and one is tempted to wonder whether it would be possible to apply a graduated scale of assessment instead. There is, of course; the theoretical objection that such a measure would promptly label land revenue as a tax. But I cannot help thinking that the Government of India's record shows that it is strong enough to look this difficulty boldly in the face and pass it by.

To turn from these points to noteworthy differences in practice elsewhere, it may be remarked that the principles of survey, record, and valuation are common ground. In Oudh, however, where land-owning is often on the grand scale, and where revenue is assessed on the aggregate of the sums received by a single landlord as rent from a number of villages forming his estate, attention is paid more to actual rents than to general rates of rent that ought to apply to soils. In the Central Provinces, there is an ingenious system in force by which the value of the different soils is reduced to a common denominator, and the proper rent-scales determined thereby for purposes of revenue assessment. We can deal more conveniently with the peculiar features of this system when we turn to matters of tenancy practice.

In the great cultivated areas, as for instance in Madras and Bombay, the task is a little simpler. In dealing with the actual occupant of each field, there is no need to do more than value and assess the field correctly ; the determination for rights of tenure, and the distribution of assessment over the property-group as undertaken in the Punjab drops out. In Southern India we find villages arranged in groups, corresponding to the Punjab circles, but a broad division is observed according as the land depends for its water-supply on irrigation, or on rainfall supplemented by wells. Assessment of course is based on an exhaustive scrutiny of the possibilities of the various soils.

Before I leave the subject of revenue rights and assessment, I should add that the revenue claim is held to extend to urban areas as well as to other. In a resolution of 1879, it is stated that the Governor-General in Council is 'aware of no reason why land revenue should not be levied upon lands attached to private residences or covered with buildings as much as upon arable or pasture lands.' In general, land that is cultivated for profit in these areas is assessed in the ordinary on a share of the produce ; land used for private amenities or other like purposes is assessed according to the usual rate for the description of soil, although there are provisions making for leniency in dealing with this kind of property. It is interesting to find that in the United Provinces there are rules under which areas covered by groves are exempt from revenue payment unless and until the groves are cut down. Lands taken up by a municipality for public purposes are generally speaking exempt, unless they are devoted to objects, such as establishment of markets, from which income is raised. I do not think it is necessary to deal with local rates or cesses, except to say that they are usually levied on the basis of revenue assessment unless in particular cases they take special forms.

Premier Partner in Land.

If I may try to sum up in the broadest terms the feature of the ground we have so far covered, I would repeat that the Government of India has succeeded to the position of premier partner in the land, with not only the rights but the corresponding duties of that position. I have shown how, in the areas under a temporary settlement, it has been able to take in the form of revenue a large share of the unearned increment of the land ; this is, of course, devoted to public purposes, the benefit of which is ultimately shared by the agriculturists. But the State's concern for subordinate interest is shown directly as well as indirectly. There is, for instance, a general practice of ensuring that favour shown to the landlord by way of reduction or remission of revenue in a bad season shall be passed on in some degree to the tenant in the matter of rent. There is, too, a special circumstance which has led the Government of India, to quote the words of Sir J. Bampfylde Fuller, 'to intervene and to use its proper functions of controlling and moderating the struggle for life.' By the moderation of its assessment the British Government has raised the selling value of landlords' estates from next to nothing to over 300 millions sterling, says the same authority; and the result has been a strengthening of the power of the landlords and a weakening of the poorer cultivators which has been met with fearless and sometimes drastic treatment. We are told now and then that the Government of India contents itself with the function of looking after the interests of those who have either fallen from a higher estate or have enjoyed the protection of preceding rulers, or for other reasons have historical claims upon the State. This may have been the case in the early days of British rule, but the facts show that since then the Government has moved step-by-step in the direction of what we should call benevolent interference. Nowhere is this better exemplified than in the systems of tenant law and practice for which I should now like to ask your patience.

I will take first as an illustration the policy that has been followed in Bengal and in Agra. Two classes of tenants among others were found; those who represented the old land-holders, and those whose position was really, though perhaps not demonstrably, due to contract. The first of these clearly had theoretical claims to perferential treatment, but great difficulty was found in drawing a working distinction between the two. The difficulty was summarily met by enacting that, where any tenant had continuously held the same land for twelve years, he should be regarded as a privileged or 'occupancy' tenant, endowed with a hereditary right and secured against rack-renting and arbitrary eviction. Landlords found it easy to forestall the acquisition of occupancy tenant right, either by evicting and reinstating the tenant or by inducing him to change some part of holding before the twelve years ran out. These devices were met later by specific checks in the case of Agra and by an enactment in Bengal that the tenant need merely prove that he had held land in his village for twelve years continuously. In the Punjab, the Central Provinces, and Oudh, it was an easier matter to distinguish a class of privileged land-holders, who were recognised as 'sub-proprietors to their land lords, and there was consequently the less need in theory to extend the protection of Government indiscriminately to all classes of tenants. Even so, the Oudh Rent Act of 1886 gives certain privileges to all tenants in the matter of seven years' term without ejectment or further enhancement. In the Central Provinces, individual landlordships were created at one time for special reasons by grant of Government, and as a set-off the State has exercised itself even more directly than elsewhere to maintain the rights of the tenants. At the time of the Settlement the revenue officer does not stop short at comparing the rent-rolls with the result of valuation ; he is empowered by law to fix for a term of years the actual rents payable by the tenants to the landlords, in order to ensure that the general incidence of rent, and with that of revenue may as far as possible be equal. It will not be out of place to mention an interesting episode that occurred in the Central Provinces before power was taken to fix rent under law. At a time when the wheat export trade was expanding, the landlords took to demanding their rents in grain instead of in cash, and at ruinous rates, in order to gain control of the produce of the tenant class that was then unprotected by law. When revenue came to be assessed on the rent-rolls as they stood, the landlords complained that these were fictitiously high, whereupon the Government offered to reduce its revenue demands on condition that rents were lowered to a realisable standard and fresh leases were issued. Since then, as we have seen, the State has intervened by direct legislation and there has been the less need to rely on the check of revenue assessment. That is to say, the Stat has tended to emphasise its position rather as the arbitrator between classes than as merely the predominant partner in the land ; and I think it would be pedantic to have to postulate the latter position before venturing to exercise the functions of the former. Generally speaking, the privileged or occupancy tenants still enjoy special measures of protection as regards fixity of rent and tenure which are not as a matter of principle conceded to ordinary tenants ; that is to say, rent enhancement, ejectment, and distraint are largely taken out of the hands of the landlords in the former but not in the latter case. Yet ordinary tenants are protected by Government against harshness on the part of the landlords in exercising their powers, and the barrier between the two classes is not insurmountable. In the landlord areas of Madras, where the influence of middlemen on the land has been much less marked than in Northern India and the tenant's position is of a simpler kind and has been safeguarded by tradition, the latest Act, passed in 1908, is of a striking nature. It declares that every cultivator or ryot, 'now in possession or who shall hereafter be admitted by a landlord to be in possession of ryoti-land' (that is, land on an estate other than the home farm land in the special possession of the proprietor) shall have a permanent right of occupancy in his holding. The tenant's right is hereditable and transferable ; he can make improvements and claim compensation for them in the event of dispossession ; his rent cannot be raised except by decree of court, and then only to the extent of 12½ per cent. Such are the typical rights guaranteed by Government to privileged tenants, not only when their status is historical, but when they have been raised to that status, as they not infrequently are, by express enactment.

Over and above these special cases it is important to remember that as a matter of general practice the revenue officers of the Government, where they are not actually empowered to fix rents by law, can and do use their discretion to settle the rates that ought to be paid; in fact, they play the part of the good land agent to the superior landlord—the State in this case—intervening actively in matters of dispute between tenant and sub-tenant. Moreover, when there is occasion for rent or tenant ceases to be taken into court for decision, they go in most of the provinces before special revenue courts, or at any rate tribunals of revenue officers composed of men who have kept in close working touch with the problems on which they have to adjudicate. The Government of India are not content to leave these matters to the ordinary and perhaps inexpert processes of civil law.

PROTECTION OF TENANTS.

I should like to refer to two sets of arguments against the possibility of applying principles of Indian land administration to English conditions. In the first place, it is sometimes said that the right of appeal to judicial authority in matters of rent and tenure is confined on principle to the privileged tenant-class in India, while ordinary tenants are properly left to depend on the bargains that they can derive with their landlords; and it is argued that the indiscriminate extension of the right in England would be a dangerous innovation. I think it is fair to say that the State protection of the privileged tenants goes as a matter of fact a good deal beyond that right. As to the ordinary tenants, it has to be remembered that the State has helped them on occasions, as I have mentioned, either by interposing the check of revenue assessment upon excessive rent demands, or by raising the tenants' status bodily to that of the privileged class; and this apart from the good offices, as I have just said freely rendered by its revenue officers. It does not seem to me that measures such as these are any less drastic in principle than the comparatively mild expedient of allowing the right of appeal in question. If the State in India is ready to take the most convenient form of protecting the weaker interests, why should not we in England be prepared to follow their example?

The second contention is that the tenant in India, without State intervention, is so much more at the mercy of his landlord, by reason of the keenness of competition and the absence for the most part of alternative industries, and the difficulty of transplantation to other districts, that a far greater of State protection is justifiable than would be the case in England. To this I would answer that where the strain on the tenant in England is removed as is so often the case, by the simple process of shifting it on the class below him, the case for State intervention on behalf of that class is no less urgent. And if the State in securing higher rates of wages for the labourer finds it necessary to re-impose the burden on the tenant, it is surely no less its duty to lighten that burden by the most expedient means, that is, as I have said, by the principle of working from the foundation upward. It is in the light of this principle that I have tried to put before you the leading methods of tenant protection in India.

If your patience is not already exhausted, I should like to take up as briefly as possible some feature of the land system lying outside the two great spheres of land revenue and tenancy. There are for instance one or two points of interest connected with lands under the direct control of the State in India. These fall mainly into two classes. There are properties which have passed by various ways into Government lands, whether because the title of succession has lapsed or been forfeited, or because estates have been taken over (though very rarely in recent times) for arrears of revenue. I have already mentioned how these came for the most part to be handed over to cultivators working directly under State, which managed by this means to secure protection for the agriculturist at the same time a valuable training ground for young revenue officers. In the second place, Government claims the ownership of all waste lands. Some of these are held by the State as forest reserves or (in the Punjab) as fuel areas ; some are gradually made over to villages for cultivation as the demand spreads ; and in the north-west of India large arid tracts have been brought under irrigation by means of monumental engineering works, and are being parcelled out to colonists with the double object of extending the area of cultivation and of raising the pressure on the land elsewhere. These canal colonies are worked by cultivators directly under the State ; land revenue is payable on the usual basis, but the assessment is very light during the early years of occupancy when the outlay is heavy and the return is small. While we are on this subject we can conveniently refer to the powers of Government to acquire land when necessary for public purposes. Procedure under the latest Land Acquisition Act, that of 1894, is simple and satisfying. The Government notifies the areas which it wishes to exercise the right of taking over, and the right is incontestable at law ; a State officer values the lands and estimates the compensation payable at market rates to the holders ; and the latter may, if they wish, appeal to the Civil Courts against the amount of compensation assessed. But the courts are expressly debarred by Statute from taking into consideration any rise in the value of the property that may have taken place since the date on which the Government notified its intention of acquiring the land. The expedient is so direct and so wholesome that it needs no comment; it is comforting to know that we shall not have long to wait before municipalities in this country are empowered to get to work in similar lines. I will only add that in the course of the latest and in the most extensive proceedings under the Act—I mean the Acquisition of Land for the new Imperial Capital at Delhi extending back to the early part of 1912—it is being found that the original estimates for compensation are not being seriously exceeded as a result of actions at law.

The agriculturist in India, as in other countries, has always the problem of finding capital for his needs. Private money-lenders are plentiful but the rates of interest they ask, ranging from 12 to 24 per çent. or more, are not exactly conducive to prosperity, and their ambitions to secure land by mortgage are looked at askance by the Government which has found it necessary, in some parts, to curtail the peasant's ability to raise money on his land by placing restrictions on alienation. Direct State assistance is forthcoming in the grant of Government loans for the purpose of making improvements and the provision of advances to meet more temporary needs, such as the relief of distress and the purchase of seed and cattle. It is worth while remembering that Indian peasants give valuable hostages to fortune in the shape of livestock, and that fortune is often cruel in India. A second and more important form of State activity is the encouragement of Co-operative Credit Societies which are run, as far as possible, by the members themselves, but with sympathetic help and directions from Government officials. The expansion of the movement under Government guidance has been most successful, and everything points to continued growth. Apart from these measures, the State gives direct encouragement to more expenditure of capital on the land by framing rules in the various provinces under which increase of income, due to improvements made by private individuals, are exempted from revenue assessment, either permanently or for a term of years.

CASE OF ENGLAND.

No one, I trust, will imagine that I have tried to do more than give the barest outline of the Government land policy in India. I shall have succeeded if I have conveyed some impression of the methods followed by what is perhaps the most efficient administration of our times. In a land such as England, where reform moves from within, and has to depend in the long run upon the pressure of democratic opinion with its confused voices and conflicting interests, it is sometimes difficult to escape into the hard, clear atmosphere which one finds in India. In this country we broaden reluctantly with many creakings, from precedent to precedent, and every creak is hailed as a portent of revolution. Whatever on the other hand may be the defects of a bureaucratic Government, its cardinal justification should at any rate be efficiency : the unbiassed and unhesitating application of the right method to secure the right result. If India we find an example of a condition, in which the State, freed from the resourceless grib of hallowed catchwords, secures its just shares of the profits it has created, and intervenes to protect the weaker interests against the stronger, and finds its chief concern in the ceaseless maintenance of prosperity on the land—are we to say that no lesson is to be learned, no moral is to be drawn from its activities ? Can we not for once turn aside from the immemorial phrase that too often stand in the part of progress in this country ? An Indian land-holder sometimes tells the revenue officers, when he cannot account for the origin or extent of holding, that it is dadillahi, or gift of God ; but that simple utterance does not relieve the State of its rights or its duties in respect of his holding. It is hard to maintain that any equivalent formula should be allowed to have magic properties in England.

FIRST VISIT TO INDIA.

In the course of a speech to his constituents at Histon on March 28, 1913, Mr. Montagu, M.P., Under-Secretary of State for India, said :—

It is not now a suitable opportunity or place to enter into a lengthy discussion or account of the impressions I formed in India. Indeed, the duty of a Minister who has been permitted this great opportunity of investigation must largely be to use his information inside his office and not on the platform. I have only to thank you for the generous confidence which alone made it possible for me to go, and I have to tell you that I am confident of the complete success of my journey. I was met with the splendid hospitality so characteristic of those brave men and women on whose shoulders rest the heavy responsibility of a task of increasing difficulty and increasing demand. I was honoured with the confidence of British and Indian, and, in the 15,000 miles I travelled, was able to see something of the unending varieties of Indian conditions, and meet the great leaders of Indian opinion as well as our officials. I cannot find words in which to thank them for all that they did for me, and if I can prove to them that we at the India Office are anxious to appreciate the difficulties and problems of Indian administration both from the British and Indian points of view in a personal sense as well as by despatch and in replies to petitions, I hope to offer them some return for their confidence and welcome.

Courage is the attribute of the Government of India which I would place first, courage and single-purposed strength begotten of a confident belief in the humanity and essentiality of British Government. What better object lesson, what better example of this, can one have, than the splendid courage of Lord and Lady Hardinge on December 23 last, when the British Government entered the new capital of Delhi? The hideous act of a miserable anarchist led to an escape from death which can literally be calculated in fractions of an inch, and yet, by the wounded Viceroy's own orders, the procession continued, and the British Raj was firmly installed in the capital of the Great Moghuls. I do not think history records greater physical courage than was shown that day, or greater honesty of mind than was shown in the great speech I heard in January, with which the Viceroy—still with pieces of the miscreant's missile in his back—announced his unfaltering confidence in the people of India. And his courage and our policy can plead its justification in the joy with which his complete recovery has been witnessed and the condemnation of the outrage throughout the whole of India. I can only say in this connection, for I do not want to spend your time in India to-day, that the wisdom of the Durbar policy must be recognised by anyone who visits India now, but that we must not forget that anarchy exists in India, fostered from hidden sources, some possibly beyond the Empire itself, wholly independent of political agitation, yielding in no way to political treatment, and requiring the rigour of the Executive and the co-operation of all Indians in stamping it out.

In an another part of his speech, Mr. Montagu referred to the silver purchases.

He said some people had thought fit to bring against his personal honour charges of corruption based on the fact that Lord Crewe had purchased silver, to the great gain of tax-payers of India, in the normal course of business and without his knowledge—for it was not in his Department—through his brother's firm, a firm with which he happened to have no personal connection. He could only express a certain amount of family pride that his brother's firm were successful in carrying out the wishes of the Government of India, and after the speeches of the Prime Minister and the answers given to questions in the House there was no single respectable person of either political party who believed that there was anything in the charges whatever.

INDIAN ADMINISTRATION AND THE MESOPOTAMIAN COMMISSION.

[*Mr. Montagu delivered the following speech in the House of Commons on July* 12, 1917, *in connection with the Debate on the Report of the Mesopotamia Commission.*]

The first consideration which I would like to address to the House is that we are discussing the second occasion which has arisen during the War in which politicians, soldiers, doctors and civil servants come in for severe censure. This country, which started at the beginning of the War wholly unprepared for, and wholly unexpectant of a conflict of this kind, has, despite the atmosphere of self-criticism in which we live, somehow or other through all these mistakes and muddles, developed into the terror of all our enemies, and the most conspicuous enemy and the most successful enemy that Germany possesses. It does seem to me that that is a remarkable fact. When we consider the Reports of Commissions of this kind, after all, we are now discussing one phase in the most successful campaign of the War, the one campaign in which the objective has been achieved. To-day the British flag is flying at Bagdad. Where else has there been any comparable success? And these are only the early stages which played a preliminary part in that great success which has been won by General Maude. I agree with the Hon. Gentleman who spoke last and my Hon. and gallant friend (Colonel Sir M. Sykes) who spoke from the Back Bench opposite. There are many grave disadvantages in the appointment of these commissions. As my Hon. and gallant friend said they are bound by their terms of reference to act exactby as the Allies have acted throughout this War, and to consider separately little bits of the picture rather than bring it into true perspective with all the other events which are happening in other parts of the world. After all, if our conspicuous success had been continuous, if General Nixon had reached Bagdad without a reverse, would there ever have been a Mesopotamia Commission? And yet there is no comment upon the fact that just after the battle of Ctesiphon—I think I am right in the date—Gallipoli was evacuated and the whole picture was changed by the liberation of the Turkish forces in the Peninsula. That is my first criticism on the Commission, that you cannot get a true perspective by examining as an isolated thing one theatre of the world War; and the second point that I make against these Commissions has been rendered obvious by all the discussion which took place in the early part of the afternoon. As a result of the publication of the Report, necessarily without evidence, serious charges are made against individuals who have never had an opportunity of learning the evidence against them.

The result is that if you wish to take action against these individuals you are confronted with difficulties with which my Right Hon. and learned friend dealt earlier this afternoon, and I submit that if you are going to have any further proceedings it would have been far better to postpone the question until your sittings are completed, because now, whatever Court sits, it must not only have the prejudice of this discussion, but the prejudice of the public discussion upon the Report. I join with my Right Hon. and learned friend beside me in his suggestion that of the two alternatives offered that of the Right Hon. Gentleman the Attorney-General is much the more satisfactory. My third complaint against this Commission is that in the terms of reference they are asked to attach responsibility to departments of the Government, but what the Commission did was to attach responsibility not to departments of the Government, but to individuals. The house and the country are sapping in that way the service of co-operative effort and departmental responsibility in this country. Men are asking for instructions in writing, men are safeguarding themselves by letters and by minutes, men dare not give advice because they are afraid of a Commission sitting upon their action. Under the old system the Parliamentary Chief of the Department was responsible for what occurred, and under his rule he cloaked with his authority all those who worked for him. Has that gone by the board ? This man and that man may come to be censured, although working seriously and courageously to the best of his endeavours. I believe that by that means you are doing irreparable injury to our system of Government ; and you want to weigh that well against any good you can achieve on the other side.

After all, do not let us pass a verdict upon the share of these men in this story because of the fact that we know now that in this part of the campaign, at all events, they were defeated. Do not let us punish men for failure. After all, when was it that the serious defects in the equipment and the plans of the advance on Bagdad really become obvious? I do not say that there were not serious shortages, horrible shortages of necessary supplies before they could be successful, but what I do say is that if there had been no defeat at Ctesiphon and if General Nixon had succeeded in getting to Bagdad most of the evils which overtook the Army in retreat would not have occurred. Therefore, the greatest charge that you can bring against General Nixon is that he failed to obtain success and took serious risks. I do not believe that you will ever beat the Germans unless you take risks, and I think at any rate that the Press atmosphere, if not the House of Commons atmosphere, on this Report is a direct invitation to everybody to take no risks at all. Supposing—which God forbid!—we should have a similar Commission on affairs in Palestine; in the one case it would be that the advance was too quick, and in the other that the advance was possibly too slow. After all, has anybody read paragraph 9, page 18 of the Report, where it describes General Nixon going in the direction of Nasariyeh. The paragraph says:

"The heat was terrific; still General Nixon deemed it expedient to carry on the enterprise. Major-General Gorringe, who was in charge of this column, succeeded in capturing Nasariyeh on the 25th July, with 950 prisoners, seventeen guns and much booty. These operations were initiated by the General on the spot, supported by the Commander-in-Chief and the Viceroy of India, and acquiesced in by the Secretary of State. They appeared to us to be sound from both a military and political view. Our casualties amounted to 533 of all ranks."

In that cold and colourless language is described one of the most courageous and brilliantly executed exploits in all war, accomplished by General Sir John Nixon, who has served his country well, who has served it with distinction and who has played a vital part in the greater successes of his better equipped successors, and certainly he ought not to be censured and punished, and driven out of the Army on the isolated circumstances after the battle of Ctesiphon, but we should acknowledge the incomparable services which that same soldier has rendered to his country.

From Sir John Nixon I will turn to Lord Hardinge. There can be no doubt in the mind of anybody who is acquainted with recent occurrences in India, that Lord Hardinge when he left India left it by the universal opinion of all Indians, certainly by the overwhelming majority of Indians, people and Princes, as the most popular Viceroy of modern times. There have been strong predecessors of his, but when he came to India irritation was rife, public opinion had been slighted and ignored, he showed himself from the beginning to the end of his Viceroyalty to be a Viceroy upon whose sympathy and assistance Indians could rely, not only in India but in the whole world, and, as my Hon.

friend has said, through personal bereavement and attempted assassination, he stuck to his post to the end of his prolonged term, never faltering, never losing courage, and he left having achieved much for India, and now he is censured by this document, for what, for the fact that he relied too much upon those who had been chosen to give him military advice. Among many things we have never decided in this country are the relations between politicians and soldiers. On the same day you may read two newspapers : sometimes, I think, you will read in one newspaper trenchant criticisms against the Government for overruling or disregarding or attempting to hamper the action of their military advisers, and on the other hand you will find peremptory demands that they should hamper, overrule or criticise their military advisers. The two accusations are not in harmony with one another, and the true relation of the responsibility of politicians and soldiers has never been satisfactorily decided in this country, or as far as I know, by any Government. But the mistake that Lord Hardinge made, if it be a mistake, is the same mistake as my Right Hon. friend made when he relied upon Lord French and Sir Douglas Haig, and the same mistake which I presume the present Prime Minister is making when he relies now on the advice of Sir Douglas Haig. May I give an analogy of what I mean ? When we were told the other day that the defence of London against air-raids depends upon the number of aeroplanes wanted at the front, who says how many aeroplanes are wanted in France ?—the Commander-in-Chief.

Supposing a committee of inquiry sitting afterwards discovered that in a particular month—I do not make the allegation for one moment—that there were certain aeroplanes which might have been used for the defence of London lying idle in a particular part of the front, would the responsibility be that of Sir Douglas Haig or the Prime Minister? What is the alternative to a politician relying on his military advisers? If he cannot trust them, let him choose others. All I say is that Lord Hardinge's reliance upon Sir Beauchamp Duff is not different from that of my Right Hon. friend opposite. Lord Hardinge in this regard cannot be treated as an isolated figure. I think the real charge against the Indian Government is a charge in which I want to include Lord Hardinge and my Right Hon. friend opposite and his predecessor in office, Lord Crewe. It is so easy to be wise after the event. The real charge against the Indian administration seems to me to be this: At the beginning of the War I believe there was too great doubt of the loyalty and co-operation of the Indian people. The *Times* newspaper, day after day for sessions and months past, had articles pointing out that sedition was supposed to be rife. It loomed certainly much too large in the discussions of this House. It misled the Germans into thinking India was disloyal, and the deliberate policy of the Government in regard to India during the War seems to me to have been, let us make the least contribution as we dare as far from India as is possible. Keep the War away from India; we will take Indian soldiers and put them into France, and lend Indian civilians to the Home Government. India geographically as a country should be content with defending its own frontiers, and in maintaining order—a very great responsibility—inside the continent of India. Apart from that, it was to do nothing near itself in the War. The people of India were even not asked to contribute to the War, although they asked Parliament that they should be allowed to contribute. I am told that volunteers were asked for in Bengal for certain purposes, and afterwards were told they were not wanted. I am talking now of the beginning of the War. The policy was that we did not know whether India should co-operate in this War or not; we did not trust them; we dare not trust them—I am not criticising them from that point of view—let us keep the War far from India. Then events proved that the Indian people were anxious to co-operate, and the share of the Indian people in this War, from beginning to the end has always been greater than the share of the Indian Government in this War, and always more willing than the share of the Indian Government. When this atmosphere had been created, when Indian troops had been sent to France and Indian civilians sent here, and when India, as Lord Hardinge said, had been "bled white," suddenly there comes a change of policy, and we have this expedition to Bagdad, a complete reversal of policy, unaccompanied, so far as I can see, with any big enough effort to put the Government and organisation of India, which was then on a peace footing, on a war footing, for an aggressive war comparable to the change in policy. Therefore, the machinery was overturned;

there was no equipment for war, and when expeditions were sent abroad they ought to have been equipped in a way comparable to the equipment of the expeditionary forces in this country and in our Dominions. As a matter of fact, here comes what I regard a true reduction from this source. The machinery of Government in this country, with its unwritten constitution, and the machinery of Government in our Dominions has proved itself sufficiently elastic, sufficiently capable of modification, to turn a peace-pursuing instrument into a war-making instrument. It is the Government of India alone which does not seem capable of transformation, and I regard that as based upon the fact that the machinery is statute written machinery. The Government of India is too wooden, too iron, too inelastic, too ante-diluvian, to be any use for the modern purposes we have in view. I do not believe that anybody could ever support the Government of India from the point of view of modern requirements. But it won't do. Nothing serious had happened since the Indian Mutiny, the public was not interested in Indian affairs, and it required a crisis to direct attention to the fact that the Indian Government is an indefensible system of Government. I remember when I first came to the House, when my Hon. friend opposite—he will perhaps forgive me for reminding him of the fact,—and I were members, of one of those Committees which Members of Parliament form themselves into and he spent the whole of his time in trying to direct his colleagues' attention to the necessity of thinking about India. He urged people to go to the Debates about it. I was one of those whom he let to go to the early Debates, when Lord Morley took charge of its affairs. Was he successful? Does anybody remember the Indian Budget Debates before the War? Upon that day the House was always empty. India did not matter, and the Debates were left to people on the one side whom their enemies sometimes called "bureaucrats," and on the other side to people whom their enemies sometimes called "seditionists" until it almost came to be disreputable to take part in Indian Debates. It required a crisis of this kind to realise how important Indian affairs were. After all, is the House of Commons to be blamed for that? What was the Indian Budget Debate? It was a purely academic discussion which had no effect whatever upon events in India, conducted after the events that were being discussed, had taken place. How can you now defend the fact that the Secretaries of State for India alone of all the occupants of the Front Bench, with the possible exception of the Chancellor of the Duchy of Lancaster, are not responsible to this House for their salaries, and do not come here with their estimates in order that the House of Commons may express its opinion?

MR. DILLON :—I have said so over and over again in this House.

MR. MONTAGU :—I know, and I am not blaming anybody for it. What I am saying now is in the light of these revelations of this inelasticity of Indian Government. However much you could gloss over those indefensible proceedings in the past, the time has now come to alter them. Does the Hon. Member resent my advocacy of a change ?

MR. DILLON :—For twenty years a small group of us have been demanding that the salary of the Secretary of State for India should be put on the estimates and the two Front Benches always solidly combined against us.

SIR J. D. REES :—Was there not justification for that in the tone of the Debates ?

MR. DILLON :—That may be your opinion.

MR. S. MACNEILL :—You (Sir J. D. Rees) contributed very largely.

MR. MONTAGU :—The tone of those Debates was unreal, unsubstantial and ineffective. If estimates for India, like estimates for the Secretary of State for Foreign Affairs and the Colonial Secretary were to be discussed on the floor of the House of Commons, the Debates on India would be as good as the debates on foreign affairs. After all, what is the difference ? Has it ever been suggested to the people of Australia that they should pay the salary of the Secretary of State for the Colony ? Why should the whole cost of that building itself, in Charles Street, including the building itself, be an item of the Indian taxpayers' burden rather than that of this House of Commons and the people of this country ? If I may give one example of the inconvenience of the existing system, I would refer to the Indian Cotton Duties debate which occurred in this House this year. The Cotton Duties had been imposed and there was no possible way of undoing that. That is the attitude in which we always debate Indian affairs. You have got no opportunity of settling the policy. It has been sometimes questioned whether a democracy can rule an Empire. I say that in this instance the democracy has never had the opportunity of trying. But even if the House of Commons were to give orders to the Secretary of State, the Secretary of State is not his own master. In matters vitally affecting India, he can be overruled by a majority of the Council. I may be told that the cases are very rare in which the Council has differed from the Secretary of State for India. I know one case anyhow, where it was a very near thing, and where the action of the Council might without remedy have involved the Government of India in a policy out of a harmony with the declared policy of the House of Commons and the Cabinet. And these gentlemen are appointed for seven years, and can only be controlled from the Houses of Parliament by Resolution carried in both Houses calling on them for their resignations. The whole system of the India Office is designed to prevent control by the House of Commons for fear that there might be too advanced a Secretary of State. I do not say that it is possible to govern India through the intervention of the Secretary of State with no expert advice, but what I do say is that in this epoch now after the Mesopotamia Report, he must get his expert advice in some other way than by this Council of men, great men though no doubt they always are, who come home after lengthy service in India to spend the first year of their retirement as members of the Council of India. No wonder that the practice of telegrams backward and forward and of private telegrams, commented upon by the Mesopotamia Report, has come into existence.

Does any Member of this House know much about procedure in the India Office, how the Council sits in Committees, how there is interposed between the Civil Servant and the political Chiefs, the Committees of the India Council, and how the draft on some simple question comes up through the Civil Servant to the Under-Secretary of State, and may be referred back to the Committee which sends it back to him, and it then goes to the Secretary of State, who then sends it to India Council, which may refer it back to the Committee, and two or three times in its history may go backwards and forwards. I say that that is a system so cumbrous, so designed to prevent efficiency and change that in the light of these revelations it cannot continue to exist. I speak very bitterly, and I speak with some feelings on this subject, for in the year 1912 a very small modification in this machinery was attempted by Lord Crewe, and a Bill was introduced into the House of Commons. On the motion of Lord Curzon, it was thrown out on Second Reading in another place. Its authorship was attributed to me, and I was supposed to have forged it on my Noble Chief, because I found that the machinery of the India Office was not good for my own purposes. My only desire then, as it is now, was to try and find some-thing which had some semblance of speedy action. Government offices are often accused of circumlocution and red-tape. I have been to the India Office and to other offices. I tell this

House that the statutory organisation of the India Office produces an apotheosis of circumlocution and red-tape beyond the dreams of any ordinary citizen. Now I will come to one particular detail of the India Office administration before I pass from this subject. I think the Mesopotamia Report stigmatises the conduct of the Stores Department as in the one respect unbusiness-like. The Stores Department of the India Office is a Department whose sole function—a most important function certainly—is the purchase of millions of pounds worth of equipment for the Indian Army, clothing and such like. It is presided over by a Civil servant; in the year 1912 or 1913 a vacancy occurred in that office, and it was suggested then that the proper man to superintend mere purchasing operations of that kind was a business man, an institution of the policy always associated with the Prime Minister. Great difficulties appeared in the way of the appointment of a business man, and a Civil servant was appointed. But it was agreed then that the next occupant of the office should be a business man. My right Hon. Friend the Secretary of State told me yesterday that a Civil servant had again been appointed.

The Secretary of State for India (Mr. Chamberlian): I never heard of any such agreement.

Mr. Montagu: My Right Hon. Friend is not responsible for any agreement come to by his predecessor. I say it was then agreed as a policy that a businessman should be appointed to succeed the Civil servant. I am only giving this history to point out that now, after the Report of the Mesopotamia Commission, I would suggest to him that the time has come to abolish the Stores Department of the India Office, when the work that it is doing of clothing the Indian Army is comparable entirely to the work which is now being done by the Ministry of Munitions and the War Office for equipping our own Armies and the Armies of our Allies and that the sooner all these multifarious supply Departments are abolished and the whole business concentrated under one roof and under one office the more efficient will the supplies be.

I come now to the question of the Government of India from India. I think that the control of this House over the Secretary of State ought to be more real, and I would say further that the independence of the Viceroy from the Secretary of State ought to be much greater. You cannot govern a great country by the despatch of telegrams. The Viceroy ought to have far greater powers devolved to him than is at present the case. When I say that, I do submit that you cannot leave the Viceroy as it is. Are there four much more busy men in this country than His Majesty the King, the Prime Minister, who sits opposite, the Secretary of State for Foreign Affairs, and the Speaker of the House of Commons ? Yet the analogous positions of these four posts are held by one man in India, and he is expected to be responsible and closely to investigate the conduct of a great expedition like this ! You cannot find an individual who can undertake the work. Your executive system in India has broken down because it is not constituted for the complicated duties of modern Government but you cannot reorganise the

Executive Government of India, remodel the Viceroyalty, and give the Executive Government more freedom from this House of Commons and the Secretary of State unless you make it more responsible to the people of India. Really the whole system has got to be explored in the light of the Mesopotamian Commission. It has proved to be of too much rigidity. My Hon. and gallant friend opposite in his Minority Report, I think—certainly in the questions he has asked in this House—seems to advocate a complete Home Rule for India. I do not believe there is any demand for that in India on a large scale. I do not believe it will be possible, or certainly be a cure for these evils.

COMMANDER WEDGEWOOD :—I want that to be the goal towards which we are driving.

MR. MONTAGU : As a goal, I see a different picture ; I see the great self-governing Dominions and Provinces of India organised and co-ordinated with the great Principalities, the existing Principalities—and perhaps new ones—not one great Home Rule country, but a series of self-governing Provinces and Principalities, federated by one central Government. But whatever be the object of your rule in India, the universal demand of those Indians whom I have met and corresponded with is that you should state it. Having stated it, you should give some instalment to show that you are in real earnest ; some beginning of the new plan which you intend to pursue that gives you the opportunity of giving greater representative institutions in some form or other to the people of India, of giving them greater control of their Executive, of remodelling the Executive—that affords you the opportunity of giving the Executive more liberty from home because you cannot leave your harassed officials responsible to two sets of people. Responsibility here at home was intended to replace or to be a substitute for responsibility in India. As you increase responsibility in India you can lessen that reponsibility at home.

But I am positive of this, your great claim to continue the illogical system of Government by which we have governed India in the past of is that it was efficient. "It has been proved to be not efficient." It has been proved to be not sufficiently elastic to express the will of the Indian people; to make them into a warring nation as they wanted to be. The history of this war shows that you can rely upon the loyalty of the Indian people to the British Empire—if you ever before doubted it! If you want to us that loyalty you must take advantage of that love of country which is a religion in India, and you must give them that higher opportunity of controlling their own destinies, not merely by councils which cannot act, but by control, by growing control of the Executive itself. Then in your next war—if we ever have war—in your next crisis, through times of peace, you will have a contented India, an India equipped to help. Believe me, Mr. Speaker, it is not a question of expediency, it is not a question of desirability. Unless you are prepared to remodel, in the light of modern experience, this century-old and cumbrous machine, then, I believe, I verily believe, that you will lose your right to control the destinies of the Indian Empire.

SPEECH AT CAMBRIDGESHIRE.

Mr. E. S. Mantagu, Secretary of State for India, was in July, 1917, unanimously adopted as candidate for West Cambridgeshire, the Parliamentary representation of which he resigned on accepting Ministerial office as Secretary of State for India.

The offer of the position of Secretary of State for India, he said, was made to him recently, and after a few hours thought he came to the conclusion that anything a man was asked to do now for his country by those who were responsible for guiding its destinies must be done. Nothing else mattered—no personal, no political considerations. Accordingly he had accepted the heavy responsibilities and the difficult anxieties of that office.

Ever since he entered public life he had taken an absorbing interest in the Indian fellow-subjects of the King Emperor. He had served first as Under Secretary to Lord Morley, the veteran statesman who represented all that was best in English public life. He had also served under, and as colleague of Lord Crewe. If Lord Crewe had escaped some of the abuse which public men receive he certainly had escaped the credit that was due to a wise and far-seeing statesmen whose counsels were of the utmost value. He had served as a colleague of Mr. Austen Chamberlain, who in his resignation had acted froma fine sense of honour which had endeared him to the people of this country, but in doing this he had inflicted a serious loss on the counsels of the nation.

I take up the work (Mr. Montagu proceeded) where Mr. Chamberlain left it a few days ago. As a private member of the House of Commons, when I had no sort of notion that I should be asked to fill any vacancy in the India Office, I made a speech on Indian affairs. That speech embodied the opinions I held and still hold. Mr. Chamberlain told the House of Commons that the reform of the Government in India was now under discussion between him and the Council and the Viceroy and his Council and advisers in India. I take up that discussion, I hope, without interruption, where he left it, and in due course the Government will announce their policy.

There are only two issues now at stake—the successful conclusion of the war and adequate preparation for peace when it comes. For some months I have been presiding over a conference to consider the actual steps to be taken for bringing home from abroad, releasing from service, and sending back to their homes the most gallant soldiers in history. The care of those who fought and won is a first charge upon statesmanship. Our plans are nearly ready, and with the co-operation of the Ministry of Labour and the War Office our report will soon be before the Government.

Everything depends, after the war, on the rapidity with which we resume our peace vocations. The future of our returned soldiers depends largely on the rapidity with which we can start manufacturing. Has not the war taught us, revivified and made more acute as a motive power, the sense of nationality? Our country and Empire must be made secure not only in arms, but in supplies. You will, after the war as now, have to suffer hardships and inconvenience. With all the efforts that we can make, there will be a shortage of shipping in the early months of peace. That will mean shortage of all the food we might like and of raw material. Let no one imagine that these difficulties will disappear with the coming of peace! therefore, the more we produce and set ourselves to provide in the future, the better off we shall be.

You will have noticed that whenever I am asked to undertake any work I am assisted in the responsibility I assume by expressions of opinion from a certain section of the Press. That is their method, and they have time for it. What does it matter to us, after all? I do not stand alone. The present Prime Minister who is squaring up so successfully to his gigantic task; the late Lord Kitchner, to whom we owed almost everything at the beginning of the war; Mr. Balfour, whose work in America is still fresh in the mind of everybody; Viscount Grey, whose diplomacy was the machinery for rallying all the civilized nations of the world against Germany; Mr. Churchill, who mobilized the Navy on the eve of the war; Lord Haldane, who gave us the Expeditionary Force; even Mr. Asquith, whose wise leadership held the country together in unity for the first two and a half years of the war—all these, Liberals and Conservatives come in for their share.

What does it matter? The fact remains that I base

my right to serve my country upon your confidence, and while I have that I shall pay no attention to anything else. (*Cheers*).

Mr. Montagu concluded with the statement that the expressions of confidence he had received from many in that constituency and in India gave him this assurance, that it would not be from want of friends if he failed.

APPENDIX I.

THE COUNCIL OF INDIA BILL.

Mr. E. S. Montagu, M. P., the late Under Secretary for India, deals vigorously in the following letter to the "Times" of Monday (July 6, 1914) with the attack made by Lord Curzon in the House of Lords on the Council of India Bill in general, and on himself in particular :

Lord Curzon, in moving the rejection of the Council of India Bill in the House of Lords on Tuesday last, found occasion to refer to two persons of widely different fame and achievements, from whom he had nothing to fear in the course of debate. His strictures on the late Lord Minto I can safely leave to be dealt with my more competent hands, but I trust you will allow me space to reply to an observation which he did me the honour to direct at me.

In the earlier part of his speech he remarked, as reported in your columns :—" It is common knowledge that this Bill in its main features is the product of the late Under Secretary (Mr. Montagu), who during his term at the India Office found that the machinery that existed did not suit his ideas, and set about to destroy it to the best of his ability."

I fear he has attached too much importance to a compliment which Lord Crewe was good enough to pay to me in the House of Lords last July. It is, of course, easy for Lord Curzon with his wonted delicacy of touch to lift the skirt of a reforming measure in order to reveal beneath it the cloven hoof of a scheming politician, and, what is to him worse, a politician still young. I will not urge the obvious plea that the Secretary of State, by introducing the measure in the House of Lords, has completely identified himself with its scope and intentions. So far as I am concerned, I confess I feel no cause to be ashamed of any part I may have played in the initiation of the proposals now brought forward in their matured form.

"A SYSTEM PETRIFIED IN A STATUTE."

The charge, however, as it reads, is explicit. It attributes to me no better object than ruthless destruction, and no higher motive than the satisfaction of my personal predilections. As, in the event of Lord Curzon's motion succeeding, I shall have no other opportunity, I feel it is only due to myself to ask you to allow me to correct this most unfair and entirely false impression. I have no objection to stating my main motive in helping to adapt to modern conditions a system petrified in a statute founded on the conditions of more than half a century ago. It does not require argument to show that in the peculiar circumstances of Indian Government it is a grave danger that there should exist lack of sympathy between the Executive Government of India and the guiding and ultimately controlling office at home. I have long been convinced, from my knowledge of recent events and from careful enquiry in India, that such lack of sympathy as may exist is due, not to the exercise by the Secretary of State of those functions of revision and of determining policy so justly defined by John Stuart Mill in the passage quoted by the writer of your leading article on June 29, but to the intolerable procrastination, inevitable under the India Office system, and to a tendency to undue interference from home in the minutiæ of administration. Interference of this kind comes, I assert emphatically, not from the Secretary of State, who has neither the time nor the inclination for it, but from his Council, whose energies are naturally turned in this direction by their Indian-formed and regularised habit of mind. My ideas have, therefore, always moved in the direction of a smaller and at the same time more up-to-date advisory body, working on a more elastic, adaptable and speedier system.

I could not expect this line of thought to commend itself to Lord Curzon, whose every word on the subject of India since he resigned his office has underlined the essential truth stated by the *Times of India* on February 24 last, that "India is moving so fast that it is dangerous for those who have been long absent to venture on dogmatic opinions regarding current politics." I should be the last to depreciate Lord Curzon's incessant, unwearying, and uncompromising efforts to perfect administrative efficiency; but I must be permitted to hold that it is carrying indulgence for the opinions of a retired Indian administrator, however great, too far to acquiesce in his assumption that "the force of Nature can no further go" than the high-water mark of his own seven years' achievement.

In considering details of a scheme framed to meet the needs of 1914, it is difficult to be convinced by arguments based upon Lord Stanley's speeches in 1858, the experience of an Under Secretary, however superior, in 1891, and the *excathedra* pronouncements of a Viceroy of 1899-1905.

I must resist the temptation to comment upon the lengths to which Lord Curzon's passion for solid obstructiveness can carry him, as, for instance, when he makes a pathetic appeal on behalf of voiceless Indian taxpayers within a few minutes of stating pontifically that a proposal to give them a voice is utterly indefensible; it is perhaps unfair to cavil at the self-contradictions of a speaker so sadly hampered by a redundancy of superlatives. The fact is that some of his own arguments fail to escape the orgy of mutilation which followed his exhibition in the first few sentences of the corpse of the Bill hanged, drawn, and quartered.

When Lord Curzon says that in the case of the Government of India autocracy is not a blunder, but a crime, I can only humbly assent to his august and incontrovertible maxim, adding my regret that its utterance was unaccompanied by any note of personal repentance.

APPENDIX II.

THE LATE MR. GOKHALE.*

The news of Mr. Gokhale's death has come with an inevitable sense of shock, even to those of us who had feared for some months past that there was grave reason for anxiety about his health. We have lost the outstanding figure in the great transition stage of Modern India ; a man whose abilities brought him to the forefront, and whose sense of right forced him into controversies of which we have not yet seen the end. But at this moment the dominant feeling among all who were brought into contact with him is, I think, that the value of a life and personality such as his—a record of single-minded devotion to an unselfish ideal and of ceaseless labour in its service over an almost unlimited field of activity—stand above and apart from all controversy. It is with this aspect before my mind that I welcome the opportunity, as one among many of his admirers, of paying my tribute to his memory and of recalling the impressions on which in my own case it is built up.

One of the many remarkable characteristics of Mr. Gokhale was the degree to which he was able to combine enthusiasm for reform with a patient industry not too often found in close association with the first

---

* From *India*, 26th February 1915.

quality. But he never allowed his idealism and his infinite capacity for taking pains to interfere with one another ; rather, they both served as a joint inspiration to the work he set before him. The result was that, whether one agreed or disagreed with him, he gave a sense of practicalness in his dealings which seemed to sweep away half the difficulties at the outset. Like all men gifted with the spirit of reform, he was always on the alert to unearth and state the problems which others would be content to leave half-hidden beneath the weight of administrative machinery ; but it would never have occurred to him to rest satisfied with the bare statement of the problem. The vital point in his view was to arrive at the solution, and to that end he would bring to bear all the resources of his fertile mind and all the great influence of his personality. If any illustration of his way of setting to work needed, we turn most naturally, perhaps, to his visit to South Africa, the effects of which, in view of what has since happened, may well be said to be incalculable.

It is almost inevitable—and perhaps it is right—that in thinking of our great men of public affairs we recall the atmosphere of their ideals and their personality, rather than the underlying fact of their sheer intellectual power. Yet in Mr. Gokhale's case this fact claims special recognition, if only because it was so often veiled beneath the modesty and sincerity of his nature. His grasp of things, both in essentials and in details was not the least valuable of the assets which he brought to the service of his country. It is not too much to say that his annual contribution to the debate, on the budget proposals in India, to quote only one example, was one of the outstanding features of the proceedings of the Viceroy's Council, and was eagerly awaited even by those who could not see eye to eye with him in his criticisms. That a man should interest himself in the complexities of Indian economics and finance is in itself a tribute to his powers of mind; that he should master them, and should display his mastery at an age at which few people would care even to study them cursorily, was a sign of a ripening intellect and a serious endeavour which served to lay the sure foundations of Mr. Gokhale's work. And with all his comprehensiveness of judgment and mental clarity he never dropped into the academic fallacy of contempt. He impressed one as being among the most candid and unassuming of men; and he was equally ready to give or to take advice where it seemed most serviceable. His mind possessed the qualities ascribed to statesmanship without ever losing the fire of its enthusiasms or its warm human interests. We feel that his loss touches deeply not only India but the Empire and the whole world of men whose thoughts move in harmony, whether they know it or not, with the spirit of the brotherhood of "the Servants of India."

APPENDIX III.

GOAL OF BRITISH POLICY.

A Gazette of India Extraordinary issued, Simla, August 20, published the following notification :—

The following announcement is being made this day by the Secretary of State for India in the House of Commons and is published for general information :—

The policy of His Majesty's Government, with which the Government of India are in complete accord, is that of increasing the association of Indians in every branch of administration and the gradual development of self-governing institutions with a view to the progressive realisation of responsible Government in India, as an integral part of the British Empire. They have decided that substantial steps in this direction should be taken as soon as possible and that it is of the highest importance, as a preliminary to considering what these steps should be, that there should be a free and informal exchange of opinion between those in authority at Home and in India. His Majesty's Government have accordingly decided with His Majesty's approval that I should accept the Viceroy's invitation to proceed to India to discuss these matters with the Viceroy and the Government of India, to consider with the Viceroy the views of Local

Governments and to receive the suggestions of representative bodies and others. I would add that progress in this policy can only be achieved by successive stages. The British Government and the Government of India, on whom the responsibility lies for the welfare and advancement of the Indian peoples, must be judges of the time and measure of each advance and they must be guided by the co-operation received from those upon whom new opportunities of service will thus be conferred and by the extent to which it is found that confidence can be reposed in their sense of responsibility. Ample opportunity will be afforded for the public discussion of the proposals, which will be submitted in due course to Parliament.

(Signed) J. H. DuBOULAY,

Secretary to the Government of India.

INDEX.

I

HINDU RELIGION AND PHILOSOPHY.

Sri Sankaracharya.—I.—His Life and Times. By C. N. Krishnaswamy Aiyar, M.A., L.T. II.—His Philosophy. By Pandit Sitanath Tattvabhushan. Both in one volume. As. 12. To Subscribers of the "Indian Review," As. 8.

Sri Madhwa and Madhwaism.—A short Historic Sketch. By C. N. Krishnaswamy Aiyar, M.A. As. 12. To Subscribers of the "Indian Review," As. 8.

Sri Ramanujacharya.—His Life and Times. By S. Krishnaswami Aiyangar, M.A. His Philosophy. By T. Rajagopalachariar, M.A., B.L. As. 12. To Subscribers of the "Indian Review," As. 8.

The Life and Teachings of Buddha. By Dharmapala. Price As. 12. To Subscribers, "I. R.," As. 8.

Sri Sankaracharya's Select Works.—The Text in Sanskrit Devanagiri type and an English Translation. By S. Venkataramanan, B.A. Price Re. 1-8. To Subscribers of the "Indian Review," Re. 1.

The Vaishnavaite Reformers of India.—Critical Sketches of their Lives and Writings. By T. Rajagopalachariar, M.A. B.L. Price Re. 1. To Subscribers of the "I.R." As. 12.

Swami Vivekananda.—An exhaustive and comprehensive collection of his speeches and writings. *With four portraits.* Fourth Edition. Price Rs. 2. To Subscribers of the "Indian Review," Re. 1-8.

Aspects of the Vedanta. By various writers. Second Edition. As. 12. To Subscribers of the "I. R.," As. 8.

Ten Tamil Saints. By Mr. M. S. Purnalingam Pillai, B.A., L.T. Price As. 12. To Subscribers, "I. R.," As. 8.

India's Untouchable Saints. Price As. 6 To Subscribers, "I.R.," As. 4.

Essentials of Hinduism. As. 8. To Subscribers, I.R., As. 6.

Hindu Psalms and Hymns. By Mr. K. V. Ramaswami, B.A. Price As. 4.

Maitreyi: A Vedic Story. By Pandit Sitanath Tattvabhushan. Price As. 4.

The Bhagavād-Gita or the Lord's Song.—With the text in Devanagiri and an English Translation. By Mrs. Annie Besant. Third Edition. As. 2.

G.A. Natesan & Co., Sunkurama Chetty Street, Madras.

The "Friends of India" Series

This is a new Series of short biographical sketches of eminent men who have laboured for the good of India, which the Publishers venture to think will be a welcome addition to the political and historical literature of the country. These biographies are so written as to form a gallery of portraits of permanent interest to the student as well as to the politician. Copious extracts from the speeches and writings of the "Friends of India" on Indian Affairs are given in the sketches. Each volume has a fine frontispiece.

Lord Morley	*Henry Fawcett*
Lord Ripon	*Mr. A. O. Hume*
Sir William Wedderburn	*Sir Henry Cotton*
Mrs. Annie Besant	*Lord Macaulay*
Lord Minto	*Sister Nivedita*
Edmund Burke	*Rev. Dr. Miller*
Charles Bradlaugh	*Sir Edwin Arnold*
John Bright	*Lord Hardinge*

THE LEADER :—Will be a welcome addition to the political and historical literature of the country.

THE MODERN REVIEW :—On the cover of each volume is printed a portrait of the subject of the sketch and the stories are told in a lively and interesting manner with short extracts from notable speeches delivered. The series should be welcome to the public.

Foolscap 8vo. Price As. Four each.

ANNIE BESANT'S

SPEECHES & WRITINGS ON INDIAN QUESTIONS

This is the first attempt to publish in one volume a comprehensive and exhaustive collection of Mrs. Besant's speeches and writings on Indian Questions.

Second Edition:

Price Re. 1-8. To Subscribers of the "I.R." Re. 1-4.

MORLEY'S INDIAN SPEECHES.

A NEW AND UP-TO-DATE EDITION.

Revised and Enlarged.

Price Re. 1-8. To Subscribers of "I. R." Re. 1-4.

A. Natesan & Co., Sunkurama Chetti Street, Madras.

INDIAN ARTS, INDUSTRIES & AGRICULTURE

Indian Industrial and Economic Problems. By Prof. V. G. Kale, Fergusson College, Poona. Price Re. 1-8. To Subscribers of the "Indian Review," Re. 1-4.

The Swadeshi Movement.—A Symposium by Representative Indians and Anglo-Indians. Re. 1-4. To Subscribers of the "Indian Review," Re. 1.

Agricultural Industries in India. By Seedick R. Sayani. With an introduction by Sir Vitaldas Damodar Thackersey. Second edition. Revised and enlarged. Re. 1. To Subscribers of the "Indian Review," As. 12.

Essays on Indian Art, Industries and Education. By E. B. Havell, Re. 1-4. To Subscribers of the "I.R." Re. 1.

Essays on Indian Economics. (Third Edition). By Mahadev Govind Ranade. Price Rs. 2. To Subscribers of the "I.R.," Re. 1-8.

Industrial India. By Glyn Barlow, M.A. Second Edition. Re. 1. To Subscribers the "I.R." As. 12.

Lift-Irrigation. By A. Chatterton. Second Edition. Revised and enlarged. Price. Rs. 2. To Subscribers of the "Indian Review," Rs. 1-8.

The Improvement of Indian Agriculture.—Some Lessons from America. By Cathelyne Singh. Price Re. 1. To Subscribers of the "Indian Review," As. 12.

THE SWADESHI MOVEMENT

Views of representative Indians and Anglo-Indians.

Contains among others, the views of Dadabhoy Naoroji, H. H. the Gaekwar of Baroda, H. H. the Maharaja of Dharbunga, G. K. Gokhale, Dr. Sir Rash Behari Ghose, Hon. Sir Fazulbhoy Currimbhoy Ebrahim, Mr. M. K. Gandhi, Sir R. N. Mookerjea, Sir D. E. Wacha, Hon. Rao Bahadur R. N. Mudholkar, Hon. Pandit Madan Mohan, Mrs. Besant, Mr. Tilak, Mr. Surendranath Bannerjee, and also of Lord Minto, Lord Carmichael, Lord Ampthill etc.

Second Edition, Revised and Enlarged,

Price Re. 1-4. To Subscribers of "I.R," Re. 1.

G. A. Natesan & Co., Sunkurama Chetty Street, Madras.